New Business Matters

Coursebook

business English with a lexical approach

Mark Powell

with Skills Units by Ron Martínez and
Video Worksheets by Rosi Jillett

THOMSON ™

HEINLE

United Kingdom • United States • Australia • Canada • Mexico • Singapore • Spain

THOMSON

™

HEINLE

New Business Matters, Coursebook

Powell/Martínez/Jillett

Publisher: *Chris Wenger*
Director of Editorial Developmental ESL/ELT: *Anita Raducanu*
Editorial Manager: *Howard Middle, of HM ELT Services*
Developmental Editor: *Jean Pender*
Editorial Assistant: *Lisa Geraghty*
Sr. Production Editor: *Sally Cogliano*
Director of Marketing, ESL/ELT: *Amy Mabley*
Associate Marketing Manager: *Laura Needham*
Sr. Print Buyer: *Mary Beth Hennebury*

Compositor: *Process ELT (www.process-elt.com)*
Production Management: *Process ELT*
Photography Manager: *Sheri Blaney*
Photo Researcher: *Loukas Ioannou, Process ELT*
Copyeditor: *Katerina Mestheneou*
Cover/Text Designer: *Studio Image & Photographic Art*
(www.studio-image.com)
Printer: *Seng Lee Press*

Cover Images: *(main image) Matthias Kulka/CORBIS; (world map) Royalty Free/CORBIS*

Printed in Singapore.
1 2 3 4 5 6 7 8 9 10 07 06 05 04 03

For more information contact Thomson Learning, High Holborn House, 50/51 Bedford Row, London WC1R 4LR United Kingdom or Heinle, 25 Thomson Place, Boston, MA 02210 USA. You can visit our Web site at http://www.heinle.com

ISBN: 0-7593-9856-9
(Coursebook)

Photo Credits

Page 9 © Digital Vision, page 10 © PictureQuest, page 13 (top) © Najlah Feanny/CORBIS SABA, page 13 (bottom) courtesy Esther Dyson, page 15 © BananaStock, page 17 © Painet Inc, page 18 © AFP/CORBIS, page 23 © Tony Arruza/CORBIS, page 25 (top) © Antonio M.Rosario/Brand X Pictures, page 25 (bottom) & 26 (top) © Steve Allen/Brand X Pictures, page 33 © BananaStock, page 35 © J.Horton-Brand X Pictures, page 36 (top) © Coca-Cola Company, ho, page 36 (bottom) © AP Photo/Ed Bailey, page 40 © Don Carstens/Stock Connection, page 43 © Painet Inc, page 44 © D.&J.Heaton/Stock Connection, page 51 © Dynamic Graphics/CREATAS, page 52 © Jeremy Horner/CORBIS, page 55 © Craig Lovell/Stock Connection, page 56 © Corbis Images, page 57 © Burke/Triolo/Brand X Pictures, page 58 © BananaStock, page 59 © Mark Cass/Brand X Pictures, page 61 © AP Photo/Charlie Neibergall, page 64 © Painet Inc, page 65 © Digital Vision, page 67 © Painet Inc, page 69 © Bob Daemmrich/PictureQuest,

page 70 © Reuters NewMedia Inc./CORBIS, page 73 © Derek Trask/CORBIS, page 77 © AP Photo/Gurinder Osan, page 78 © Digital Vision, page 84 © Steve Gottlieb/Stock Connection, page 85 © Dynamic Graphics/CREATAS, page 87 © TM 2003 Amelia Earhart by CMG Worldwide, Inc. www.CMGWorldwide.com, page 88 © Digital Vision, page 94 © AP Photo/Adam Butler, page 95 © A.Caminada/Rex Interstock, page 96 © AP Photo/Kathy Villens, page 102 © Digital Vision, page 103 © Tom Brakefield/Stock Connection, page 104 © AP Photo/Eric Draper, page 111 © BananaStock, page 113 © Steve Allen/Brand X Pictures, page 114 © Harold Stucker/PictureQuest, page 119 © Painet Inc, page 120 © Burke/Triolo/Brand X Pictures, page 121, 122 & 126 © Painet Inc, page 127 © Steve Allen/Brand X Pictures, page 130 © AP Photo/Bernd Kammerer, page 133 (top) © AP Photo, page 133 (middle) © AP Photo/K.Rodsupan, page 133 (bottom) © AP Photo/Chad Rachman

Illustration on page 136 by Peter Standley/Process ELT.

To the student

Introduction

In New Business Matters you will find:

- four new listening-based skills units, focusing on the language of meetings, presentations, telephoning and negotiations.

- a selection of fifteen video extracts with worksheets from authentic CNN programmes.

- a new glossary of key business vocabulary

- a new Workbook, providing a substantial amount of grammar, vocabulary and writing practice and consolidation work for class or home study, also offering general relevance to the BEC Vantage exam.

A New Approach

New Business Matters is based on the latest research into the language of business. At your level of English you do not need to spend a lot of time learning more grammar or vocabulary. What you need is the ability to *combine* words, many of which you already know, into the phrases and expressions which are the basis of business English. New Business Matters is the fast-track to fluency in the special English of business.

Getting Started

Each unit of New Business Matters explores a different international business issue. You may wish to work through the book from the beginning to the end or you may choose those units which are of most interest to you and work on those first. Study the contents list on the next four pages to discover the topics and the key language taught in each unit.

If you are working in class

Take every opportunity to discuss the issues raised in your course with your fellow students and teacher or trainer. By talking about what interests you or surprises you in the articles, you will be re-cycling a lot of the language you need to learn.

Most of the exercises on the Language Focus pages can be done in class or at home.

At the end of each unit there is a fluency activity to give you the chance to use the language you have learned in the unit. Sometimes they need some preparation – just like a task at work.

If you are working alone

How much time can you realistically spend studying at home? An hour twice a week is better than eight hours once a month.

Resist the temptation to read all the articles first. Work on one at a time and do the exercises which follow it. This will keep your interest level up and help you to learn any new language in easy stages. Don't be afraid to read the exercises aloud to yourself or to summarise what you have read out loud.

You can use the separate Workbook for additional practice, also if you are studying for the Cambridge BEC Vantage exam.

The Articles

The articles at the beginning of each unit are the most important part of this course. They have been carefully written to include lots of useful language. Most of the exercises are based on them. By referring back to the articles you will find the language work easier, and you will be reading the language in context. Always refer back to the text – rather than look the answers up in the key.

Listening

All the articles, as well as the listening skills inputs, are recorded on cassette and CD. Listening to a recording of an article a few days after reading it is an excellent way of reminding yourself of the most useful language. Read an article, then listen to it. Listen to it, then read it. Leave it for a few days and listen again. The more you listen and read, the better!

The Glossary

A glossary of key business vocabulary has now been included. This will help you learn important word partnerships, as well as explain the meaning of many of the business terms used in the course.

Before Unit One

Before you start the units we recommend that you study page 8 – Before Unit One. This introduces you to several key ideas in the English of business which will help you develop your fluency. In particular, you will learn how important word partnerships are.

Contents

	Text	Language Focus
Page 9 **Unit 1:** **Career Management**	*Me plc.*	The Appointment Pages: job advertisement expressions Reading between the Lines: understanding job ads Career, recruitment and interviewing phrases
Page 17 **Unit 2:** **Enterprise**	*Entrepreneurs*	Word Grammar: expressing nouns in the adjective form Word Partnerships in the context of entrepreneurial skills Business Grammar: reporting verbs, gerund/infinitive expressions, prepositional verbs
Page 25 **Unit 3:** **E-business**	*Dot-con?*	Abbreviations: business and technology terms Find the Words Prepositions Word Partnerships: verbs and verb phrases
Page 33	**Skills Unit A: Meeting Skills**	
Page 35 **Unit 4:** **Brand Management**	*Brand Wars*	Word Partnerships: brand, market and product descriptions Business Metaphors: terms of war, sport and games, water, health and flight. Business Grammar: writing a successful sales letter
Page 43 **Unit 5:** **Prices and Commodities**	*If the price is right …*	Word Partnerships: business words, fixed expressions in the context of price and money Word Grammar: *price, trade, profit, compete* The language of trends and developments
Page 51 **Unit 6:** **Corporate Entertaining**	*Looking after the Twenty Percent*	Word Partnerships in the context of corporate entertainment Describing food and drink Expressions with *deal*
Page 59	**Skills Unit B: Telephoning Skills**	
Page 61 **Unit 7:** **Innovation**	*Bright Ideas* *The Lateral Thinker*	Word Partnerships: research, problems, ideas; adverbs Business phrases with *make* and *do*
Page 69 **Unit 8:** **Public Relations**	*True Lies*	Word Partnerships in the context of recommendations PR crises Key words for mission statements Expressions with *image* Word Grammar: *communicate, public, persuade, reputation*

Discussion Topics	Fluency Work
Do you live to work or work to live? Applying for jobs that are not as advertised	*Dream job*: interviews – what would be your ideal job?
Entrepreneurism within corporations, using intuition and ingenuity, personal success	*Business Venture*: starting a new business, drawing up and presenting a business plan
Criticisms of corporate Web sites	*Dotcom Clinic:* giving online business advice
Company names and product differentiation	*Product Development*: challenging a brand name with a competitive new product
Bargaining, profit margins, critical business indicators, factors influencing pricing policy	*Case Study: Sumitomo Bank*: the world of commodity trading
Above the line and below the line marketing, corporate gift-giving, wining and dining clients, the business lunch	*Mixing Business and Pleasure:* a business meal with a foreign host
Creativity in business, breakthroughs and backfires, dealing with problems at work, responding to change and new ideas	*Brainstorm:* defining, reformulating, and solving problems
Dealing with PR crises	*Case Study: Intel in Trouble:* holding a crisis meeting

	Text	Language Focus
Page 77 **Unit 9:** **Cultural Awareness**	*Boardroom Culture Clash*	Word Partnerships: business verbs and nouns Business Grammar: negotiations, diplomacy
Page 85	**Skills Unit C: Presentations Skills**	
Page 87 **Unit 10:** **Global Advertising**	*Going Global*	Expressions with *commercial* Word Partnerships in the context of advertising Word Grammar: *-ize, -ise*
Page 95 **Unit 11:** **Management Styles**	*She's the Boss*	Word Partnerships in the context of company organisation and management Expressions with *company* and *staff* Word Grammar: adjectives for managers Business Grammar: prepositions
Page 103 **Unit 12:** **Mergers and Acquisitions**	*Greed is Good*	Word Partnerships: verbs and nouns in the context of acquisitions and company management Word Grammar: prefixes, *finance, invest, capital, negotiate*
Page 111	**Skills Unit D: Negotiating Skills**	
Page 113 **Unit 13:** **Business and the Environment**	*Managing the Planet*	Word Partnerships: ecology and commerce Business Grammar: attitude verbs, natural and unnatural sentences
Page 121 **Unit 14:** **Finance and Credit**	*Credit Out of Control*	Word Partnerships in the context of Finance and Credit Expressions of bankruptcy Expressions with *money* and *order* Business Grammar: prepositions
Page 129 **Unit 15:** **Economic Issues**	*The Death of Economics*	Word Partnerships in the context of economic issues and political speeches Expressions with *economic* Expressions for current affairs Abbreviations and Acronyms Word Grammar: *economics, politics* Business Grammar: describing economic situations
Page 137	**CNN Video Worksheets**	
Page 153	**Answer Key**	
Page 161	**Tapescript**	
Page 169	**Glossary**	

Discussion Topics	Fluency Work
Cultural aspects of conducting meetings and prioritising business issues; meetings with native speakers of English	*The Cultural Awareness Game*: creating business solutions in a multinational environment
Attributes of market leaders, branding for different countries	*Case Study:* BA: a disastrous branding decision
Male- and female-oriented management styles, company organisation, ratio of male to female employees	*Discrimination:* evaluating job candidates
Globalisation	*Simulation: Takeover:* a media giant decides which companies to put on its 'hitlist' of acquisitions (*See also page 174*)
Environmental problems and solutions	*Business Ethics:* ethical think tanks
Cross-border trade, credit card debt	*Getting Tough:* dealing with debtors
Economic situations, political views, beliefs, hopes, memories and regrets	*Election Campaign:* economic and political prospects of an imaginary country

Before Unit One

The Power of Reading

Reading is one of the best ways of developing your English. The articles in this book have been carefully written to contain the essential business language you need. Although they contain only 12,000 words, you would have to read an enormous number of newspapers and magazines to find as much useful business English. The articles in New Business Matters are written to provide a concentration of really useful business English.

Identifying the Language

As you read, it is important to identify and record the language which is most relevant to you. Many of the activities in this book train you to do this. Make sure you recognise the following types of language.

1. Words and Phrases

New Business Matters contains words and phrases which will be new to you and which you may want to learn:

downsize	as a rule
margin	on the whole
incentive	in effect

Don't try to learn every new word you meet. Not all new words you meet will be useful to you. Choose the words you plan to learn. Do you already do this?

2. Word Partnerships

Much more important than lots of new words is learning how to combine the words you already know into word partnerships. Learning business English is learning the word partnerships of business.
You must already know the three words: *market, into,* and *break.*
But do you know the much more useful:
break into the market?
There is no point in knowing the word *market* unless you know the words you need to talk about markets. The same is true for all the most common business words – *product, sales, demand, price, money* etc.
Here are some more examples of word partnerships:

launch a product
sales prospects
meet demand
raise money
enter foreign markets

The more word partnerships you know, the more fluent you will become and the less you will have to worry about grammar! *European sales prospects* is not only much better English than *The possibility of selling our products in Europe,* it is much simpler too!
Can you match these six common words to make two word partnerships each containing three words:

management	down	slim
out	carry	research

You will learn many powerful word partnerships in New Business Matters. They are much more useful than single 'new words'.

3. Fixed Expressions

There are many expressions which are fixed – they never change. You should learn them as if they were single words. For example:

It can't be done.
You can say that again.
Funnily enough ...
As a matter of fact ...

Many common expressions are a lot more fixed than we think. Learning them can be a very efficient way of improving your English. Try to learn them in context: for example, disagreement expressions, clarification expressions, etc.
Many of the activities in the Language Focus pages deliberately contain many phrases and sentences which are fixed or nearly fixed. This means that you can use a lot of that language yourself immediately. Don't forget how useful learning something by heart can be.

This is Business English

Business English is a combination of the words, word partnerships, and fixed expressions which are used in business life. New Business Matters brings all this language together and places it at the centre of your learning.

High-flier or Wage Slave?

"It's a shame that the only thing a man can do for eight hours a day is work. He can't eat for eight hours; he can't drink for eight hours; … The only thing a man can do for eight hours is work."
William Faulkner, American novelist

We all know people for whom the above may not be true! But, in general, do we spend too much time working? Do you live to work or work to live? Where would you place yourself on the scale below?

Get ahead   **Get a life**

Work with a partner. Discuss the following questions.

- Would you take a job you didn't like in order to get the experience you need?
- Would you take a pay cut to do something you really enjoy?
- Would you relocate to a foreign country if the package was tempting enough?
- Would you give up a steady job to take a chance on a new enterprise?
- Would you accept a top job offered only on a temporary basis?
- Would you keep changing jobs until you got exactly what you wanted?

For an analysis of your answers see page 153.

Now read the article, *Me plc*.

Me plc.

Hired Guns

What do Steve Jobs, CEO of Apple Computers, Karl von der Heyden, former CFO of PepsiCo., and twenty other top executives at Fortune 500 companies have in common? The answer is they have all been 'interim managers', hired on a temporary basis to come in and revitalise a firm with their own special brand of magic. And then leave. In fact, such short-term employment contracts are now becoming the norm at all management levels. And if they're good enough for the likes of Jobs, they're good enough for the rest of us.

Employability

Provided you can stand the insecurity, there has never been a better time to get a job. The old 'smokestack industries' of mining, shipbuilding and steel may be gone, but with the arrival of the New Economy, what we're now increasingly seeing is highly paid project teams created for particular assignments for a specific period of time. Once the project is completed, the team is simply disbanded. No hard feelings – just thanks and goodbye. There's no promise of more work, but if you've done a good job, you've added to what human resources people call your 'employability'. You've enhanced your career prospects with another firm on a similar short-term basis.

The Corporate Ladder

In the past it was different. You worked hard, pleased an insufferable boss - you had a job for life. True, you were little more than a wage slave, but if you stuck to the dress code, played by the rules and made a few powerful friends along the way, you could climb to the top of the corporate ladder by the age of fifty, take early retirement at fifty-five and drop dead at fifty-six.

Re-engineering

Then along came the 're-engineered' 90s and changed all that. According to Jerry Yoram Wind and Jeremy Main at the world-leading Wharton School of Management, big companies like AT&T "finally woke up in 1995 and said 'Oh my goodness, we have 40,000 people too many'." Mass redundancies followed. In April 1997 Newsweek ran a cover story entitled 'Corporate Killers, the Public is Scared as Hell'. The killers were giants like General Electric and IBM. Now managers were kicked out at fory-five and on the scrap heap at forty-six.

Empowerment

The tables have turned. The forty-three million jobs lost in the United States alone since 1979 are more than compensated for by the 70.2 million jobs created in the same period. Now it's our employers who are afraid we'll take our expertise elsewhere. With so many job opportunities, severe skills shortages in many industries, fewer barriers to entrepreneurship and easier access to start-up capital, we've never been so empowered. Never mind the corporation. What about me?

Telecommuters

In a study carried out for Management Today by RHI Management Resources, sixty-seven per cent of managers put a job for life at the bottom of their list of priorities. Amongst the under-35s the figure was seventy-seven per cent. Ninety-one per cent of those younger managers said career development was the responsibility of the individual. Fifty-five per cent of them wanted to retire at fifty-five or younger. All of them wanted the flexibility to work from home or even telecommute. All of them said they would dump their present company in an instant if they were offered something 'sexier' by another employer.

The Rat Race

Mark Albion, founding partner of You & Co., and co-founder of Students for Responsible Business, approves of this new opportunism. "You learn where you fit in by not fitting in," he says. "You learn what you want to do by doing what you don't want to do. If you're offered a 'big' job, take it. You might love it. But you might not find it as satisfying as you'd hoped, and it will be a jumping-off point for what you really want to do." His simple message seems to be: "Don't get really good at something you don't want to do." And remember to get a life along the way. For, as comedian, Lily Tomlin once put it: "The trouble with the rat race is that even if you win, you're still a rat".

Crosschecking

Which of the following viewpoints support the opinions expressed in the article? Compare your answers with a partner.

1. *"To make a living is no longer enough. Work also has to make a life."*
   Peter Drucker, management guru

2. *"In the past we said to employees, 'Do as you're told and you have a job for life.' Then we betrayed them."*
   AT&T manager who preferred not to be named

3. *"Ambitious young people should be reasonably patient and hold the success of the company as more important than their own success."*
   Sir John Egan, British executive

4. *"No longer can one expect to sell 100,000 hours of one's life to an organization."*
   Charles Handy, business writer and thinker

Which opinion do you most agree with?

Against the Clock

Without looking at the article, try to complete all the expressions below in under five minutes. Use the clues in brackets to help you. Then look at the article to check your answers.

1. Hired on a te … basis. (opposite of permanent) (paragraph 1)

2. Short-term employment co … . (what you sign when you join a company) (paragraph 1)

3. Once the project is completed, the team is simply dis … . (broken up) (paragraph 2)

4. You've enhanced your career pr … with another firm. (chances of being successful) (paragraph 2)

5. You worked hard, you had a job for li … . (until retirement) (paragraph 3)

6. True you were little more than a wa … slave. (the money your employer pays you) (paragraph 3)

7. Managers were k … o … at forty-five and on the scrap heap at forty-six. (fired) (paragraph 4)

8. So many job op … . (openings) (paragraph 5)

9. Severe skills sh … . (opposite of surplus) (paragraph 5)

10. Sixty-seven per cent of managers put a job for life at the bottom of their list of pr … . (essential requirements) (paragraph 6)

Language Focus

The Appointments Pages

Do you look at the appointments pages in the newspapers - just in case there's something really interesting?

Complete the following extracts from job advertisements using the words in the box which fit best.

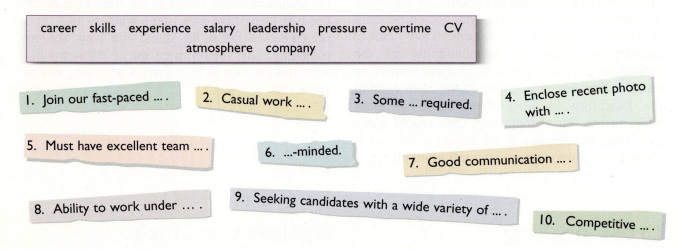

career   skills   experience   salary   leadership   pressure   overtime   CV
atmosphere   company

1. Join our fast-paced … .

2. Casual work … .

3. Some … required.

4. Enclose recent photo with … .

5. Must have excellent team … .

6. …-minded.

7. Good communication … .

8. Ability to work under … .

9. Seeking candidates with a wide variety of … .

10. Competitive … .

Reading between the Lines

Be careful! Not all job ads are what they seem. Match the extracts above to what they can really mean.

a. We stay competitive by paying less than our competitors.

b. If you're old or ugly, we'll tell you the post has been filled.

c. You'll need it to replace the different jobs of the three people who just quit.

d. You will not start a family while you are working for us.

e. So fast we have no time to train you.

f. You can wear jeans one Friday in the month.

g. Some each evening and some each weekend.

h. We tell you what to do; you work out what we mean and do it.

i. You'll have all the responsibilities of a manager, without the pay or respect.

j. You'll need to be able to work in a very stressful environment.

Have you ever applied for a job that turned out to be very different from the way it was advertised?

Quotes

Using the words in the shaded circles, complete the advice of four American business leaders on how to get ahead in business.

William Raduchel

"Don't pick a job. Pick a ... . Your first boss is probably the biggest ... in your career ... . A boss who doesn't trust you won't give you ... to grow."

William Raduchel has held senior positions at companies such as AOL Time Warner, Inc. and Sun Microsystems.

Shaded circle words:
- options
- boss
- team
- factor
- economy
- standard
- opportunities
- success

Lisa Gansky

"Make mistakes early and often. Try out lots of different ... early in your career. For most jobs, especially those in the digital ..., there is no objective ... for being 'qualified'. If you and the ... you're working with think you're qualified, you are."

Lisa Gansky was founder and CEO of Global Network Navigator, the first commercial site on the Web. It was acquired by America Online in 1995.

Simon Roy

"The smartest route between two points is not a straight line. Take a ... . The only ... you'll regret are the ones you didn't have. Always work with people who know more than you do. They're the best source of new ..., and they help you make great ... down the road."

Simon Roy's career has included the position of CEO at Accrue Software.

Shaded circle words:
- thing
- skills
- experiences
- trouble
- work
- connections
- adventure
- detour

Esther Dyson

President, EDventure Holdings

"Be careful about getting too good at one ... . The world around you keeps changing and if you can't change with it, you're in ... . Look for ... . If you feel as if you can't get much better at something, do something else. If you're not enthusiastic about your ... , you won't be very good at it anyway."

Esther Dyson is one of the world's most influential commentators on technology and business.

Work in groups. Whose advice seems the most sensible to you?

Write your own 'secret of success'. Compare with the others in your group.

Language Focus

Recruitment

What procedure does your company or a company you know go through to recruit executive staff? Do they advertise or are most posts filled internally?

Work with a partner. Add the following stages in the recruitment procedure to the checklist below.

> **Invite applicants to a first interview.**
> **Send out rejection letters.**
> **Draw up a job description.**
> **Conduct in-depth interviews.**
> **Compile a shortlist of the best candidates.**
> **Offer the post to the successful applicant subject to satisfactory references.**
> **Place a job advertisement.**

1. Identify required skills and qualifications.
2. …
3. Produce an ideal candidate profile.
4. …
5. Screen applicants.
6. …
7. Conduct preliminary interviews.
8. …
9. Invite selected applicants to second interview.
10. …
11. Conduct aptitude tests.
12. …
13. Check references.
14. …
15. Appoint the successful applicant to the post.

Interview Skills

How many job interviews have you been to? What would you say are your strengths and weaknesses as an interviewee?

Work with a partner and compare strengths and weaknesses. Do you agree with their self-assessment? What advice would you give them if they were about to apply for a job?

Listen to a careers consultant giving her 'Top Ten Tips' on how to be successful at interviews and put the points she mentions in order.

a. showing you've done research on the company
b. selling yourself to the company
c. making a good first impression
d. talking about your weaknesses
e. dressing to impress
f. showing loyalty to previous employers
g. projecting the right attitude
h. talking about your strengths
i. avoiding sounding self-congratulatory
j. talking about your career history

Phrase-building

All the phrases below were in the advice you just listened to. Complete them using the pairs of words in the box.

> make + references   put + ease
> build + humour   don't + CV
> do + company   give + examples
> dare + chances
> don't + ex-employers   ask + questions
> conduct + presentation

1. … the interviewer at …
2. … your homework on the …
3. … informed …
4. … the interview as a …
5. … in a bit of …
6. … say negative things about …
7. … concrete …
8. … sure you have great …
9. … try to cover up gaps in your …
10. … to take a few …

What, for you, was the most useful piece of advice?

Who Said It?

Look at the list below of things that were said at a job interview. Who do you think probably said them - the interviewer or the interviewee?

1. Take a seat. Coffee?

2. Could I ask you what attracted you to the position?

3. I'm looking for something with much more managerial responsibility.

4. I feel I'm ready for more of a challenge.

5. To be honest, I think I work better under pressure. I thrive on chaos!

6. Would I be allocated my own budget?

7. I imagine a fair amount of travel is involved, is that right?

8. How do you think your colleagues would describe you?

9. I think this is a company to which I could make a real contribution.

10. Where do you see yourself five years from now?

11. I'd like to be in your position by then.

12. Are there any other questions you'd like to ask me?

13. In our line of work, it's important to be able to work as part of a team.

14. The whole package includes health insurance, a contributory pension plan and share options.

15. Do you mind if I ask you why you left your last job?

16. There was a clash of personalities.

Look at the interviewer's questions again.

Which do you think would be the most difficult to answer?

Look at the interviewee's remarks. Are there any you think he shouldn't have made?

Phrases and Expressions

Can you remember these phrases and expressions from the interview extracts you just read? They are in the order they appeared.

1. m ... responsibility

2. ready for a c ...

3. work better under p ...

4. t ... on chaos

5. be allocated your own b ...

6. make a real c ...

7. the whole p ...

8. health i ...

9. p ... plan

10. a c ... of personalities

Fluency Work

Dream Job

What would be your ideal job? Imagine you are about to be interviewed for it.
First write your dream job description, completing the following advertisement.

> As one of the leading ... , we ... .
>
> Current expansion means that we are now looking for a ... .
>
> This is a unique opportunity for the right person to ... .
>
> Ideally, you will ... .
>
> ... would also be an advantage.
>
> Above all, you will be able to bring ... to this dynamic, growing company.

Now prepare a set of questions you would expect to be asked at the interview.
The question starters below may help you. The words in parenthesis are only
suggestions.

- What exactly/in particular (attracted to you this position)?
- What, would you say, (are the main challenges facing this industry)?
- What do you consider to be (the most important qualities for a manager)?
- What particular strengths could you bring to (this job/ department/company)?
- How would you describe (the ideal manager/present state of the market)?
- Do you mind if I ask you (why you left your last job)?
- How do you see yourself (fitting in here/managing in a foreign country)?
- Where do you see yourself (five years from now/in ten years' time)?
- How would you feel about (being posted abroad/reporting to two different line managers)?
- Can you give me an example of a time when you (had to make a difficult decision/take a calculated risk)?
- Suppose (your budget was halved). How would you react/ respond to that?
- In a word, can you sum up (the job/role of a manager)?

Now get a partner to interview you, using the questions you prepared as the
basis of their interview. Ask them what they thought of your answers. Would
they have given you the job?
If they think they could have done better, swap roles and you interview them for
the same job.

'How to Make a Million'

Room at the Top

What are the easiest routes to making your first million? Intelligence? Hard work? Inheritance? An outstanding education? Luck? A tough childhood? Good looks?

Work with a partner and list your ideas. Then compare them with those in the article below. Are you at all surprised by what you read?

Trying to make your first million? Then forget about drive, initiative and ingenuity. And don't let anyone tell you it's about putting in an 18-hour day, having a sudden stroke of genius or beating the system as you work your way to the top. Statistically speaking, your chances of making a fortune will largely depend on how fortunate you are in the first place. According to all the surveys, here are four sure-fire ways of getting rich:

1. START OFF RICH.

It's depressing but true that half of Britain's 95,000 millionaires were born into wealthy families, and so were a quarter of those who head the country's largest corporations. When you're rich already it takes a special kind of person not to get richer.

2. DO BADLY AT SCHOOL.

Richard Branson, the founder of Virgin, is the classic case, leaving school at sixteen to start a mail-order record company and ending up running his own airline, publishing, broadcasting, construction and holiday empire. He's not alone. Almost two-thirds of the UK's top earners finished their education early. And the studious graduate is less likely to be found staying at the Hilton Hotel than applying for a job in its kitchens.

3. LOSE A PARENT.

Amazingly, only five per cent of successful entrepreneurs had both parents present throughout their childhood. Perhaps a lack of parental control gives you the toughness, resilience and independence you need to make it on your own.

4. BE BEAUTIFUL.

Silly as it sounds, good looks really do get you places, both in terms of career and marital prospects. If you are too pretty, however, people may tend to assume that you're nice but stupid and pass you over for promotion.

So what can you do if you're born poor and ugly, pass all your exams and have parents who look as though they'll make ninety…?

Now read the article, *Entrepreneurs*.

Entrepreneurs come in all shapes and sizes - the dynamic, the cautious and the greedy. But all of them hold an equal fascination for us. How do they do it? What's their secret? Some of the world's biggest corporations would like to know, too. For entrepreneurism is in. And these days everyone wants to be an entrepreneur.

Entrepreneurs

"The ultimate risk

advance. You get there one sale at a time.

In the beginning, only the entrepreneur needs to see the goal, nobody else. And the goal is quite simple: you get an idea; you identify your customer; you make a sale. Then you make another and another and another until your office in the spare bedroom has turned into the tower block in Manhattan you always wanted. Forget about marketing strategy at this stage. What you need first is a steady cashflow. Bide your time. Focus on the little things. That's how it works. Big companies are just small companies that got bigger.

Take Richard Branson, for instance. For the founder of Virgin, the first ten years were a struggle, with his company suffering some cashflow problems until as late as 1980. By then, the Virgin Group was running eighty different operations, none of them making large amounts of money and some of them losing money hand over fist. Yet in 1992 Branson's music business alone sold for £560 million.

Or take Nicolas Hayek, the man who invented the Swatch and brought the Swiss watch-making industry back from the dead. Hayek took on Japanese market leaders, Seiko and Citizen, and

But an entrepreneur is not what you are, it's what you become, and real entrepreneurs exist only in retrospect. At first, nobody takes them seriously. They're crackpots, dreamers, unemployables. And by the time they've finally earned the respect of the business community, they've already made it. So cancel the classes on entrepreneurship and throw out your business plan. For the road to entrepreneurial success can't be mapped out in beat them on quality and price. Today the Swatch Group, which includes many famous names such as Omega, Longines, Calvin Klein and Tissot, sells 114 million watches a year. With annual sales of over four billion Swiss francs and a twenty-five per cent share of the global market, the group is now by far the largest manufacturer and distributor of finished watches in the world. The

is......... not taking a risk."

Swatch was a 20th century icon and some of the highly collectable early designs are now classed as art and fetch more than £20,000 – not bad for a plastic watch!

So what is it that makes a good entrepreneur on the scale of a Bill Gates, a Jeff Bezos or a Michael Dell? Clearly, not the same thing that makes a good manager. For good managers tend to come from fairly conventional backgrounds. They're the bright kids everyone knew would do well, born organizers, who rise through the ranks to reach the top of large corporations. But the budding entrepreneur is more likely to be an outsider, a troublemaker, a rebel who drops out of college to get a job, discovers a flair for building companies from nothing, gets bored quickly and moves on. Most of all, the entrepreneur will be a master of risk-management. For risk doesn't mean the same thing to the entrepreneur as it does to the rest of us. The king of corporate raiders, Sir James Goldsmith, summed it up best: "The ultimate risk," he said, "is not taking a risk." And that's probably how he got to be a dollar billionaire.

Information Check

Which of the following topics does the article discuss?

1. The hero-status of the entrepreneur
2. How to get rich quick
3. goal-setting
4. perseverance
5. enterprising managers

Interviews

In groups, spend 10 minutes preparing a set of questions about the article to ask the other groups. Use these question starters:

1. What exactly . . .?
2. What should you . . .?
3. According to the article, how would you go about . . .?
4. What's the reason behind . . .?
5. What's wrong with . . .?
6. What problems . . .?
7. Do you happen to remember . . .?
8. In what ways . . .?
9. What's the connection . . .?
10. What do you understand by . . .?

Find the Expressions

Look back at the article. Find the words and expressions which mean:

1. popular, fashionable (paragraph 1)
2. looking back (paragraph 2)
3. mad or eccentric person (paragraph 2)
4. succeeded (paragraph 2)
5. losing money rapidly (paragraph 4)
6. revived (paragraph 5)
7. fought against (paragraph 5)
8. a classic image of the time (paragraph 5)
9. climb the corporate ladder (paragraph 6)
10. the developing entrepreneur (paragraph 6)
11. a natural skill or talent (paragraph 6)
12. a person who launches hostile takeover bids (paragraph 6)

In the text, find:

13. three words you want to use more often.
14. three word partnerships you need with their equivalents in your own language.
15. three longer expressions with their equivalents in your own language.

Language Focus

Word Grammar

Put the following entrepreneurial qualities into what you consider to be their order of importance.

To be an entrepreneur you need:

a. drive

b. intuition

c. determination

d. ingenuity

e. dynamism

f. initiative

g. dedication

h. guts

i. faith

j. the killer instinct

Which of the above can you express by using an adjective?

To be an entrepreneur you need to be …

Match five of the nouns above with the definitions below.

1. To be an entrepreneur you need to have energy and motivation.

2. To be an entrepreneur you need to have courage.

3. To be an entrepreneur you need to come up with ideas and make decisions on your own.

4. To be an entrepreneur you need to be prepared to destroy your competitors if necessary.

5. To be an entrepreneur you need to believe in yourself.

Word Partnerships 1

Without referring back to the article, put the following advice on how to become an entrepreneur into the right order. The first and the last parts are in the correct order.

a. **If you want to make it to**

b. sale at a time. You will, of course, need to take many calculated

c. the top, forget about putting in an 18-hour

d. biggest cause of business failure. Make sure you clearly identify your

e. established. That's not how you beat

f. risks on the way to making

g. cashflow. For money problems in the early years are the single

h. target customers and settle for making one

i. your time and focus

j. market leaders until you're well

k. for success, so throw out your business plan, bide

l. strategy at this stage and should concentrate instead on achieving a steady

m. day or carefully mapping out your career in advance. There's no simple recipe

n. your first million, but there's no point in thinking you can take on the

o. on the little things to begin with. You can do without a marketing

p. **the system.**

Discuss

These days a lot of companies try to encourage the entrepreneurial spirit inside their organisations. They talk about the 'intrapreneur' or enterprising manager with the intuition and nerve to take their company into the 21st century. Do you think entrepreneurism can work within a corporation? Can a manager ever be an entrepreneur?

Word Partnerships 2

Do you have what it takes to be an entrepreneur? Complete the 'Entrepreneurial Indicator' below using the following words.

plan	make	open	dealing	reliant	stamina	building	goals	cope
taking	starter	sacrifices	thrive	handle	minded	adapting	suggestions	

THE ENTREPRENEURIAL INDICATOR

Score yourself according to how true the statements below are for you:

YES..............NO

1. I like to ... all my own decisions.	5	4	3	2	1	0
2. I am a self-	5	4	3	2	1	0
3. I am totally self-	5	4	3	2	1	0
4. I ... on competition.	5	4	3	2	1	0
5. I'm good at ... to change.	5	4	3	2	1	0
6. I always ... well ahead.	5	4	3	2	1	0
7. I have a flair for ... teams.	5	4	3	2	1	0
8. I'm quite capable of ... with complex issues.	5	4	3	2	1	0
9. I can ... a fair amount of stress.	5	4	3	2	1	0
10. I can ... with uncertainty and ambiguity.	5	4	3	2	1	0
11. I have the physical ... to work long hours.	5	4	3	2	1	0
12. I am quite single- ... about my work.	5	4	3	2	1	0
13. I'm no stranger to risk-	5	4	3	2	1	0
14. I'm always ... to other people's... .	5	4	3	2	1	0
15. I'm prepared to make ... to achieve my	5	4	3	2	1	0

Work out your score and check it in the answer key. How did you do?
Does the test above take a different view of entrepreneurial skill from the article?

Quotes

Complete the following quotations on success.

1. Success is getting what you want. Happiness is ... what you ... .
2. Success comes to those who are too ... to look for it.
3. Success is one ... inspiration and ninety-nine ... perspiration.
4. There are no rules to success that will work ... you do.

Do you agree? Do you have a favourite quotation of your own?

Language Focus

Business Grammar 1

Reporting verbs help you to summarise later something you have already heard said. Match what was actually said to the later report.

What was said		Report	
1.	It's absolutely vital that we expand.	a.	She raised the issue of expansion.
2.	If you ask me, it'd be madness to expand.	b.	He stressed the importance of expansion.
3.	Can we look at the possibility of expanding?	c.	She questioned the need for expansion.
4.	So, just to sum up . . .	d.	He outlined the proposed plans for expansion.
5.	Very briefly, what we plan to do is this . . .	e.	She argued that expansion would be disastrous.
6.	Are you sure this expansion is absolutely necessary?	f.	He recapped on the main points of the plan.

Match the following ways of reporting in a similar way.

7.	Actually, it's true that we've gone some way already.	g.	He reaffirmed his position on expansion.
8.	I'm afraid I'm still not convinced.	h.	She demanded to know how far their plans had gone.
9.	OK, OK. Nobody said it was going to be easy.	i.	He confirmed that the programme was already underway.
10.	Look, just how far have you gone with this?	j.	She conceded that the plan was well-researched.
11.	You've done your homework, I'll grant you that.	k.	She still doubted whether any expansion was possible.
12.	I can only repeat that expansion is essential.	l.	He admitted that expansion would be difficult.

Look carefully at the word which follows a reporting verb: confirm *that*, doubt *whether*.

Business Grammar 2

Now work with a partner to report the following remarks made by the Finance Director (FD) or the Managing Director (MD). Use the language given.

1. MD: It's crucial that we form a strategic alliance with the Japanese.
   (stress / importance)

2. FD: Look, what I want to know is how the project is going to be financed?
   (demand / know)

3. MD: Are you certain we need to raise extra capital?
   (question / need)

4. FD: OK, I grant you it's going to take an injection of cash at the outset.
   (concede / injection of cash)

5. MD: Let me say again how important it is that we team up with the Japanese.
   (reaffirm / position)

6. MD: OK, I'll just run through the main points.
   (recap / main points)

How many word partnerships can you find in the sentences above?

Business Grammar 3

In English, verbs are frequently combined to make more complex expressions. To do this you need to know how to form the second verb. For example:

They **refused to buy** from us.

They **delayed buying** from us.

We **persuaded them to buy** from us.

I **recommend you buy** from us.

Complete the following sentences using the appropriate form of the second verb.

1. We can't afford . . . (take) any risks.

2. We risk . . . (lose) everything if we fail.

3. We can't really avoid . . . (involve) the shareholders.

4. I'd recommend . . . (concentrate) on cashflow to begin with.

5. I tend . . . (agree) with you.

6. We used . . . (work) in different departments, but now we work together.

7. Are you used . . . (take) the initiative or do you wait to be told what to do?

8. I strongly advise you . . . (get) professional advice.

9. Have you considered . . . (draw) up a provisional business plan?

10. I suggest we . . . (meet) at eleven.

11. We stopped at eleven . . . (have) a break.

12. Thankfully, they've stopped . . . (send) us their damned publicity leaflets.

13. Don't forget . . . (do) that report.

14. I'll never forget . . . (meet) them for the first time.

Which of the fixed expressions do you think you could use yourself?

Discuss

Can you think of a time when you had to use your intuition and ingenuity to accomplish something that couldn't be worked out logically?

Business Grammar 4

Now try these. You'll need to decide on the connecting preposition and use the correct form of the verb.

1. Actually, I'm thinking . . . the company. (leave)

2. Thank you . . . to meet us at such short notice. (agree)

3. Fortunately, we succeeded . . . the deadline. (meet)

4. I don't believe . . . too much notice of our competitors. (take)

5. Let's just concentrate . . . what we do best. (do)

6. I don't blame him . . . up on his own. (start)

7. I won't prevent you . . . ahead if you want to. (go)

8. I warned you . . . on too much work too quickly. (take)

9. Success depends . . . in the right place at the right time. (be)

Identify the whole verb phrase in each example.

Discuss

To be successful, how important is it to be in the right place at the right time?

Fluency Work

Business Venture

How would you like to launch your own business? Work in small teams to come up with a good idea for a new small or medium-sized enterprise (SME). Your objective is to persuade the other members of your class (your financial backers) that your venture is the most likely to succeed. You can use your own professional experience or dream up something totally new.

Step 1

Use the checklist below to help you draw up a provisional business plan. You don't need to include all these points, but make sure you cover the basics. Don't worry too much about precise figures at this stage. Decide which members of your team are going to deal with which points and try to anticipate some of the questions you may be asked.

Step 2

Give your presentation. Try to 'sell' your idea in less than ten minutes. When the other teams present their business plans, use your list of anticipated questions as the basis for questioning THEM on THEIR ideas. Make sure they explain anything which is unclear and give further details if necessary.

Step 3

Hold a short meeting with the rest of your class to decide which business venture should get the financial backing. The meeting should end in a vote. Obviously, no-one can vote for their own idea, but should choose the best idea from amongst the other presentations.

BUSINESS PLAN CHECKLIST

THE NATURE & OBJECTIVES OF THE BUSINESS

- What will be your main business activity?
- What is your own professional background?
- Roughly how will the business be structured?
- Do you have an overall vision for the company?

THE PRODUCT/SERVICE IN RELATION TO THE MARKET

- What is the state of the market? Growing, static, seasonal?
- How will your products/services be positioned? Up or downmarket?
- Who will be your target customers?
- Who will be your major competitors?
- How will you market your products or services?
  Trade press? Television? Internet? Web ring communities? Radio? Billboards? Word of mouth?

PERSONNEL

- Approximately how many people will the company employ and in what capacity?

PREMISES

- Where will the company be located? Why?
- What kind of property will you require? Offices or factories? Leased or purchased?

EQUIPMENT REQUIRED

- What general trading equipment, if any, will you require? Vehicles, computer hardware?
- What manufacturing equipment, if any, will you require? Machinery, tools?

FINANCIAL PLAN

- How much capital do you require initially?
- What will this pay for?
- Will you need more capital later on? How much?
- How soon do you expect the business to break even?
- Do you intend to float the company on the stock exchange at some point?

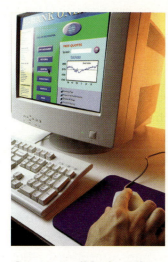

Nethead or Web-hater?

"The Internet is so big, so powerful and so pointless that for some people it is a complete substitute for life."
Andrew Brown,
Web site designer

Are you a 'Nethead' or a 'Web-hater'? Discuss the following with a partner.

1. How much time do you spend surfing the Internet?
2. Do you ever join online discussion groups or chat rooms?
3. Do you book things like flights and hotel rooms on the Net?
4. Have you ever bought goods over the Net—books, CDs, software?
5. Would you search for a job on the Internet?
6. Do you bank online? If not, would you?
7. Would you consider looking for a partner in cyberspace?

Look at the e-businesses below and right. What products or services do you think they offer (or offered - some of them may have gone out of business)? Discuss with a partner.

Which of these Web sites would you be curious to visit?

Dot.Con?

Hype

The IT industry has a tendency to exaggerate. Take Y2K, the supposed 'Millennium Bug'. It was widely predicted to wipe out seventy-five per cent of the world's computers in the very first second of the 21st century. Planes were going to fall from the sky, hospitals to be thrown into chaos and anarchists to take to the streets as the lights went out on the stroke of midnight in the civilised world. Over an eighteen-month period of corporate panic, programming experts, called in to debug doomed mainframes, amassed vast fortunes in consultancy fees. In the end, little more than minor technical problems were reported with two pocket calculators and a Gameboy.

E-volution

So it came as no surprise when those same experts announced the death of business as we know it and the arrival of the New, Weightless, Wireless, Connected Economy. 'Welcome to the Age of the Network' declared *Fortune* magazine. 'E-business: What Every CEO Needs to Know' said *Business Week*. There followed a frenzy of financial speculation not seen since the American Gold Rush. For a while, it seemed like every post-adolescent with a laptop and a business plan written on the back of a rock concert ticket could get access to unlimited venture capital. Popular domain names like business.com and houses.com were snapped up for millions of dollars. Then came a flood of more exotically named start-ups like ScreamingMedia, Egghead and AtomicTangerine.

Dot.bomb

Bust followed boom. In the race to outgrow the competition, most e-businesses burned up capital and never turned a profit. At one point e-shopping site, letsbuyit.com was getting through three and a half million dollars a month. Normally conservative organizations like Goldman Sachs, who had poured $850 million into groceries-by-Net company Webvan, saw their investment reduced to zero in two years. The prestigious Janus Mutual Fund lost a similar amount on health site WebMD. Hungry for further capital, the more dynamic dotcoms decided to issue shares. The stock market flotation of lastminute.com, to take one example, raised $175 million overnight and made the company's founders multi-millionaires. But shareholders were less fortunate. On April 14th 2001 more than one trillion dollars in market capitalisation was lost in six and a half hours of corporate madness on Wall Street. The dotcom phenomenon was over.

Return of the Dotcom

Or was it? Some say the dramatic fall in share prices reflected more the instability of the market than the commercial potential of the dotcoms themselves. New technology always leads to some kind of market correction. The same thing happened when the railways first went public. The truth is that of the 10,000 start-ups to attract major funding in the late 90s, 9,500 are still in existence. Some have 'morphed' into new companies with new names and new management. Significantly, those whose success is built on technological superiority have survived. So too have those who added 'bricks' to their 'clicks' like banco1.net, Brazil's first virtual bank, which finally decided to open conventional highstreet branches in response to customer demand.

B2B

Part of the dotcom disaster was that the media focused on the retailers, or e-tailers, like eBay and Amazon. But worries about security have prevented most of these e-tailers from ever breaking even. Less than one per cent of consumer sales are currently conducted through the Internet. In the US people spend more on dog-food than they do online! Only seven per cent of SMEs even attempt to carry out online transactions. Consumer sales, B2C, were never going to be exciting. The real growth area was always B2B. Business-to-business trading between suppliers, manufacturers and distributors over the Internet is forecast to reach $20 trillion by 2010 and, for once, the forecasts may be right. For production and logistics departments the 'friction-free' environment of the Internet is the answer to their prayers.

E-pitaph

But what about all the dotcoms that have failed? A successful industry has grown out of them, too. At NetSlaves, for example, you can visit a virtual museum of dead dotcoms. Steve Shah, the co-founder of e-business 'health-checker' DotCom Doom.com says business has never been better. And at dotcomfailures.com you used to be able to buy up dotcoms on the verge of bankruptcy, but unfortunately that is no longer possible. A short while ago dotcomfailures.com itself ... failed.

Recall

Work with a partner. Without referring back to the article, can you remember in what context the following figures were mentioned?

1. 75%
2. $175 million
3. 2001
4. 9,500
5. $20 trillion

Search in the text for the ones you have forgotten.

Crosschecking

Which of the following viewpoints support the opinions expressed in the article?

1. *"Unless the total online shopping environment - sites and payment mechanisms - is made more secure, some customers will never have the confidence to explore the opportunities."*
Anna Bradley, National Consumer Council

2. *"The compelling and main reason for e-commerce is simply and ultimately more revenue ... it's all about sales."*
Aaron Goldberg, vice-president and principal analyst for Ziff-Davis

3. *"The exciting reality is that e-commerce is in its infancy. It is today where the Wright brothers were in aviation. The Web is still an infant technology."*
Jeff Bezos, founder and CEO of e-tailer, Amazon.com

Response

What are your immediate reactions to the article you've just read?

- I'm amazed that …
- I agree with what it says about …
- But I'm not so sure about …
- I think it over-stresses the importance of …
- And underestimates the significance of …
- I don't quite understand the point about …
- And I'm not sure I believe the point about …
- Overall, I think what the article says is absolutely right/more or less right/biased/misleading/completely wrong.

Language Focus

Abbreviations

What do the following abbreviations stand for? They are all used in the article.

> IT   SME   B2C   B2B

Computer Speak

What do you think the following terms from the article mean? Check in the article if you need to.

1. debug (paragraph 1)
2. domain names (paragraph 2)
3. morphed (paragraph 4)
4. bricks (paragraph 4)
5. clicks (paragraph 4)
6. friction-free (paragraph 5)

Find the Words

Find the words in the article which mean the following. The first and last letters are given.

1. a habit or repeated action (paragraph 1)
   > t...y
2. a period of wild excited activity (paragraph 2)
   > f...y
3. a large number of (paragraph 2)
   > f...d
4. economically depressed (paragraph 3)
   > b...t
5. respected, admired (paragraph 3)
   > p...s
6. a spectacular event (paragraph 3)
   > p...n
7. the possibility to develop or achieve something in the future (paragraph 4)
   > p...l
8. only exists on the Internet (paragraph 4)
   > v...l
9. companies that sell direct to the consumer (paragraph 5)
   > r...s
10. deals, exchanges of money (paragraph 5)
    > t...s

Prepositions

The sentences below summarise different parts of the article. Complete them using the prepositions in the box. All the expressions are used in the article. Look carefully at the words on either side of the spaces before making your choice. The words in brackets ( ) explain the meaning of the more difficult phrases.

> **in** (x3)   **out** (x2)   **up** (x2)   **on** (x2)
> **through** (x2)   **to**   **for**   **between**

1. Y2K was predicted to **wipe ... three-quarters of the world's computers**. (destroy)
2. Computer programmers were **called ... to debug mainframe computers**. (hired)
3. Young entrepreneurs could **get access ... unlimited venture capital**. (obtain)
4. Popular domain names were **snapped ... for millions of dollars**. (bought quickly)
5. Most e-businesses just **burned ... capital**. (wasted)
6. Letsbuyit.com **got ... over three million dollars** a month. (spent)
7. **Hungry ... further capital**, some dotcoms issued shares. (wanting)
8. The dramatic **fall ... share prices** reflected an unstable market. (drop)
9. E-businesses whose success was **built ... technological superiority** have survived. (the result of)
10. Brazilian banco1.net opened banks in the highstreet ... **response to customer demand**. (because of)
11. A tiny fraction of total consumer sales are **conducted ... the Internet**. (made)
12. Only 7% of small and medium-sized companies **carry ... online transactions**. (do)
13. Business-to-business **trading ... firms** is forecast to grow exponentially.
14. At dotcomfailures.com you could buy dotcoms ... **the verge of bankrupty**. (close to)

Check your answers in the text if you need to.

Word Partnerships 1

Complete the following using the verbs and verb phrases in the box.

ensures
is linked
monitors
is able to receive
recognises and welcomes
is registered
manages
is managed

A good e-business Web site:

1. ... with the major search engines like Google, Yahoo and HotBot.
2. ... to other sites of interest.
3. ... on a 24-hour basis.
4. ... orders and payments online.
5. ... digital security for payments.
6. ... the number of hits the Web site receives.
7. ... registered visitors who return to the site.
8. ... stock control electronically.

Discuss

Below are some common criticisms of corporate Web sites. Which things mentioned annoy you most when you click on a Web site?

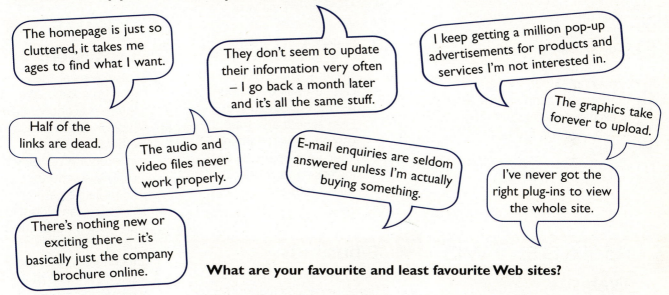

The homepage is just so cluttered, it takes me ages to find what I want.

They don't seem to update their information very often – I go back a month later and it's all the same stuff.

I keep getting a million pop-up advertisements for products and services I'm not interested in.

Half of the links are dead.

The audio and video files never work properly.

E-mail enquiries are seldom answered unless I'm actually buying something.

The graphics take forever to upload.

I've never got the right plug-ins to view the whole site.

There's nothing new or exciting there – it's basically just the company brochure online.

What are your favourite and least favourite Web sites?

Case Study: Microsoft Under Attack

As more and more business is done electronically, security risks inevitably increase. Listen to the story of how hackers gained access to confidential files at one of the world's most successful companies. Then answer the questions with a partner.

1. Do you think big companies are more or less vulnerable to this kind of attack?
2. Are you surprised the hackers were able to remain undetected for so long?
3. Do you know of any similar incidents where organisations were actually blackmailed by hackers?
4. How would your company deal with a crisis like this?
5. After the World Trade Center attack on September 11th 2001, some American politicians pressed for sentences of life imprisonment for all acts of terrorism, including corporate terrorism like computer hacking. Do you think such measures are justified?

Language Focus

Internet Evolution?

Read the following step-by-step e-business guide published by Cisco Systems. At what stage are most businesses in your country do you think?

THERE ARE FIVE STAGES TO INTERNET EVOLUTION.

HOW FAR HAS YOUR BUSINESS EVOLVED?

STAGE ONE

E-mail

Distributing letters, memos and even large data files can be almost instantaneous. E-mail delivers an immediate boost to your efficiency, making global communication as easy as exchanging data with the computer on the next desk.

STAGE THREE

E-commerce

When customers can place orders via your Web site they are engaging in e-commerce. With an e-commerce strategy, your business can be trading 24 hours a day, 365 days a year. Even service and support can be delivered online. Your sales opportunities increase and your cost of sales tumbles.

STAGE FIVE

Ecosystem

Businesses at the leading edge of the Internet economy have highly integrated infrastructures that incorporate customers, suppliers and other key alliance partners. Processes and logistics are largely automated using Internet technology, creating a seamless chain of communication and management that delivers unprecedented standards of customer service.

Business e-fficiency solutions from Cisco mean higher productivity, lower costs and increased sales opportunities.

STAGE TWO

Web site

Publishing your own Web site makes the Internet work harder for your business. As well as serving as a shop window to the world at large, your Web site can enable customers to communicate with you at any time, from anywhere. A Web site gives even the smallest local business a global presence.

STAGE FOUR

E-business

This is where your business processes are increasingly driven by Internet technology. Through secure Intranets and Extranets, your remote workers, customers and suppliers can be given access to areas of your internal network, delivering a major boost to your productivity and dramatically reducing your operating costs. At the same time, you have greater control of every stage of the business process.

Word Partnerships 2

Match the following words from the text to form word partnerships. Refer to the text only if you need to.

a.	exchange	orders via a Web site
b.	publish	customers to communicate
c.	enable	data
d.	place	a Web site

e.	engage in	operating costs
f.	trade	e-commerce
g.	deliver	24 hours a day
h.	reduce	service and support

Find the Expressions

Find words and phrases in the text which mean:

1. a dramatic increase (Stage 1)
2. allows your product or service to be noticed (Stage 2)
3. the general public (Stage 2)
4. a place in the world market (Stage 2)
5. over the Internet (Stage 3)
6. falls substantially (Stage 3)
7. an in-company network (Stage 4)
8. a network between a company and its main customers or suppliers (Stage 4)
9. tele-workers or people who work from home (Stage 4)
10. the most advanced or sophisticated businesses (Stage 5)
11. highly important (Stage 5)
12. the organisation of supplies and services in a complex process (Stage 5)
13. using machines (Stage 5)
14. unbroken (Stage 5)
15. never seen before (Stage 5)

Which Stage?

Match the following remarks to the first four stages of 'Internet Evolution'.

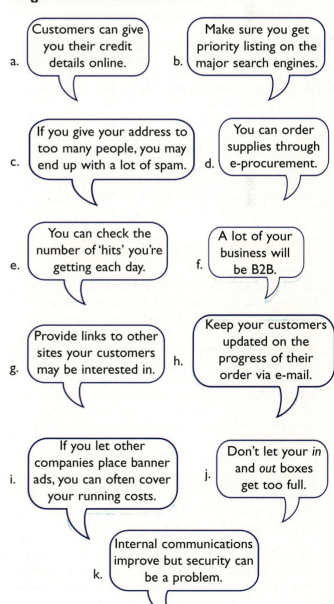

a. Customers can give you their credit details online.

b. Make sure you get priority listing on the major search engines.

c. If you give your address to too many people, you may end up with a lot of spam.

d. You can order supplies through e-procurement.

e. You can check the number of 'hits' you're getting each day.

f. A lot of your business will be B2B.

g. Provide links to other sites your customers may be interested in.

h. Keep your customers updated on the progress of their order via e-mail.

i. If you let other companies place banner ads, you can often cover your running costs.

j. Don't let your *in* and *out* boxes get too full.

k. Internal communications improve but security can be a problem.

Fluency Work

Dotcom Clinic

Work in groups. You are the directors of a small e-business consultancy, Expertise.com. You promote your services by offering initial recommendations to potential clients on the basis of a short online interview with them.

What advice would you give to the following struggling dotcoms? Draft a short e-mail to each.

Case Study 1

onecarefulowner.co.uk is a British-based e-business specialising in selling second-hand cars over the Net. Though it's had some success at the luxury end of the market selling used Jaguars and BMWs at heavily discounted prices, after two years in business, it has yet to make an overall profit. It seems buyers are reluctant to commit themselves to such a significant purchase without a test-drive.

Case Study 2

BiblioFiles.com is a US-based publisher and retailer of e-books (mostly fiction), which can be purchased on their Web site and downloaded using free software by the purchaser. Though e-books are supposed to be the next big thing in publishing, most people still seem reluctant to read long texts on-screen and e-book reading hardware has failed to catch on in a big way. There is also the problem of illegal copying.

Case Study 3

Meeeow.com is an e-tailer of pet food and supplies. Based in California, it was one of the pioneers in this line of business, but since them a flood of competitors have entered the market, making it increasingly difficult to maintain brand recognition. Though the 'clicks' side of the business runs fairly smoothly, there have been some problems on the 'bricks' side – warehousing and delivery, both of which are outsourced to other companies.

Case Study 4

dreamtree.nl is a manufacturer of environmentally-friendly and cruelty-free cosmetics based in the Netherlands. Dream Tree normally distributes its high quality and expensively packaged products through chemists, airports and the more upmarket supermarkets. The e-commerce branch of the company is relatively new but so far the response has been disappointing. A state-of-the-art Web site has failed to attract sufficient customers to break even in the first six months.

Case Study 5

saber.es is a Spanish Web site offering vocational training in secretarial skills, paralegal studies and languages for business online. A large percentage of the company's seed capital was spent on developing the software to deliver the courses designed by saber's commercial partner The Vocational College of Navarra. Spaniards are often reluctant to travel to receive education and the company expected to capitalise on this, but they wonder if they should be offering different courses. Another problem is the perception that online courses are not as good as 'the real thing'.

Case Study 6

informatech.co.uk is a specialist information service based in London. The company operates by buying access to archives and databases all over the world, organising the information in a user-friendly way and selling access-time to clients in business, legal and scientific communities. A recent heavily publicised breach of the informatech security system by hackers, who were never traced, has resulted in a loss of confidence amongst users, many of whom are concerned about their own research becoming public knowledge.

Case Study 7

clevermoney.com is a US-based financial consultancy offering advice to private and corporate investors online. Though it's a highly competitive market, business has so far been good, with the company poised to move into profit in the next 18 months. The main problem is a 'braindrain' of talent amongst the staff to rival companies. Generous salaries and bonuses do not seem to be stemming this. Some of the company's best advisers are also losing confidence in dotcoms altogether and taking jobs on Wall Street.

Meeting Skills

The Language of Meetings

Language Focus

Which statements about meetings do you agree with?

> They tend to go on forever.

> They allow people to express opinions and issues.

> I hate meetings. They're a waste of time.

> It's important to have interdepartmental meetings.

> It's essential to have an agenda and stick to it.

> They're a vital part of a company's operations.

> The most important meetings are the ones you have one-on-one, on a daily basis.

Discuss your opinions with the class.

Listening

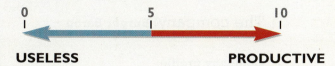

Listen to the meeting held at a company called Hands-On Software. Give the meeting a score from 1 to 10.

```
0               5              10
|               |               |
←────────────────────────────────→
USELESS                  PRODUCTIVE
```

Discuss the score you gave the meeting with the class.

Key Language

1. **These are useful expressions you heard in the meeting. Listen again and match them.**

1.	Can we get …	a. when I say …
2.	As I'm sure you're …	b. I have to disagree.
3.	I'd just like to …	c. started?
4.	I think I speak for everyone …	d. say that …
5.	That's an issue to be dealt with …	e. favor of …
6.	All in …	f. at another time.
7.	I'm sorry, but …	g. all aware, …
8.	The first order of …	h. what Paul said about …
9.	Sorry, I just …	i. second, please.
10.	Just a …	j. thoughts on that, actually.
11.	I'm sorry, I'm not sure …	k. but …
12.	Going back to …	l. wanted to say that …
13.	I have some …	m. I follow.
14.	Sorry to interrupt, …	n. business is …

2. **Now match the expressions above with the following.**

a. You want to ask a question.
b. You want to return to an earlier point.
c. You want to begin.
d. You want to disagree.
e. You want to gather support.
f. You want to give your opinion.
g. You want to interrupt.
h. You want to stay on track.

Case Study

Study the situation below.

The company: Burger Baron

Company profile:

Over 600 restaurants worldwide, including Asia, all of Europe and most of the Americas. Burger Baron specialises in fast food, mostly hamburgers, French fries, milkshakes, etc., operating almost exclusively in shopping malls.

The problem:

Over the last 3 years, Burger Baron has seen its market share declining rapidly and has had to shut 42 restaurants during the same period. The head office blames the main competitors, McDougal's and Winnie's, who have been increasing meal sizes and decreasing prices.

The competition have also added 'fat-free' and 'reduced fat' options to their menus, responding to growing consumer concern over weight problems. To make matters even worse, there has recently been a global disease-related meat scare, and Burger Baron is one of several fast-food chains that have been targeted in a media-hyped class-action lawsuit, claiming that the restaurant is responsible for increasing rates of serious health problems like diabetes and heart failure.

Hold a meeting using the expressions you heard in the meeting in the listening.

Today's meeting: Develop a plan of action on all fronts to protect Burger Baron's image and regain losses in market share.

Divide the class into the following departments to prepare for today's meeting.

Management
Shareholders want to see quick action or you know some heads are going to roll. Your job will be to make changes while still keeping costs down.

Marketing
You are being accused of a terrible job of brand management. Put together a plan to rebuild the company's image.

Product Development
The pressure is on you to come up with solutions on the product level. Can changes be made to the menu?

After preparing, sequence the meeting like this:

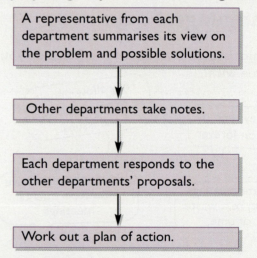

A representative from each department summarises its view on the problem and possible solutions.

↓

Other departments take notes.

↓

Each department responds to the other departments' proposals.

↓

Work out a plan of action.

Follow Up

Discuss these questions as a class.

- Do you think the meeting was productive? Why?
- Could the meeting have been more productive/efficient? How?
- Which department had the best performance in the meeting? Why?
- Were there any other expressions (not studied in this book) that came up during the meeting?
- What would be a polite way of stopping someone from interrupting you during a meeting?
- If you have something important to say, but others talk over you, what can you do or say?

Brand Management

UNIT 4

A Follower of Fashion?

What do the following terms mean to you? Discuss them with your colleagues.

- brand loyalty
- brand-awareness
- brandstretching
- own label products
- me-tooism
- subliminal advertising
- lookalike products
- market saturation

How important is image to you? Are you very choosy about the kind of clothes you wear, the sort of car you drive, the make of watch you have? Are you as fussy when it comes to the coffee and cornflakes on your breakfast table?

Creating an Image

To find out how selective and loyal a consumer you are, try the following extract from a market research questionnaire. In each section, choose the statement you prefer, a or b.

1
a. Coke and Pepsi really do taste better than other colas I've tried.

b. One fizzy drink is pretty much the same as another to me.

2
a. I wouldn't wear a cheap watch or cheap jewellery because they're a reflection of your personality.

b. I wear a watch to tell the time and jewellery for fun. I don't care what they cost if they look all right.

3
a. I wouldn't be seen dead wearing one of those Mickey Mouse fake Rolexes.

b. I'd definitely wear a fake Rolex or Omega watch if it looked just like the real thing.

4
a. I like my Audi, but if I could afford the same sort of Mercedes, I'd buy one of those instead.

b. For me, the most important thing is a car's performance and economy, not its make.

5
a. I'd pay a lot more for a garment with a famous label in it because quality always shows.

b. I'd never waste money on a silly label when you can get the same garment for half the price elsewhere.

6
a. Cheap coffee tastes horrible. I don't cheat myself by saving a few pence.

b. It all tastes the same after the first three cups!

7
a. I usually stick to the same brand of cigarettes and I wouldn't dream of switching.*

b. I'll smoke anything, as long as it doesn't taste of fresh air.*

Non-smokers needn't answer this question.

Compare your answers with those of your colleagues. Then read the article, *Brand Wars*.

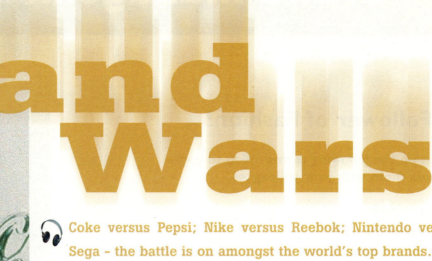

Brand Wars

🎧 **Coke versus Pepsi; Nike versus Reebok; Nintendo versus Sega - the battle is on amongst the world's top brands.**

Aggressive comparative advertising has now reached fever pitch; extra millions are pouring into R&D, and the market leaders are under constant pressure to slash their prices in a cut-throat struggle for market domination. When Philip Morris knocked 40c off a packet of Marlboro, $47-and-a-half billion was instantly wiped off the market value of America's top twenty cigarette manufacturers. Lesser brands went to the wall. And that's just one example of how fair competition within a free market has rapidly escalated into all-out brand war.

Own-Label Products

Yet, in spite of the efforts of the corporate heavyweights to win market share, when it comes to fast-moving consumer goods, more and more consumers are switching to the supermarkets' own-label products. And brand loyalty is fast becoming a thing of the past. The once unchallengeable Nescafé and Kellogg's are actually losing sales, as their higher price is no longer automatically associated with higher quality. And in many supermarkets across Europe and the States own-labels now account for over fifty-five per cent of total sales. Their turnover has never been higher.

Lookalike Coke

Of course, the big brands are not giving in without a fight. When British supermarket chain, Sainsbury's, led the attack on Coke by launching its own similarly packaged product, it managed to secure fifteen per cent of the total UK cola market in just two months. But Coca-Cola was quick to respond. Sainsbury's was told to change its packaging fast or Coke would cut its prices to rival supermarkets and leave Sainsbury's hopelessly overpriced. Some people say the Sainsbury's cola tastes as good as Coke. But they're the ones who underestimate the power of the brand.

Big Brands - Big Business

Brand names are still the reason Omega can put a 300% mark-up on their watches, the reason Nestlé spent a fortune buying Perrier, the reason investors are prepared to pay up to twelve times the book value for a company's stock. Big brands remain big business in the City.

Brandstretching

Brandstretching is another way in which the household names are fighting back. By putting their familiar trademark on attractive and fashionable new products, companies can both generate additional revenue and increase brand–awareness, hence Pepsi Maxwear, Virgin Cola, Camel Adventure Gear clothing and even jewellery by Cadbury! The high–life image suits companies like Philip Morris, for whom, as the restrictions on tobacco ads get tougher, brandstretching is the perfect form of subliminal advertising.

Buyer Beware

So much for the high-street brands. Further upmarket, the luxury branded goods manufacturers are facing an even greater enemy of their own, namely, the pirate brands. And as the trade in lookalike products increases, companies like Ray-Ban and Reebok, Yves Saint Laurent and Armani are calling for a crackdown on the pirates. In Europe over ten per cent of clothes and footwear sold are said to be fakes, costing the firms who make the real thing nearly $7 billion a year. For a fraction of the recommended retail price you can pick up fake Gucci, fake Lacoste, fake Lego, fake Disney, fake Nintendo, fake anything. But buyer beware! Your case of Möet et Chandon will probably turn out to be cider and your bottle of Calvin Klein more like industrial cleaner than perfume.

Market Saturation

But, brand wars aside, the single biggest threat to the market remains saturation. For it seems there are just too many products on the shelves. In the States they call this 'product clutter' and it is currently the cause of a strong anti-consumerism movement. In fact, product proliferation and widespread 'me-tooism' mean that some Boots stores actually stock seventy-five different kinds of toothbrush and 240 types of shampoo. It would take you over twenty years to try them all, assuming you even wanted to! And that's just got to be crazy when you think that eighty to ninety per cent of new brands fail within their first six months.

Recall

Without referring back to the article, can you remember in what context the following companies were mentioned?

1. Philip Morris / Marlboro
2. Nestlé
3. Coca-Cola
4. Omega
5. Cadbury
6. Möet et Chandon
7. Calvin Klein
8. Boots

Response

Having read the article, what can you now say about the marketing terms you discussed earlier?

brand loyalty   brand-awareness
brandstretching   own label products
me-tooism   subliminal advertising
lookalike products   market saturation

Find the Expressions

Look back at the article. Find the expressions which mean:

1. has now reached a ridiculous level (paragraph 1)
2. to cut drastically (paragraph 1)
3. fiercely competitive (paragraph 1)
4. took 40c off (paragraph 1)
5. went bankrupt (paragraph 1)
6. major companies (paragraph 2)
7. total sales before costs are deducted (paragraph 2)
8. profit margin (paragraph 4)
9. pay a lot of money for (paragraph 4)
10. official value of an asset (paragraph 4)
11. extra income (paragraph 5)
12. severe measures against law-breakers (paragraph 6)

Language Focus

Word Partnerships 1

Match each of the words in the first column with a word from the second column to make twelve word partnerships from the article. There are some alternative partnerships, but there is only one way to match all twelve.

1.	aggressive	a.	names
2.	household	b.	products
3.	me-	c.	advertising
4.	lookalike	d.	tooism

5.	retail	e.	goods
6.	supermarket	f.	market
7.	branded	g.	chain
8.	free	h.	sales

9.	subliminal	i.	consumerism
10.	anti-	j.	retail price
11.	fair	k.	advertising
12.	recommended	l.	competition

Discuss

- Is your company a household name?
- To what extent do your company's products or services rely on your name?
- Are they upmarket or downmarket?
- How do you differentiate them from those of your competitors?

Word Partnerships 2

The following nouns form strong word partnerships with the word *market*. Find five more in the article you have just read.

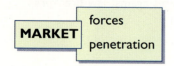

Word Partnerships 3

The following nouns form strong word partnerships with the word *brand*. Find three more in the article you have just read.

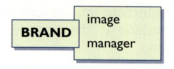

Discuss

A common criticism of target-marketing is that there are just too many identical products crowding the marketplace. Do you agree? Does your company have a problem with product proliferation?

Word Partnerships 4

Which 8-letter word can come before all the following words?

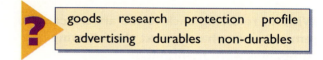

Now match these word partnerships with the following definitions:

1. commercials aimed at the end-user
2. goods used shortly after purchase such as food, newspapers, etc.
3. products purchased by a member of the public
4. goods which last a long time such as cars, televisions, etc.
5. laws to defend buyers against unfair trading
6. market study of buyer behaviour patterns
7. description of a typical buyer according to age, sex, social status, etc.

Word Partnerships 5

Without referring back to the article, complete the information flowchart with appropriate words.

 Now listen to the recording again and check your answers.

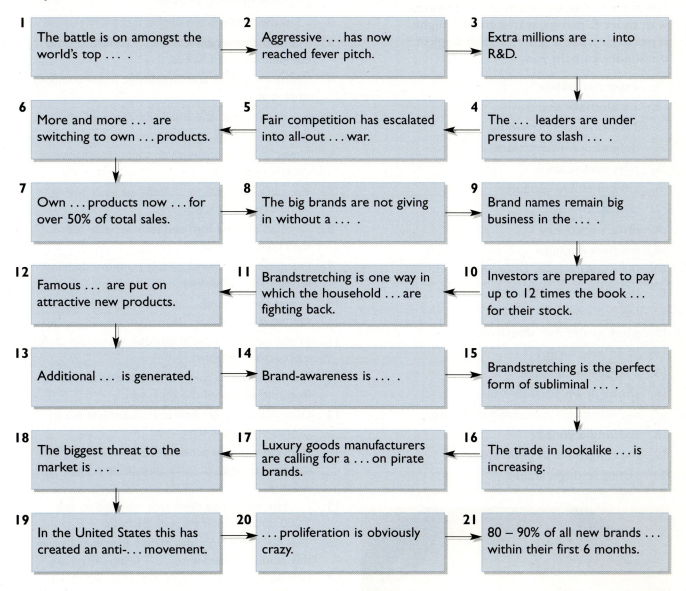

1 The battle is on amongst the world's top . . . .

2 Aggressive . . . has now reached fever pitch.

3 Extra millions are . . . into R&D.

6 More and more . . . are switching to own . . . products.

5 Fair competition has escalated into all-out . . . war.

4 The . . . leaders are under pressure to slash . . . .

7 Own . . . products now . . . for over 50% of total sales.

8 The big brands are not giving in without a . . . .

9 Brand names remain big business in the . . . .

12 Famous . . . are put on attractive new products.

11 Brandstretching is one way in which the household . . . are fighting back.

10 Investors are prepared to pay up to 12 times the book . . . for their stock.

13 Additional . . . is generated.

14 Brand-awareness is . . . .

15 Brandstretching is the perfect form of subliminal . . . .

18 The biggest threat to the market is . . . .

17 Luxury goods manufacturers are calling for a . . . on pirate brands.

16 The trade in lookalike . . . is increasing.

19 In the United States this has created an anti-. . . movement.

20 . . . proliferation is obviously crazy.

21 80 – 90% of all new brands . . . within their first 6 months.

Presenting

Use the completed flowchart above to give a team presentation of the information in the article. Hand over to another presenter after every three pieces of information.

You will need to link the main points together with some of the following words and phrases:

> ok   so   and   but   however   although   whereas
> in fact   on the other hand   with the result that

Language Focus

Business Metaphors

A lot of the language of business and marketing is full of metaphor. Group the following business expressions according to where you think the words in bold originally come from. Choose from the following: war, sport & games, water, health, flight. If necessary, use a good English-English dictionary to help you.

1. a takeover **battle**
2. a **stalemate** situation
3. a few orders are **trickling in**
4. **defend** our market share
5. sales have **soared**
6. a **flood** of new products
7. take **a time out**
8. make a **recovery**
9. the **flow** of capital
10. the company really **took off**
11. the company is **suffering**
12. the economy is **in freefall**
13. **pour** money into advertising
14. be an easy **target**
15. a **strategic alliance**
16. **shoot down** someone's idea
17. the market has completely **dried up**
18. **backing a winner**
19. the company is **in good shape**
20. playing for **high stakes**

Use the Expressions

Now use the expressions to complete the following sentences.

1. It was a ... – neither side in the negotiation was prepared to move an inch!
2. ... in the 1990s when profits increased tenfold.
3. The two companies formed ... to fight off the competition from Korea.
4. We're ... , Ladies and Gentlemen – the company itself is at risk.
5. In a ... it's often the small shareholders who decide who wins.
6. Never ... until you've given them the chance to explain what it is.
7. We can't continue to ... until we start seeing some sign that it's working.
8. ... to an all-time high and look set stay high for the rest of the year.
9. I'm afraid ... – there's simply no more demand for this kind of service.
10. Perhaps we should ... and meet back here in, say, ten minutes?
11. In our current financial position we would ... for a predator company.
12. Poor turnover is partly due to the fact that ... from the effects of the recession.
13. Liberalising the markets in Ecuador just led to ... out of the country.
14. In giving this new product the go-ahead, believe me, you're really ... – it's sure to be a huge success.
15. ... , but, when you think that we used to sell 1,000 units a day, frankly it's pathetic.
16. This big order from the Middle East is just what this company needed to ... – finally things are looking up.
17. ... has made it impossible for us to rely on brand loyalty from our customers – there's simply too much choice.
18. In spite of media reports to the contrary, ... and ready to break into new markets with this product.
19. We clearly need to ... if we are to remain the market leader.
20. Inflation is running at 66%, unemployment is up nearly 30%, our trade deficit is enormous and, to be honest, ...

Business Grammar

For many companies successful marketing begins with the successful sales letter. Read through the following text on how to write the perfect sales letter. Choose a suitable word for each blank. Then listen and compare your answers.

Do you (1) ... stop to think about what happens (2) ... your sales letters after they leave your desk? You (3) ... spend hours drafting and redrafting them. But do you give a moment's thought to how your reader (4) ... react to them when they arrive? If (5) ..., don't write another word until you do.

Before you write your next letter, put (6) ... in the shoes of the customer. Make it reader-friendly. The majority (7) ... sales letters get filed, lost or binned. The reader-friendly letter stands (8) ... better chance.

Rule number one: never insult your reader with what is (9) ... a mass-mailed letter. True, mass mailing is the quickest way (10) ... reaching hundreds of potential customers. It's also the safest way of ensuring that your letter ends up in the bin. A short personalised letter, (11) ... gets to the point and clearly demonstrates (12) ... knowledge of the customer's needs, will invariably be better received.

As a general rule, the more important (13) ... person, the shorter your letter (14) ... be. Managing Directors are deluged with mail. They rarely have time to do (15) ... than glance at it and are unlikely to respond (16) ... your letter themselves. So in writing to MDs be brief. Junior managers, on the (17) ... hand, are generally looking for ideas they can pinch and present to the boss (18) ... their own. (19) ... them long and informative letters.

(20) ... to Mark McCormack, author of *What They Don't Teach You at Harvard Business School*, different levels of management (21) ... responsive to different sales approaches. Senior management is usually (22) ... for strategic solutions to long-term problems which fit in (23) ... their corporate goals. Middle managers want tactical answers (24) ... departmental problems which will (25) ... their lives simpler and which they (26) ... easily justify to their bosses. What junior executives (27) ... is technical help to tackle immediate problems. Adapt your proposal accordingly.

If you've (28) ... three proposals to make to a customer, send three short letters (29) ... of one long one. It saves the reader having to wade through a lengthy document and it obviously (30) ... it easier to pass the proposals on to the appropriate people. Above (31) ..., it makes an impression. It shows style.

Some of the best sales letters don't look (32) ... sales letters at (33) ... . Get someone in your research department to write (34) ... a memo outlining how, with your help, your prospect's company (35) ... be improving its business. Then send the memo on to the company explaining how you thought it might (36) ... of interest. Make your sales letter (37) ... like 'inside information' and you'll make it compulsive reading.

Remember, there's no (38) ... thing as a good sales letter that nobody reads. And (39) ... the meaning of the message is the response it gets, you can go a long (40) ... towards anticipating the response you'll get before you write a single word.

How many word partnerships can you find in the text above?

Discuss

What do you generally do with the sales letters that arrive on your desk? Do you ever read them or do they tend to be filed in the wastepaper basket?

Fluency Work

Product Development

Work in pairs or small groups to develop a competitive new product to challenge an established brand name.

1. Identify a household name. You should choose a product either in one of the fast-moving consumer goods markets such as food, soft drinks, alcoholic drinks, cigarettes, or cosmetics. Alternatively, choose a product from the luxury branded goods market such as perfume, watches, or fashion.

   TARGET BRAND: ...

2. Investigate the popularity of the brand name. Identify three factors which contribute to the universal appeal of the product. Is it a unique product? If so, what are its special characteristics? If not, to what does it owe its popularity? Is it quality, image, availability, or price?

   MAIN SELLING POINTS
   1. ...   2. ...   3. ...

3. Come up with an idea for a new product to compete with the brand name. Consider the following: market positioning (upmarket or downmarket?), pricing strategy, main selling points in comparison with the brand name, packaging, advertising.

   DETAILS & FEATURES: ...

   NAME OF NEW PRODUCT: ...

4. Produce a consumer profile of the customer you are trying to attract. You need to take account of age, sex, socio-economic group, and lifestyle.

   CONSUMER PROFILE: ...

5. Devise a simple slogan to promote the product.

   SLOGAN: ...

Finally, present your idea to the others as one of the following:

An R&D team – seeking the go-ahead for the new product from the board.
Sales managers – briefing your reps on the new product.
Sales reps – highlighting the features of the new product to the purchasing department of a major retail outlet.

Value for Money

Which of the following points of view is nearer to your own?

"It is not the aim of this company to make more money than is prudent."
Lord Rayner, Marks and Spencer

"Pan Am takes good care of you.
Marks and Spencer love you.
At Amstrad we want your money."
Alan Sugar, founder of Amstrad.

Compare your views with those of your colleagues.

Since the only legitimate object of doing business is to make a decent profit, few things can be as important as the price tag you put on what you sell. But price is actually one of the hardest things to determine, and it's not so much a question of what a thing is worth as how much you can reasonably expect to get for it.

How do you think the general public think prices are fixed?

How would **you** define price?

- As a true reflection of value?
- Costs plus mark-up?
- Whatever the market will stand?

Now read the article, *If the Price is Right*.

If the Price is Right ...

A personal computer wouldn't cost twice as much in the UK as it does in the States and you wouldn't need to take out a bank loan to buy a coffee in the Champs-Elysées. Of course, strictly speaking, the computer is tradeable and the coffee non-tradeable. For tradeable goods are exported all over the world, but non-tradeables have to be consumed where they are produced. And, since a café noir halfway up the Eiffel Tower can only be purchased in Paris, frankly, they can charge what they like for it. But, tradeable or not, as every salesperson knows, "The price of a thing is what it will bring." And when it comes to price, the buyer is his own worst enemy. Show me a high price and I'll show you too many customers prepared to pay over the odds.

The truth is, people pay the price they deserve. A massive twenty per cent mark-up does not stop people buying a billion cans of Coke a day. And with profit margins of up to a phenomenal fifty per cent, Philip Morris can still gross around $100 billion a year, making the makers of Marlboro cigarettes the most profitable company in the world.

In fact, product-pricing lies at the very heart of the marketing process itself. Its impact is felt in sales volume, in the product's contribution to overall profits and, above all, in the strategic position the product occupies in the marketplace. For a higher price will often raise a product's profile and a high product profile commands a higher price. Product profile is basically the difference between a Rolex and a Timex, a bottle of Chanel No.5 and a bottle of Boots No.7. So, of course, is price.

But it isn't as simple as that. Economic, as well as market forces are at work. If they were not, we might expect international competition to equalise prices everywhere, but in spite of all the talk of a single market, a borderless Europe and a common currency, prices remain alarmingly elastic. And what goes for a song in one country can cost a bomb in another.

For one thing, most commodities, particularly agricultural products, are usually heavily subsidized. So, in the absence of free trade, food will tend to be cheap in the USA, cheaper still in Central and South America, expensive in Europe and outrageously so in Japan. Trade barriers compound the problem. For sadly, those who took part in the last round of GATT could barely reach general agreement on where to have lunch.

So how do you put a price on things? An everyday supermarket item in one country might be a luxury item in another and cost considerably more. Scotch, for instance, is a mass market product in Aberdeen but understandably a niche market product in Abu Dhabi. No prizes for guessing where it's cheaper.

Then, of course, there are taxes. By imposing wildly different rates of tax on otherwise homogeneous commodities like petrol, governments distort prices even further. If you're driving through Europe, you'd certainly do better to fill up in Luxembourg than in Italy. Tax is also the reason why a Jaguar car costs less in Brussels than in Britain, where it was built.

So buy your car in Belgium, your fridge and other 'white goods' in the UK; stock up on medicines in France and on CDs in Germany. That way you'll be sure to get the best deal. For where you spend your money is almost as important as what you spend it on, but neither is as important as the fact that you're prepared to spend it. In the words of film actor Cary Grant, "Money talks, they say. All it ever said to me was *Goodbye.*"

Recall

Without referring back to the article, how much can you remember about:

1. computers
2. Coca-Cola
3. Marlboro cigarettes
4. Rolex and Chanel
5. food
6. GATT
7. Scotch whisky
8. Jaguar cars
9. fridges
10. CDs

Find the Expressions

Find the expressions in the article which mean:

1. to be absolutely accurate (paragraph 2)
2. pay more for something than it's worth (paragraph 2)
3. money will get you anything (paragraph 9)

Read the text again. Find:

4. three words you want to use more often.
5. three word partnerships you need, with their equivalents in your own language.
6. three longer expressions, with their equivalents in your own language.

Language Focus

Word Partnerships 1

The following business words appeared in the article in the order in which they are listed. How many of their word partners can you find in just five minutes?

BUSINESS WORD	WORD PARTNERS	BUSINESS WORD	WORD PARTNERS	BUSINESS WORD	WORD PARTNERS
1. tradeable	. . .	6. strategic	. . .	11. free	. . .
2. profit	. . .	7. product	. . .	12. trade	. . .
3. product	. . .	8. market	. . .	13. luxury	. . .
4. sales	. . .	9. borderless	. . .	14. mass	. . .
5. overall	. . .	10. common	. . .	15. niche	. . .

Choose the eight most useful word partnerships and find an equivalent for them in your own language.

Cheap or Expensive?

Decide whether the following expressions mean *expensive* or *cheap*.

1. It cost the earth.
2. It cost a bomb.
3. It was going for a song.
4. It cost peanuts.
5. It cost a fortune.
6. They were practically giving it away.
7. It cost an arm and a leg.
8. It was a real bargain.
9. It cost a packet.

Word Grammar

In each example, use the word in CAPITALS to make another form of the word, which will fit in the sentence.

1. TRADE
   . . . goods are exported all over the world.

2. TRADE
   China is rapidly becoming one of the world's main . . . nations.

3. PROFIT
   Unfortunately, the product didn't turn out to be very . . . .

4. PROFIT
   The ratio of net profit to sales will give us an idea of the company's overall . . . .

5. PROFIT
   I think we have all . . . from a sharp increase in demand.

6. COMPETE
   We've lost market share because our products are no longer . . . .

7. COMPETE
   In the oil industry our main . . . are obviously the Arabs and the Americans.

8. COMPETE
   With so many similar products available already, the . . . is very stiff.

9. PRICE
   It's high time we had a thorough review of our . . . policy before we . . . ourselves out of the market.

10. PRICE
    Some of their products are a bit . . . . We can get the same thing cheaper elsewhere.

Discuss

- What is the most expensive thing you've ever bought for cash?
- What's the best bargain you've ever picked up? Have you ever been badly ripped off?

Word Partnerships 2

All the words below form strong partnerships with the words *prices* and *price*, but the vowels are missing from each word. How many can you work out?

VERB + *price(s)*	ADJECTIVE + *price(s)*	*price* + NOUN
1. c _ t		15. c _ t
2. f _ x	9. f _ x _ d	16. w _ r
3. s l _ s h	10. c _ m p _ t _ t _ v _	17. r _ s _
4. r _ d _ c _	11. r _ _ s _ n _ b l _	18. r _ d _ c t _ _ n
5. r _ _ s _	12. _ t t r _ c t _ v _	19. s _ n s _ t _ v _ty
6. q _ _ t _	13. _ l _ s t _ c	20. _ l _ s t _ c _ty
7. f r _ _ z _	14. _ n b _ _ t _ b l _	21. _ n d _ x
8. _ q _ _ l _ z _		22. h _ k _

Word Partnerships 3

Now complete the following using some of the word partnerships above.

1. If we accept your offer, we will expect you to . . . prices at their present level for the next 12 months.

2. If we all keep reducing our prices, we'll end up with a price . . . on our hands.

3. You can't buy cheaper. Our prices are not just . . . , they're . . . .

4. We more than cut our prices – we . . . them by 35%!

5. The price of most things is pretty . . . . It depends on where you buy them and what the demand is.

6. Talk about a price . . .! They've practically doubled their prices every six weeks!

7. We think the price you've . . . us is very reasonable. You've got yourself a deal.

8. Acute price . . . has prevented us from raising our prices.

Discuss

• What's the difference between mark-up and profit margin?

• Roughly, what are the profit margins for the products or services you're most closely involved with?

Money Expressions

Rearrange the following to make useful business expressions. The first word is in the right place.

1. Let's figures talk.
2. Just a look figures take the at.
3. Can us you a figure rough give?
4. How these at did arrive you figures?
5. Where these did from come figures?
6. The speak figures themselves for.
7. The encouraging not very are figures.
8. Can it you a on put figure?

Which of the above expressions mean:

a. you want an approximate figure?
b. the figures are bad?
c. the figures need no explanation?
d. you're not sure you believe the figures? (two expressions)
e. you want a fairly precise figure?

Discuss

What kind of figures are the critical indicators in your own line of business?

• economic statistics
• market figures
• demographic trends

Language Focus

Word Partnerships 4

Now match the following words and phrases to complete these notes on the article you read earlier. Referring back to the text will help you. The first sentence has been done for you as an example.

SUBJECT	VERB	COMPLEMENT
1. Tradeable goods	are consumed	to pay over the odds.
2. Non-tradeables	are prepared	all over the world.
3. Too many customers	are exported	where they are produced.
4. People	lies	the price they deserve.
5. Product pricing	is felt	in sales volume and profits.
6. Its impact	pay	at the heart of the marketing process.
7. Every product	usually commands	a product's profile.
8. A high price	occupies	a higher price.
9. A high product profile	often raises	a strategic position in the marketplace.
10. Economic and market forces	are heavily	at work.
11. Prices	are also	subsidised.
12. Most commodities	remain	elastic.
13. Trade barriers	distort	on homogeneous commodities.
14. Different rates of tax	compound	prices even further.
15. Governments	are imposed	the problem.

Can you link these notes together to produce a short summary of the article? You will need extra words and phrases to connect up the facts. The first sentence has been done for you

but	because	for	whereas	in fact
the fact is	for example	for one thing	so, basically	by

Whereas tradeable goods are exported all over the world, non-tradeables are consumed where they are produced. But in both cases too many customers . . .

Discuss

- What are the main factors influencing the price of the products or services you offer?
- How do government taxes and subsidies affect your prices?

Trends 1

Which graph illustrates the movement described in these sentences?

1. The market is showing some signs of growth.

2. The market is extremely volatile.

3. The pound slipped back against the dollar.

4. The Swiss franc is staging a recovery.

5. The Euro lost ground slightly.

6. There's been a dramatic downturn in the market.

7. There's been an upsurge of interest in gold.

8. The share price bottomed out at 115p.

9. Sugar peaked at $400 a tonne.

10. Profits will level off at around £1.1bn.

11. Sales hit an all-time low.

12. There hasn't been much movement in the price of tin.

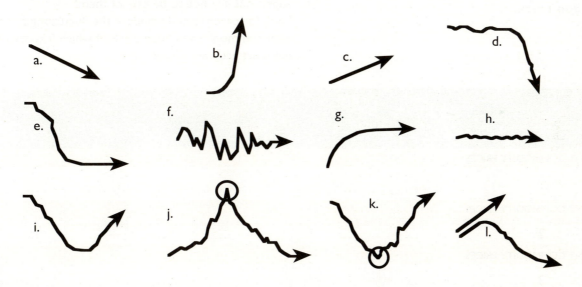

Trends 2

The financial press is full of expressions of change and development.
Match each verb below with the type of change it describes.

slump	rise	recover	plunge	pick up	plummet
drop	soar	bounce back	take off	climb	rally
fluctuate	fall	stabilise	slide	flatten out	crash
hold steady	escalate	decline	rocket	dip	

Fluency Work

Case Study: Sumitomo Bank

Listen to the story of the famous Sumitomo Bank copper scandal and answer the questions.

1. Why is investing in commodities such a high-risk business?

2. Who was Mr 5%?

3. How much money did he lose the Sumitomo Bank?

4. Why do you think it took so long for the bank to find out what was going on?

You are about to compete in the dangerous world of commodity trading. Work in small groups. You will start off with US$100,000,000 of capital to speculate with and may buy, sell or hold any or all of the seven commodities in which you trade.

 Information Updates

Every ten minutes you will hear an information update detailing the current commodity prices and giving you an up-to-the-minute forecast on likely changes in trading prices for each commodity. On the basis of this information you should agree on what to buy, sell or hold during this trading session. Keep a record of all your transactions. There are eight trading sessions in all.

Your Objective

Your objective is to make as much money as possible by the end of the final session. You may not borrow extra capital and may therefore need to fund purchases of a commodity whose price you believe to be going up by selling your holdings in a commodity whose price you think may be about to fall. Be careful – not all the forecasts are accurate!

Beware!

Remember, 85% of all commodity speculators get wiped out. Try not to be one of them!
Look for patterns and trends in the fluctuating price of each commodity and keep track of which forecasts are the most accurate. Good luck!

TRADING SESSION	CAPITAL	GOLD $/troy oz	SILVER $/troy oz	COPPER $/tonne	TIN $/tonne	COFFEE $/tonne	SUGAR $/tonne	OIL $/barrel
Start	$100,000,000	0	0	0	0	0	0	0
CURRENT COMMODITY PRICES								
1		...	...	...	...	...	...	...
CURRENT COMMODITY PRICES								
2		...	...	...	...	...	...	...
CURRENT COMMODITY PRICES								
3		...	...	...	...	...	...	...
CURRENT COMMODITY PRICES								
4		...	...	...	...	...	...	...
CURRENT COMMODITY PRICES								
5		...	...	...	...	...	...	...
CURRENT COMMODITY PRICES								
6		...	...	...	...	...	...	...
CURRENT COMMODITY PRICES								
7		...	...	...	...	...	...	...
CURRENT COMMODITY PRICES								
8		...	...	...	...	...	...	...
TOTAL ASSETS:								

What's your Price?

Some companies seem only too happy to spend enormous sums of money on their best clients in order to 'keep them sweet'. Does this make good business sense or is it just another form of corruption? When is a gift a bribe? And where do you draw the line?

Can you be bought? To find out how 'open to persuasion' you are, try the following test:

1. **One of the suppliers tendering for a contract with your company invites you out for lunch at a top-class restaurant in London to 'talk things over'. Do you ...**
   a. Insist that you cannot be bought and remove the supplier's name from your shortlist?
   b. Politely refuse, saying that you never mix business with pleasure?
   c. Take advantage of the situation by ordering a more expensive meal than you usually have?
   d. Give yourself a real treat – caviar, lobster, vintage champagne, the best brandy?

2. **You have been asked to choose a venue for your company's annual conference. The manager of one of the hotels you are considering mentions that there could be a week's holiday in it for you and your family. Do you ...**
   a. Report him to his regional manager?
   b. Smile and point out that free holidays are not a condition for winning the contract?
   c. Gratefully accept a large en suite room with minibar and a view of the bay?
   d. Ask him if he could manage a fortnight and include the use of a car?

3. **The father of an applicant for a post in your company sends you a Rolex watch and a case of Bollinger champagne for Christmas. Do you ...**
   a. Send them back with a note saying: 'Thanks, but no thanks'?
   b. Return the watch, drink the champagne and forget the name of his son?
   c. Give his son the job immediately and ask him if he has any other children looking for work?
   d. Write him a letter saying you never received the matching Rolex he obviously intended for your partner?

For an analysis of your answers see page 155.

Looking after the
Twenty Percent

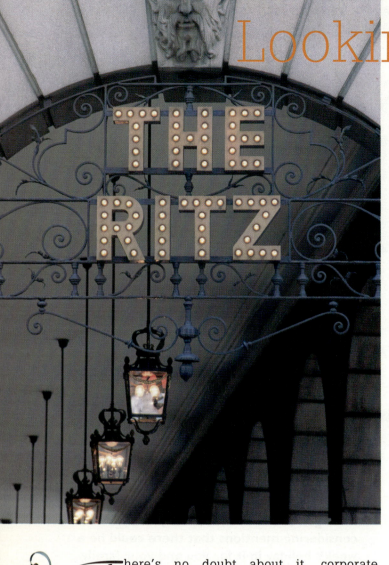

To some, corporate entertainment is merely an expensive and perhaps unnecessary luxury. To those who take a dimmer view, it's nothing short of bribery. But the truly corrupt corporate entertainer is relatively rare. Famous fraudsters, the Bank of Credit and Commerce International, did indeed specialise in 'sweetening' their most valued clients - frequently international terrorists, drug barons and Third World dictators - with shopping sprees in London and endless lines of credit at Las Vegas casinos. But this is a million miles away from an everyday business breakfast at the Hilton or a power lunch at the Savoy. For most successful business people would agree that goodwill is a crucial part of clinching lucrative deals and these days goodwill costs more than a smile.

A few years ago, the Ritz Hotel, recognising the major contribution made by executive diners to its restaurant turnover, invented the award of Business Luncher of the Year to honour, in their words, "the executive who does most to help the recovery of the economy by lunching out". Only those who spent in excess of £5,000 a year stood a chance of winning, but there was no shortage of candidates willing to compete.

There's no doubt about it, corporate entertainment is big business. In Japan, for example, where relationship-building is a fundamental part of business life, a staggering £40 billion of marketing expenditure goes on corporate entertainment annually. That's roughly equivalent to Romania's GDP or Venezuela's total foreign debt. The infamous Recruit Group, which has been the subject of repeated scandals in Japan, once paid $15,500 for a single meal for a dozen executives at a favourite restaurant. So it's easy to see how the money the Japanese spend in a year on wining and dining important clients could add up to the cost of 365 brand-new jumbo jets!

What the Ritz was acknowledging is that business lunches are an important part of corporate culture, whether to consolidate professional relationships between colleagues and charge it to expenses or to manipulate over-cautious clients into an immediate agreement. After all, it's rather difficult to reject your host's proposal (however unspeakable) when you have just eaten a hundred dollars' worth of their entertainment budget!

How cost-effective it really is for Fiat to own an art gallery so it can take customers on special conducted tours or for the German Neckermann company to have a whole department organising weekends in the Mediterranean for important clients is, of course, open to question. Certainly in Austria, where corporate entertaining is tax-free, offering Mozart festivals to music-lovers and Klosters to corporate skiers seems to promise a good return on an initial investment. But can it legitimately be considered part of a company's overall marketing effort?

It can. What more and more companies are realising is that across-the-board marketing doesn't work. Marketing in the future will have to be more clearly focused. And it may turn out that big above-the-line marketing campaigns prove less effective in moving goods than simpler strategies for getting the client on your side. Of course, in times of recession, corporate hospitality looks extravagant and doesn't make for good public relations. But it still makes sense to target your best clients. For if the so-called Pareto Principle is true and eighty per cent of your business really does come from twenty per cent of your customers, then shouldn't you be looking after the twenty per cent?

Response

1. **What in the article did you personally find most amusing, interesting, surprising, and shocking?**

   What amused me was . . .
   What interested me was . . .
   What surprised me was . . .
   What shocked me was . . .

2. **Was there anything in the article that annoyed you or you thought was wrong? Was there anything you didn't know?**

   It annoyed me that . . .
   I wasn't aware that . . .
   I'm not sure about . . .

Expand

Without referring back to the text, can you expand on the following facts and figures mentioned in the article?

1. $40 billion
2. Romania and Venezuela
3. $15,500
4. 365
5. BCCI
6. The Ritz
7. Fiat and Neckermann
8. Tax
9. Above-the-line marketing
10. The Pareto Principle

Language Focus

Summary

Now complete the following summary of the first half of the article using the words below. Referring back to the text will help you. Listen and check your answers.

culture	scandals
part	entertainment
marketing	contribution
luxury	clients
hospitality	extravagant

A lot of people regard corporate (1) … as an unnecessary (2) … , but not the Japanese! As far as they are concerned, it makes a major (3) … to a company's overall (4) … effort, and they spend a staggering $40 billion a year looking after their most important customers. That's roughly equivalent to Romania's GDP!

And, though there have been repeated (5) … in Japan involving the most (6) … companies, extending (7) … to your most valued (8) … remains a crucial (9) … of Japanese corporate (10) … .

Without changing the meaning too much, which of the adjectives in the summary above could be replaced by the following words?

a. significant   c. phenomenal

b. total   d. vital

Find as many word partnerships as you can in the summary above.

Word Partnerships

Re-arrange these 'word dominoes' in the right order so that each makes a strong word partnership. Make a list of the words pairs you create. The first and last domino are half-blank.

1.		corporate
2.	effort	public
3.	on an investment	marketing
4.	lunch	lunch
5.	and dining	sweeten
6.	out	consolidate
7.	to expenses	a return
8.	valued clients	power
9.	building	wining
10.	relationships	charge it
11.	entertainment	relationship
12.	relations	

Discuss

• What do you understand by the terms *above-the-line* and *below-the-line* marketing?

• Can corporate entertaining really be considered a below-the-line marketing strategy?

Describing Food

Describing food and drink to someone who doesn't know much about your local cuisine is not always an easy thing to do. Match each noun from the box with the groups of words below to form strong word pairs. Note that each noun will be paired individually with every word in a group.

> meat salad dish red wine food
> meal steak beer white wine vegetables

1. light   heavy   quick   vegetarian
2. rich   spicy   plain   fast
3. traditional   unusual   exotic   local
4. roast   stewed   cold   sliced   minced
5. rare   medium   well-done   fillet
6. fresh   frozen   crisp   seasonal
7. green   side   chicken   mixed
8. light   full-bodied   robust
9. dry   medium   sweet   crisp   fruity
10. strong   bottled   export   draught

Discuss

Does your firm do any kind of corporate entertaining? What about corporate gifts? Have you received gifts from companies for whom you're a major client?

Which of these gifts would you be happy to receive?

- a travel clock-radio
- golf balls with your name on them
- a case of red Bordeaux
- a leather briefcase with your initials embossed in gold
- a personalised pen set

Which of these gifts have you received?

- a cheap biro with your supplier's logo on it
- a desk diary with adverts for your supplier running through it
- a calendar featuring photographs of your supplier's factories
- a mousemat with your supplier's logo on it

Expressions with *deal*

Divide the following expressions into two groups – those which mean *We reached a deal* and those which mean *We failed to reach a deal*.

1. We clinched the deal.
2. We wrapped up the deal.
3. We blew the deal.
4. We struck a deal.
5. We swung the deal.
6. The deal fell through.
7. We screwed up the deal.
8. The deal's off.

Discuss

- How often do you eat out on expenses in a month? What's the most you've ever spent on wining and dining an important client? Was it worth it?
- Have you ever clinched a deal over a meal? Or don't dinner and business mix?
- Does 80% of your business really come from 20% of your clients or do you think that's an exaggeration?

Language Focus

The Business Lunch

Rearrange the following to make complete sentences. The first word is in the right place.

1. There's new a nice Italian corner just the restaurant round.

2. There's Thai pretty restaurant a good go we where usually.

3. There's popular little a very restaurant has which opened just.

4. There's restaurant nice a quite fish you like might which.

5. There's vegetarian wonderful a does excellent restaurant which an lasagne.

Discuss

- What sort of food do you like? Do you have a favourite place you take people to for lunch or dinner?

- Do you ever have working breakfasts? Do you have to give up many of your evenings to socialising with business contacts? If so, does this affect your home-life?

- Have you ever had to attend a business meal which you really did not want to be at?

- Have you ever had to pretend you were enjoying some food that you really did not like?

Spoken English

During a meal out with a client or colleague, when would you expect to hear the following? Match each expression with its meaning.

1. What can I get you?
2. That sounds nice.
3. How's yours?
4. Just a drop, thanks.
5. It's an acquired taste.
6. Nothing to start with, thanks.
7. No, I'm all right, thanks.
8. Don't wait for me.
9. Where's the loo here?
10. This one's on me.
11. No, no, I insist!

a. From your description, I think I'm going to like this dish.
b. Can you tell me where the toilet is?
c. No thank you. I don't want any (more).
d. I'll have just a little more wine, thank you.
e. Please start.
f. You must let me pay!
g. What would you like to drink?
h. It's unusual and you may not like it at first.
i. I'll pay.
j. What is your meal like?
k. I don't want a first course, thank you.

Fluency Work

Mixing Business and Pleasure

Write out part of a restaurant menu which would be typical of the city or town where you live. Two or three starters, main courses and desserts should be sufficient. Try to include a few local specialities if you can. Don't translate the names of the dishes into English – write them in your own language. Look at the box *Describing Food* (on the right). Look up any extra vocabulary you'll need to describe the dishes.

Describing Food

> It's a kind of ... .
> It's a bit like ... only more / less ... .
> It's fairly / quite / rather ... .
> It's made from ... with ... and cooked in ... .
> It's served with ... .
> I think you'll like it.
> You may not like it.
>
> grilled   boiled   roast   stir-fried
> poached   stewed   baked   fried

Business over Dinner

A supplier and client are going to have dinner. Work in pairs. Decide who is going to be the supplier and who is going to be the client in the following conversation. Here is the information for the supplier. The information for the client is on the next page.

The Supplier

You are in a local restaurant with a foreign client. As they don't speak your language very well, you're both speaking English.

1. Try to relax them by asking them how they like your town/city. Ask them if they'll have time to see much of it during their stay. If so, make a few recommendations as to what they might see and do. Keep the conversation going by talking a little about current affairs, sport, the weather, holidays, your family, their family (if culturally appropriate).

2. Ask them what they'd like to eat and drink, using the menu you have just created above. If necessary, try to explain some of the things on the menu. Remember to make the dishes sound appetising and appealing.

3. Your main objective during lunch is to do some business. So, once you've established a friendly atmosphere, try to get the conversation round to the subject of the contract your company has with theirs for the supply of electrical components. You know you are not the only supplier your client uses, but you believe it would be mutually advantageous if you were. For one thing, if you had an exclusive arrangement with your client, you might be able to double the discount you offer them to 11%. Be careful not to sound too pushy, but take every opportunity to talk business during the meal.

The Client

You are in a foreign restaurant with a local supplier. As you don't speak their language very well, you're both speaking English.

1. Answer your host's questions and talk about your impressions of their town/city so far. Ask them what there is to see and do in the city and remember to respond enthusiastically to some of their suggestions. If you don't like the suggestions, be diplomatic! Keep the conversation going by talking a little about current affairs, sport, the weather, holidays, your family, their family (if culturally appropriate).

2. Decide what you'd like to eat and drink. If there are things on the menu you don't understand, you could ask your host to explain them to you. If you're not sure what to choose, perhaps your host can recommend something. Remember to sound interested in the food.

3. Your host's company is one of three which supply yours with electrical components and you are quite happy with this arrangement. You really don't want to re-negotiate your contract with them and, anyway, you don't believe in mixing business and pleasure. Without being rude, avoid getting into any discussions about business. If business does come up, try to change the subject.

Telephoning Skills

The Language of Telephoning

Language Focus

Talk with your classmates. What are some problems that irritate you when telephoning? Look at the list of complaints. Put them in order from 1 to 5 (5 being the most irritating).

Five most common complaints about telephoning:
* waiting on hold for too long
* not being get through
* not being able to see facial expressions
* having to repeat the same information to different people
* talking to rude operators

Now discuss the list with your classmates. Do they agree?
Add three or more new complaints to the list.

Listening

🎧 **You will hear three different types of telephone calls.**
Listen and match the calls you hear with the types of calls in the list below. (One is extra):

contact call: getting in touch with a business contact

information call: calling to get information

voice mail call: calling and leaving a message on a machine

appointment call: contacting a business to arrange a meeting/appointment

Call 1. ...   Call 2. ...   Call 3. ...

Key Language 1

Complete these sentences from the listening using the pairs of words below.

how / help	calling / because	let / transfer
call / later	speak / please	this / speaking
name / from	mine / referred	sorry / was
afraid / in	put / down	remember / met
wondering / help	time / reach	I'll / message

1. ... can I ... you?
2. I'm ... ... I need some information.
3. ... me ... you to Sales.
4. Would you like to ... back ... ?
5. My ... is Chris Robb ... York Paper.
6. A colleague of ... , Liz Peterson, ... me to you.
7. I'm ... she's not ... this week.
8. I could ... you ... for Friday afternoon.
9. ... , your name ... ?
10. I'd like to ... to Mark Chin, ...
11. ... is Mark ... .
12. You may not ... me – we ... last year.
13. I was ... if you could ... me.
14. ... give him the ... .
15. What's a good ... to ... you?

Listen to the calls again and check your answers.

Key Language 2

These are some common and useful telephone questions. Match the endings with the question starters. (More than one combination is sometimes possible.)

1. ... leave a message?
2. ... take a message?
3. ... transfer me to his voice mail?
4. ... have your phone number?
5. ... know what this regarding?
6. ... help you?
7. ... ask what this is regarding?
8. ... speak to Stuart Tipps, please?
9. ... 555-7434?
10. ... ask who's calling?
11. ... repeat that please?
12. ... ask him to call John Donson?
13. ... speak up a little, please?
14. ... a good time?
15. ... ask when he'll be back?
16. ... call back later?
17. ... something I could help you with?

a. Would you like to ... ?
b. May I ... ?
c. Could you ... ?
d. Does s/he ... ?
e. Is this ... ?

Telephoning Skills

Making Business Calls

Practise using the models below. Take turns playing the roles.

The Appointment Call

THE COMPANY: Kickbacks Construction

CALLER
You want to build a small shopping centre in your city – Mexico City.
A colleague, Jamie, refers you to Kickbacks Construction.
Problem: You are calling from your cell phone – the connection is terrible.
You are only available on Fridays.

RECEPTIONIST
You are the receptionist.
The problem: Marion White is not in this week.
Try to make an appointment.
Marion is only available on Mondays.

Receptionist answers phone.
Caller asks for Marion White.
Receptionist informs Marion not in.
Caller tries to make appointment.
Receptionist negotiates a date with Caller.

The Contact Call

THE COMPANY: Cellu-Lite Mobile Phones

CALLER
You own a small electronics shop in Tokyo, Japan.
You want to call Chris, Director of Cellu-Lite Mobile Phones.
You met 3 years ago at a trade fair.
You need to know if he can offer a discount on the new "XL-200".

CHRIS WEST
You are the director.
The problem: You cannot offer discounts – only Jamie can, who is in Sales.
Jamie is on vacation

Receptionist answers phone.
Caller asks for Chris West.
Receptionist transfers call.
Chris answers phone.
Caller identifies him/herself and says what s/he wants.
Chris explains the problem.
Caller and Chris come to a resolution.

The Information Call

THE COMPANY: Aroma Coffee

CALLER
You are a coffee importer in Italy.
You want information on Aroma's line of coffees – especially prices.

TERRY SHORT
You are a sales representative.
You really need to make a sale.
The problem: The computers are down – the price list is not available.

Receptionist answers phone.
Caller describes what he wants.
Receptionist transfers call.
Terry answers phone.
Caller identifies him/herself and says what s/he wants.
Terry explains "the problem".
Caller and Terry come to a resolution.

Follow Up

Speaking in a foreign language is even more difficult on the phone. Here are some hints to help people in telephone conversations. Which three do you think are most useful?

- Don't panic.
- Rehearse the call.
- Predict what the other caller might say.
- Ask questions if you don't understand.
- Keep a pen handy and take notes.
- Don't be afraid to ask the caller to slow down.
- Check your understanding, repeating back important information.
- Don't call from your cell phone.

Now discuss the three you chose with your classmates. Do they agree? Can you think of any more to add to the list?

Innovation

How Creative Are you?

Do you consider yourself to be creative? Are you the sort of person who gets sudden flashes of inspiration or are you more of a methodical problem-solver?

To find out how good you are at thinking your way around a problem, try this: connect all the circles below with the minimum number of straight lines without lifting your pen from the paper.
When you have finished, check the answer key on page 156 for possible ways to solve this problem.

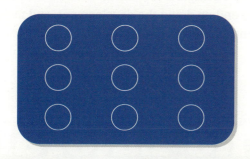

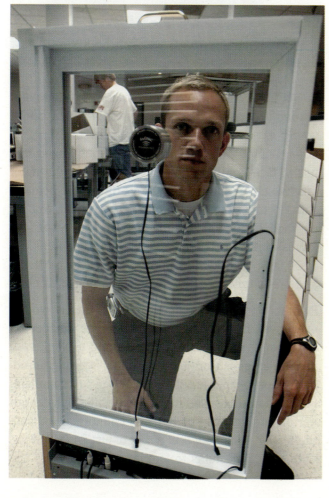

Discuss

How important is creativity in business? Are creativity and innovation the same thing?

Some suggest that luck plays a major part in any innovative breakthrough. Below is a list of tips on how to maximise your chances of striking it lucky, taken from Tom Peters' bestseller, *Liberation Management*. Which piece of advice strikes you as:

- the most useful?
- the cleverest?
- the silliest?

1. Listen to everyone. Ideas come from everywhere.
2. Don't listen to anyone. Trust your inner ear.
3. Constantly reorganise. Mix, match, try different combinations to shake things up.
4. Read odd stuff. Visit odd places. Make odd friends. Work with odd partners.
5. Disorganise.
6. Get out of your office.
7. Get rid of your office.
8. Nurture intuition.
9. Forget the same tired meetings, talking with the same tired people about the same tired things.
10. Get fired. If you're not pushing hard enough to get fired, you're not pushing hard enough!

Do you have a strategy of your own for coming up with new ideas?

Work in two groups. One group should read the article entitled *Bright Ideas*; the other should read the one entitled *The Lateral Thinker*.

Bright *Ideas*

The scene is the boardroom of a multinational cosmetics company at the end of an exhausting all-day meeting. The conference table is littered with screwed up papers and empty Perrier bottles. The financial controller is tearing his hair out and the director of R&D is no longer on speaking terms with the head of marketing. The launch of a new shampoo has backfired badly. All decisions have had to be deferred until the next meeting. Nobody even wants to think about the next meeting.

At this point a young marketing consultant cuts in. "Ladies and gentlemen, I have an idea which is guaranteed to double sales of your new shampoo. Now, believe it or not, my idea can be summed up in just one word and for $30,000 I'll tell you what it is." Naturally, objections are raised, but the chairman finally agrees to the deal. "Here is my idea. You know the instructions you put on the back of the shampoo bottle? I suggest you add one word to the end. And the word is: 'repeat'."

Not all good ideas are this simple, but in business a surprising number of them are. At least, they seem simple after they've been thought of – the secret is to think of them in the first place. As someone once remarked, "If you can't write your idea on the back of your business card, you don't have an idea."

So what are the conditions for creativity in business? And is there a blueprint for having bright ideas? Here's what the psychologists think:

1. Be a risk-taker. Those who are reluctant to take risks don't innovate.
2. Be illogical. An over-reliance on logic kills off ideas before they have a chance to develop.
3. Let yourself be stupid from time to time. Great ideas often start out as stupid ideas.
4. Regularly re-think things. Problem-solving frequently involves breaking up problems into parts and putting them back together again in a different way.
5. Take advantage of lucky breaks. The most creative people never ignore an opportunity.

They say the West creates and the East innovates, and there may be some truth in this. Take British entrepreneur, Sir Clive Sinclair, the great electronics inventor of the 70s, whose C5 electric car flopped when people found it quicker to get out and walk. Then take Akio Morita, the chairman of Sony, who has seen his company claim eighty-five per cent of the world personal stereo market with the much imitated Sony Walkman – a masterly innovation which merely took advantage of existing technology. The comparison speaks for itself.

And maybe one reason high-technology companies seek to merge multinationally is so that they can combine both creative and innovative strength. For anything that won't sell isn't worth inventing and it's an expensive waste of time coming up with ideas you can't exploit. But it's even more expensive if your competitors can exploit them. And there's not much point doing the research if another company is going to end up doing the development, and making the profit.

The Lateral *Thinker*

In his book on creative problem-solving, *'Breaking Through'*, Tom Logsdon tells the story of a bright young executive hired to manage a San Francisco hotel. One of the first problems the young executive has to face is a flood of complaints about the hotel lifts, which are infuriatingly slow. Guests are actually starting to demand rooms on lower floors. But an upgrade of the lift system is ruled out when the lowest estimate for reconstruction comes to $200,000. Clearly something else has to be done, and pretty quickly, before people start checking out.

Finally, a creative solution occurs to the young executive. The key to the problem, he decides, is boredom. With only the lift doors and a blank wall to stare at, guests are understandably getting bored, and when people are bored they tend to complain. So instead of speeding up the lifts, full-length mirrors are installed both inside and directly outside the lifts on each floor – at a cost of just $4,000. Now, with their reflections to look at when they use the lift, people stop complaining, thereby saving the hotel $196,000.

This is what Edward De Bono called lateral thinking, and it's the result of looking at the problem in a different and unusual way. Indeed, reformulating and redefining a problem is just one of the ways in which you can create a climate for creativity in business. And an increasing number of companies now see such creative strategies as vital to their survival.

At 3M, for example, employees spend as much as fifteen per cent of their time on new ideas and twenty-five per cent of every manager's product portfolio consists of products that are less than five years old. At Hewlett-Packard more than half their orders in 1992 are for products introduced in the previous two years. It's a similar story at Glaxo, ICL and SmithKline Beecham. For it's no coincidence that in research-driven industries, like computers and pharmaceuticals, an innovative lead creates the market leaders. Management guru, Tom Peters, talks nowadays of a company's whole culture being creative. But creativity would be useless without innovation, and the two terms should not be confused.

According to the team running creativity courses at the Cranfield School of Management, creativity is essentially about generating, not judging, ideas. Innovation, on the other hand, is the successful implementation of those ideas on a commercial basis. In a brainstorming session, you don't criticise ideas before they're fully formed. That would be counter-productive. Evaluation comes in at the innovation stage, where you're turning good ideas into a commercial proposition. It follows that you cannot be both creative and innovative at the same time.

For making a discovery is one thing; exploiting it quite another, as the Xerox Research Centre found out to its cost when its system for making personal computers easier to use was copied by Apple Macintosh. Apple led the market for almost ten years with the enormously successful desktop system it 'borrowed' from Xerox. But Apple had the foresight to copyright the system. Xerox didn't. Originality, it seems, is the art of concealing your source, and too many companies fail to see an opportunity until it ceases to be one.

Summary

1. The first two paragraphs of the article you have just read were actually a true story. Without looking back at the text, exchange stories with someone who read the other article. What do you think is the moral of their story?

2. Work with a partner who read the same article as you to produce a 60-word summary of the rest of the text. You need only mention the important points, but you must use **exactly** 60 words.

3. Read your summary out to someone who read the other article. Answer any questions they may have.

4. Quickly read through the other article to see if the summary you were given is accurate.

Find the Expressions

Look back at the article *Bright Ideas*. Find the words and expressions which mean:

1. is frustrated (paragraph 1)

2. has gone wrong (paragraph 1)
3. a master plan (paragraph 4)
4. unexpected opportunities (paragraph 4)
5. failed badly (paragraph 5)
6. is obvious (paragraph 5)

Look back at the article *The Lateral Thinker*. Find the words and expressions which mean:

7. a creative environment (paragraph 3)
8. it's not by chance that (paragraph 4)
9. management expert (paragraph 4)
10. idea-generating meeting (paragraph 5)
11. viable enterprise (paragraph 5)
12. not telling people where you got the idea (paragraph 6)

From the articles list:

13. three words you want to use more often.
14. three word partnerships you need, with their equivalents in your own language.
15. three longer expressions with their equivalents in your own language.

Language Focus

Word Partnerships 1

Complete the presentation extract below by matching the two halves of each sentence. Referring back to the articles may help you.

1. As you know, in our view, too many companies fail to see . . .

2. So what we try to do is to create . . .

3. Indeed, we see such creative strategies . . .

4. Nevertheless, you don't need me to tell you that the launch of our latest product . . .

5. And, no doubt, you'd like to know why we haven't been able to turn what looked like a great idea . . .

6. Well, the main difficulties we've had . . .

7. And the key to . . .

8. You see, this new product is extremely advanced, and clearly, we should have taken . . .

9. The ideal solution would have been to simply add new features to our old system, and it's . . .

10. With hindsight, we know what we did wrong, but, as always, the secret is . . .

a. . . . to think of these things in the first place.

b. . . . the whole problem really is technology.

c. . . . a climate for creativity in everything that we do.

d. . . . advantage of existing technology instead of redesigning the whole system from scratch.

e. . . . into a commercial proposition.

f. . . . an opportunity until it ceases to be one.

g. . . . to face have been technical.

h. . . . as vital to our survival.

i. . . . a pity this didn't occur to us sooner.

j. . . . has backfired badly.

Discuss

- What impact has your company made on the market it operates in? Has it made any breakthroughs in its field?
- Has the launch of any of your company's new products or services ever backfired?

When do you Say . . .?

1. Believe me, we've really done our homework on this one.
2. Look, let's not make a mountain out of a molehill.
3. Well, we'll just have to make the best of a bad job.
4. Well, we'll just have to make do, won't we?

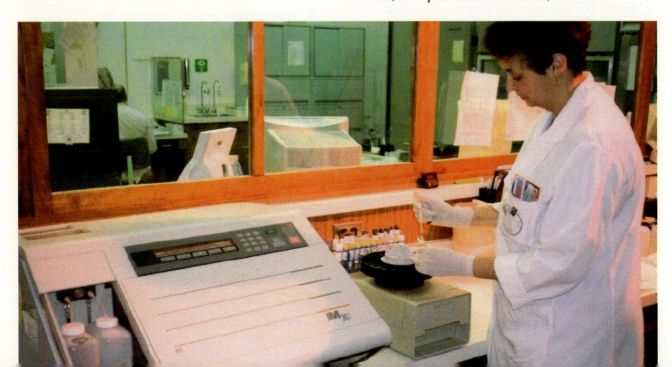

Word Partnerships 2

Group the following verbs according to whether they form strong word partnerships with *research*, *problems* or *ideas*. Some of them belong to more than one group.

solve	fund	implement	carry out	generate
create	put money into	face	develop	brainstorm
tackle	promote	define	come up with	have
come up against	cut back on	cause		

Word Partnerships 3

Now complete the following using some of the verbs from the previous exercise:

Companies who are prepared to (1) ... research know that it will be money well spent. Many research-driven companies will even go so far as to invest up to 20% of their turnover in new research in the hope that their R&D team can (2) ... at least one new idea which will ensure the company's future profitability. And companies who, in times of recession, decide to (3) ... research are probably making a big mistake.

These days it is the business of all departments within a company to (4) ... as many ideas on improving the business as possible, some of which, if (5) ... further may turn out to be major breakthroughs, for the R&D department is not always in the best position to (6) ... a particular problem, let alone (7) ... it. Of course, you may have to toy with an idea for quite some time before you can see a way to actually (8) ... it, and it is this implementation stage which is the test of a really good idea.

How many word partnerships can you find in the paragraph above?

Language Focus

Make and Do

**There is a guide to the basic use of these two words in English.
You *do an activity*, but you *make a product*. Look at these two examples:**

- Have you done the copying?
- Have you made the copies?

**As well as this basic use, both words are used in fixed expressions which you
need to learn.**

Word Partnerships 4

**You can make lots of useful business phrases with the verbs *make* and *do*. But
do you know which ones to use? Which of the following words are used with
make and which with *do*? A few of them can be used with both, but the meaning
sometimes changes:**

business	an effort	a decision	a profit
research	a loss	money	a report
progress	a phone-call	a project	a rush-job
tests	a proposal	a survey	arrangements
a breakthrough	recommendations	a mistake	an excuse
an impact	a presentation	a deal	an improvement
a discovery	an appointment	a good job	a comparison
a comment	a feasibility study	an offer	

Word Partnerships 5

Which adverbs, if any, do not fit?

1.   New patent registrations declined →   sharply/considerably/encouragingly/disappointingly.
2.   The old model was phased out →   dramatically/gradually/suddenly/eventually.
3.   R & D expenditure rose →   promisingly/steadily/significantly/tremendously.
4.   Eurotunnel shares fluctuated →   slightly/wildly/slowly/noticeably.

**Eurotunnel, connecting the UK and France, was a triumph of engineering innovation.
What will be the next great innovative project?**

Fluency Work

Problem-solving

Put the following stages in the problem-solving process into the most likely chronological order. Are there any alternative orders?

STAGE 1 → STAGE 2 → STAGE 3 → STAGE 4 → STAGE 5 → STAGE 6 → STAGE 7

a. Reformulate the problem in different ways.
b. Implement your idea.
c. Break the problem down into parts.
d. Eliminate non-starters.

e. Define the basic problem.
f. Select the best possible solution.
g. Brainstorm possible solutions.

Discuss

- What kind of problems do you have to face on a daily basis at work?

- What's the biggest headache in your job? How do you deal with it?

Idea Killers

The following 'idea killers' should sound familiar. They are the kind of objections people always raise when new ideas are presented. The words are mixed up. Can you rearrange them? The first word is in the right place.

1. It cost much would too.

2. It too would take long.

3. Our would that for go customers never.

4. We work that it before tried and didn't.

5. I never boss agree get to the it could to.

6. Now time isn't to the trying be new anything.

7. Don't we've thought already think you that of?

8. It's nice but get never it idea a we could work to.

Discuss

- How would you deal with each of these objections? Have you ever 'killed off' someone else's idea and later regretted it, or had an idea of your own rejected which you still believe would have worked?

- Do you personally like change at work, or in your private life, or do you prefer a steady world, where things go on in the same old way?

Fluency Work

Brainstorm

"The best way to get good ideas is to have lots of ideas," Linus Pauling, Nobel prizewinner.

Thanks to a computer error, your company's production plant has managed to manufacture three million useless plastic discs by mistake! The 5cm cubes are white in colour, rigid, and hollow. Unfortunately, it would not be economical to reprocess them and they are not recyclable. Minor modifications could be made, however.

Form yourselves into 'thinktanks' of three or four members and give yourselves ten minutes to brainstorm as many possible uses for the cubes as you can. Write them all down. Select the best idea you can come up with and present it to the other groups. Vote for the overall best solution.

- Define the problem.
- Can it be broken down and reformulated?
- Brainstorm as many ideas as you can in 10 minutes.
- Eliminate non-starters.
- Present your best solution.

Discuss

Do you like brainstorming or do you prefer to work things out alone?

How about ...?

Couldn't we ...?

Suppose we ...

We could try ...

In what way could we ...?

How could we change ...?

What if we ...?

What would happen if ...?

Wouldn't it be fun if ...?

It's just an idea, but why don't we ...?

Public Relations

The Power of the Media

"Love them or hate them, the media are now an indispensable part of modern business. No major corporate action is complete without a press release and a series of interviews. Some executives seem to spend more time with profile writers than in their offices. They know that reputations are what history remembers of us."
Stuart Crainer, business journalist

**How much do you think a company's reputation influences its performance?
Do you believe what you read about companies in the papers and see on TV or the Net?**

Complete the following headlines using the names or terms below:

> NIKE SUMITOMO LEWINSKY BARINGS INTEL BEEF MICROSOFT

... ON TRIAL

... SWEATSHOPS IN ASIA

LEESON BRINGS DOWN ...

COLLAPSE OF ... BANK

... AFFAIR THREATENS CLINTON

EU BAN ON BRITISH ...

... PENTIUM CHIP DEFECTIVE CLAIMS US PROFESSOR

Do you remember any of these stories? How do you think they were handled in the media? How effectively did the companies and individuals concerned respond?

With a partner, make a list of the things a company can do to maintain or improve its image. Then read the article, *True Lies.*

We get poorer 'cause Gates gets...

MICROSO
GENTRIFIE
SEAT

True Lies

reputation. Faced with a corporate crisis, it's the PR team that the CEO will increasingly call in first. In the words of business journalist Stuart Crainer, "They are on their mobile in the boardroom while you are crying in the corridor."

Global Communications

These days, thanks to electronic communications, a minor problem at a plant on the other side of the world can rapidly escalate into a major scandal. A back-page story in a local newspaper suddenly hits the front pages of the international press and then gets posted on the Internet, where it spirals out of control.

Knowledge Management

A partial solution is knowledge management. Edelman, one of the the world's largest PR firms, not only has its own 24-hour newsroom, it also offers clients something it calls i-Wire – a monitoring service that allows you to trace, download and evaluate anything written about your company on the Internet by anyone, anywhere, anytime.

Web Talk

But for a company in real trouble there's now nowhere to hide. For all the official statements made at the Department of Justice trial about Microsoft's anti-competitive activities, it was the leaked e-mails and sustained personal attacks on Bill Gates on the Net that did the company most damage. Facts were less important than 'cyberbuzz' – the continuous 'chat' among Internet users in newsgroups and online forums. For in cyberspace your customers are talking about you all the time. It's not word of mouth but 'word of web'. And it can be devastating.

A Wave of Bad Publicity

Sports clothing manufacturer, Nike, realized just how devastating when human rights campaigners picked up on the huge discrepancy between the $20 million Michael Jordan got to endorse Nike trainers and the twenty cents an hour workers in the Far East got to actually make those shoes. Within weeks, pressure groups were demonstrating against the

Networking

She seldom eats lunch and when she does, you pay. She knows your boss's name, his golf handicap and his favourite scotch. She knows your wife's name, your kids' names, your dog's name. She knows the names of virtually everyone she has ever met – their life stories carefully keyed into her PalmPilot. She knows pretty much everything about you. You, on the other hand, know almost nothing about her. Who is she? Your public relations consultant.

The Age of PR

There was a time when PR was just about a couple of well-timed press releases, a sponsored event and the occasional television interview. Not anymore. In the media age, the new generation of PR professionals can often make or break a company's company in US cities and unsold inventory was piling up in the warehouses.

Responding to Adverse Publicity

To protect its corporate image, Nike responded with a well-publicised 'greening' of the company. Its mission statement, "To experience the emotion of competition, winning and crushing competitors" was replaced by the more caring, if less inspiring, "Nike will share responsibility with our manufacturing partners to continually improve the workplace for every worker manufacturing Nike products." Nike now apparently champions better working conditions in the Developing World, but is this a genuine turnaround or a triumph of PR?

Being 'On Message'

Perhaps it's all a question, as PR people put it, of being "on message", identifying and communicating your company's unique value, raising industry awareness, educating the customer, building brand image and differentiating yourself from your competitors. For the fact is, in sophisticated high-tech cultures, mass marketing doesn't work. We simply know too much. What works isn't global advertising but tightly focused public relations.

An Invisible Force

Unlike advertising, PR is an invisible force subtly persuading us that Microsoft plays fair, that Nike really cares – so subtly that sometimes it's hard to tell reality from public relations. May the force be with you.

Crosschecking

Which of the following viewpoints support the opinions expressed in the article?

1. *"Good PR is invisible."*
   Peter Bradshaw, business journalist

2. *"Perception is reality."*
   Donald Trump, property tycoon

3. *"Price is crucial. Image isn't. You can't sell a new logo."*
   Gerald Ratner, whose career was ruined by bad publicity

4. *"Bad publicity is good publicity."*
   Malcolm McLaren, rock impresario

5. *"There is only one thing in the world worse than being talked about, and that is not being talked about."*
   Oscar Wilde, writer and wit, destroyed by being talked about

Recall

Without looking back at the article, how much can you remember about the following?

1. i-Wire
2. Cyberbuzz
3. Nike's mission statement
4. High-tech cultures

Find the Expressions

Look back at the subheadings in the article. Find the expressions which mean:

1. making business contacts through social activities.

2. identifying and manipulating external sources of information about a company and expertise within it.

3. a series of negative stories about a company in the media.

4. successfully presenting to the public the image of your company that you would like them to have.

Language Focus

Word Partnerships 1

Put the following recommendations from the PR officer of a company in crisis into the right order by numbering the 16 parts below. Some of the sentences are already in the right place. Then listen and check.

1) Right, the first thing is not to panic. I suggest we issue a **press**

   event. For now, let's just concentrate on getting ourselves back **on**

   conditions in all our overseas factories and that, no matter what these **pressure**

   world. Later on, we should give some thought to sponsoring an appropriate **charitable**

   public awareness of how we've actually championed worker's rights in the **developing**

4) **groups** are saying, we simply do not exploit our workers. I recommend we arrange a **television**

   the Internet and taking swift action if necessary to counteract what we expect to **be a wave of**

   TV9. We spend $10 million a year with them on advertising. So, believe me, our **corporate**

8) **solution.** We also need to be downloading everything written about us **on**

   release this afternoon stating quite clearly that we carefully monitor **working**

   bad publicity. It may be time to take a fresh look at our **mission**

   interview as soon as possible to make our position absolutely clear on that. I've just **been on to**

12) **competitors** very effectively, but it wouldn't do any harm to **raise**

   image means as much to them as it does to us! Now, press and TV coverage are only a **partial**

   statement as well. The one we have is strong on brand and differentiates us from **our**

16) **message.** And, Sir – please calm down, there's a group of reporters outside waiting to see you!

Making Recommendations

In the previous exercise there are eight expressions used to make recommendations. Can you find them?

1. The f ...
2. I s ...
3. Let's j ...
4. We s ...
5. I r ...
6. We a ...
7. It m ...
8. It w ...

Word Partnerships 2

Combine the words in boxes one and two below to make twelve PR crises a company may face. Then match each crisis with the best course of action in box three. The first one has been done for you as an example.

P. R. CRISES

COURSES OF ACTION

Serious	takeover bid
A hostile	accident
Adverse	financial problems
An industrial	publicity

Call for calm as the situation is brought under control.
Suppress company accounts while a rescue plan is devised.
Discredit your critics and put the other side of the story.
Urge shareholders to hang on to their stock.

Corporate	sabotage
Insider	redundancies
Mass	trading
Product	restructuring

Explain the greater efficiency of the new system.
Promise to thoroughly investigate the allegations.
Express deep regret and stress there was no option.
Recall all products unconditionally.

Product	investor confidence
A major	failure
A top management	court action
Loss of	clear-out

Set up customer helplines and offer refunds.
Issue an official statement through your lawyers.
Emphasise the need for new leadership.
Publish a set of favourable end-of-year figures.

Discuss

Work in small groups.

1. Each person in the group chooses a different PR crisis from the previous exercise and spends a few minutes inventing further details.

2. When they are ready, each person explains their situation to the rest of the group, answering questions if necessary.

3. The group offers suggestions and recommendations.

4. Each person draws up a short action plan for dealing with their crisis.

Language Focus

Mission Statements

Certain key words are always popular with the PR teams who write mission statements. Work as a group to complete the key words bellow.

ADJECTIVES	NOUNS	VERBS
1. s_cc_ssf_l	1. _xc_ll_nc_	1. s_t_sfy
2. r_sp_ct_d	2. t_ _mw_rk	2. s_st_ _n
3. s_p_r_ _r	3. qu_l_ty	3. _mpr_v_
4. _nn_v_t_v_	4. r_sp_ns_b_l_ty	4. s_rv_
5. gr_w_ng	5. pr_f_t_b_l_ty	5. _nsp_r_
6. pr_m_ _r	6. g_ _l	6. b_n_f_t
7. _ _tst_nd_ng	7. v_l_ _	7. _cc_mpl_sh
8. _n_qu_	8. v_s_ _n	8. _ch_ _v_

Which of the adjectives above could come in front of:
company, service, products, market, achievement?

Which of the verbs above could come in front of:
growth, quality, customers, consumers, objectives?

Do-it-yourself Vision Maker

Write a mission statement for your own company or a company you know using some of the words above and the model below. First match the phrases in the boxes.

STEP ONE		STEP TWO	
Our vision is to be a ...		company that provides ...	
world-	breaking	high-	oriented
market-	edge	cost-	quality
cutting-	class	client-	friendly
ground-	leading	user-	effective

STEP THREE		STEP FOUR	
products and services to ...		in the ...	
serve the global	value	rapidly	competitive
create shareholder	customers	highly	connected
satisfy our	technology	electronically	borderless
advance the frontiers of	marketplace	increasingly	changing
		automotive/engineering/financial services/telecommunications/pharmaceutical industry.	

Word Partnerships 3

All the verbs below can be used with the word '*image*'. Put them into pairs with similar meaning. The first pair has been done for you as an example.

> ~~create~~   change   preserve   project   ~~develop~~   harm   maintain
> present   strengthen   damage   reinforce   update

create and develop
....

Now complete the following using the correct tense of some of the verbs above.

1. The recent wave of bad publicity has seriously … our image.
2. I just don't think we're … the right image. Customers don't know what we stand for.
3. We're starting to look very old-fashioned. It's time to … our image.
4. We already have a strong corporate image, but we should be … it through advertising.
5. The image we're trying to … for this new product is one of energy and excitement.
6. We must … our image at all costs - our reputation is our most valuable asset.

Word Grammar

In each example, use another form of the word in capitals to complete the sentence. You may want to use a good English-English dictionary.

1. COMMUNICATE
   Thanks to modern global … , nothing stays secret for long.

2. COMMUNICATE
   The PR officer wasn't very … at the press conference.

3. PUBLIC
   Their record on human rights violations received a lot of adverse … .

4. PUBLIC
   Bill Gates's charity work has been very well … .

5. PERSUADE
   PR is about the truth. Advertising is about … .

6. PERSUADE
   I'm afraid I found their arguments mostly … .

7. REPUTATION
   The information came from a fairly … source, so it can't be relied on.

8. REPUTATION
   The CEO is … to have taken bribes.

Fluency Work

Read the quote from the public relations firm Edelman.

"A company's test of strength is judged during moments of crisis, and a company is held accountable as much for how it responds as it is for the ultimate outcome. This is more vital today because we operate in a new media environment in which information travels the globe in a matter of seconds, and a company's response is reflected in its financial situation almost immediately."

Case Study: Intel in Trouble

 1. Listen to part one of the case study about Intel. Then discuss the questions which follow.

- What fault did Professor Nicely find?
- Why was being so well-branded a problem for Intel?
- What was Intel's initial reaction to Nicely's discovery?
- How did the rumours about the Pentium chip spread so fast?
- How could IBM have taken advantage of the situation?

2. Work in two groups: the Intel Board of Directors and a group of Edelman PR consultants brought in to solve the problem. Using the role cards, prepare to hold a crisis meeting. But feel free to explore more creative ideas of your own.

INTEL BOARD OF DIRECTORS

What do you think Intel should do?
- Issue a press statement.
- Give presentations to reassure corporate users.
- Offer a free upgrade to the new Pentium chip.
- Give technical support to the small number of customers who may actually be affected.

As a group, elect a chairperson and decide on the questions you want to ask the PR consultants.

You are very concerned about Intel's reputation as the market leader in microchip technology, but you are also anxious to minimise cost to the company.

EDELMAN PR WORLDWIDE

What do you think Intel should do:
- set up a user helpline?
- put the record straight on their Web site?
- replace all defective machines?
- withdraw the product altogether to conduct thorough lab tests?

As a group, decide on the recommendations you are going to present to the Intel board.

You realise that the problem is mostly 'media hype' rather than technical inefficiency, but you want to protect Intel's image in the long-term.

3. Hold the meeting. Here is a suggested agenda:

The Pentium Controversy PR Battle Plan
AGENDA

- Outline of the current crisis, summary of the background to the problem. (Chairperson)
- Presentation of initial recommendations. (Edelman team)
- Question and answer session. (all)
- Immediate action plan. (all)
- Consider longer-term strategies to prevent a similar crisis happening again. (all)

 4. Now listen to the rest of the case study to find out what Intel actually did. Did they follow your recommendations?

Your Preconceptions

How much of your business is international? Do you travel abroad on business much? Have you noticed any differences in the way meetings are conducted in other countries? What nationalities do you tend to associate with the following characteristics?

1. They insist on sticking to a strict agenda.

2. They can't see any further than next month's sales figures.

3. They like to get to know you before they do business with you.

4. They're generally pretty disorganised.

5. They avoid confrontation at all costs.

6. It takes a while to win them over.

7. They keep changing their minds.

8. They say what they mean and they mean what they say.

9. They seem to argue for the sake of arguing.

10. They tend to dominate meetings.

11. They see meetings as an opportunity to exchange information and share ideas.

12. They see meetings as an opportunity to get things moving.

How dangerous is it to stereotype people in this way? Now compare your opinions with those in the article, *Boardroom Culture Clash*.

Boardroom Cultu

The US Perspective

For instance, most Americans will insist on the hard sell. It's not enough that you want to buy their products, you must let them sell them to you. They have to report back to superiors who will be as interested in how the deal was struck as the result. Systems and procedures matter to Americans.

The Spaniards Trust You

The Spanish, on the other hand, are unimpressed by the most meticulously prepared meeting and pay much more attention to people. In this they are more like the Arabs or the Japanese. In the Middle and Far East, business is built on trust over a long period of time. Spaniards may come to a decision about whether they trust you a little sooner.

Animated Italians

Italians, too, tend to feel that the main purpose of meetings is to assess the mood of those present and reinforce team-spirit. There may well be a lot of animated discussion at a meeting in Italy, but the majority of decisions will be made elsewhere and in secret.

Scandinavians Want Results

Strangely enough, Scandinavians are rather like Americans. They value efficiency, novelty, systems and technology. They are firmly profit-oriented. They want results yesterday.

Succeed with the Germans

Don't be surprised if the Germans start a meeting with all the difficult questions. They want to be convinced you are as efficient and quality-conscious as they are. They will be cautious about giving you too much business until you have proved yourself.

An Unpredictable Affair

Try to put pressure on a Japanese in a negotiation and you will be met with stony silence. Hold an informal fact-finding meeting with a German and you can expect a battery of searching questions. Disagree with the French on even a minor point and they will take great pleasure in engaging in spirited verbal combat. Doing business across culture can be an unpredictable affair.

Cultural Awareness

Most of us prefer to do business with people we like. And it should come as no surprise that the people we like tend to be like us. So whilst we may dispute the accuracy of cultural stereotypes, it is generally agreed that good business relationships are built on cultural awareness. Across national frontiers 'nice guys' do more business than nasty ones. But what constitutes nice-guy behaviour in a boardroom in Miami is not necessarily what they expect in Madrid.

re Clash

They will demand prompt delivery and expect you to keep your competitive edge in the most price-sensitive market in Europe. Succeed and you will enjoy a long-term business relationship.

Adversarial Meetings

The French will give you their business much more readily. But they will withdraw it just as fast if you fail to come up with the goods. Meetings in France tend to be adversarial. Heated discussion is all part of the game. Germans will be shocked to hear you question their carefully prepared arguments. The Spanish will offer no opinion unless sure of themselves, for fear of losing face. But French executives prefer to meet disagreement head on, and the British tendency to diffuse tension with humour doesn't go down too well.

Prisoners of Our Culture

Ask yourself whether meetings are opportunities to network or get results. Is it more important to stick to the agenda or generate new ideas? Is the main aim of a meeting to transmit or pool information? It all depends on where in the world you hold your meeting and whether you belong to an individualistic business culture like the French, Germans and Americans or to a collective one like the British, Japanese and Greeks. Indeed, who knows to what extent our views are our own and to what extent culturally conditioned? For in business, as in life, "All human beings are captives of their culture."

Crosschecking

Which of the following points support the opinions expressed in the article?

1. In meetings the French tend to be more aggressive than the Germans.
2. The Arabs have nothing in common with the Japanese.
3. The French generally don't appreciate the British sense of humour.
4. The Spanish are rarely hesitant in cross-cultural meetings.
5. The Americans and Scandinavians value a methodical approach.
6. The Germans want quality at any price.
7. The British tend to be more individualistic in business than the Germans.
8. In business the Italians are more or less like the Spanish.

Response

What are your own views on each of the above points?

Well, personally, I think . . .

Well, if you ask me . . .

Well, I reckon . . .

Find the Expressions

Look back at the last three paragraphs in the article. Find the expressions which mean:

1. be made to believe (paragraph 7)
2. earned their respect (paragraph 7)
3. compare favourably with your competitors (paragraph 7)
4. do as you promised (paragraph 8)
5. being made to look stupid (paragraph 8)
6. react strongly to differences of opinion (paragraph 8)
7. is not popular (paragraph 8)

Language Focus

Word Partnerships 1

The following business verbs appeared in the article in the order in which they are listed. How many of their word partners can you find in just five minutes?

Business Verb	
1. hold	9. question
2. disagree on	10. offer
3. build	11. diffuse
4. report back to	12. get
5. strike	13. generate
6. come to	14. transmit
7. reinforce	15. pool
8. withdraw	

Choose the eight most useful word partnerships and find an equivalent for them in your own language.

Discuss

- How do people generally prefer to conduct meetings in your country?

- Use as many of the word partnerships above as you need to talk about exchanging information, opinion giving, voicing disagreement, making decisions, getting results, sticking to agendas, diffusing tension, etc.

Word Partnerships 2

Complete the sentences below using words from the following list. Referring back to the article will help you with some of them.

> **market   price   client   cost   profit   quality   technology**

1. We're a firmly . . . -oriented company, so the bottom-line for us is not how big our market share is but how much money we're going to make.

2. Even at low prices, inferior products won't sell in such a . . . -conscious market.

3. The market's far too . . . -sensitive to stand an increase in service charges.

4. We're constantly forced to respond both to changing customer needs and to what our main competitors are doing in a . . . -driven business such as this.

5. The customer always comes first. We're a very . . . -centred company.

6. In a . . . -led business, such as ours, it's vital to plough profits back into R&D.

7. If the price of materials goes up any more, production will no longer be . . . -effective.

Discuss

Put the following into what your company considers to be their order of importance.

a. market trends

b. the price factor

c. client needs

d. profit levels

e. quality control

f. technological lead

g. cost control

Is this what you consider to be their order of importance or would you personally rate them differently?

Business Grammar 1

Obviously, in a delicate negotiation you do not always say exactly what you think! You need to be able to express yourself diplomatically, to make your point firmly but politely.
Match what you think with what you say.

What you think

What you say

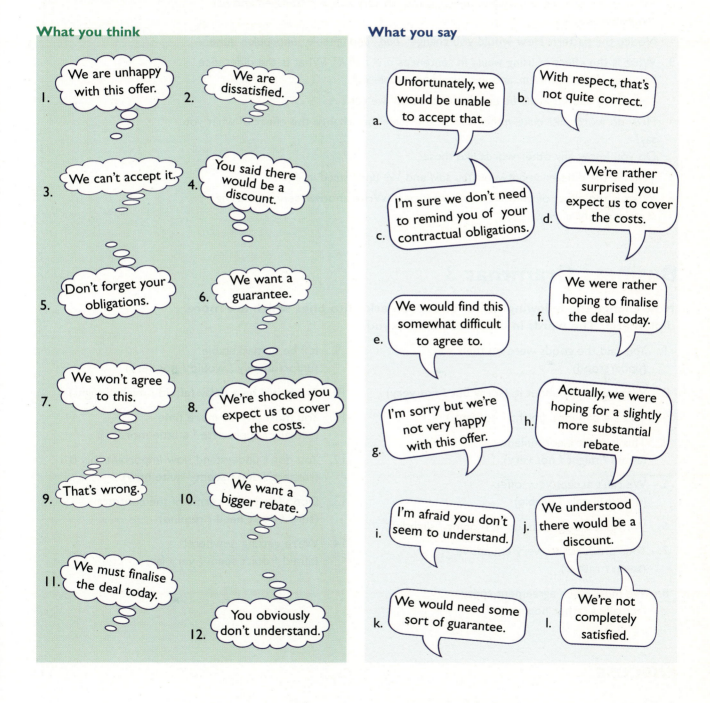

1. We are unhappy with this offer.
2. We are dissatisfied.
3. We can't accept it.
4. You said there would be a discount.
5. Don't forget your obligations.
6. We want a guarantee.
7. We won't agree to this.
8. We're shocked you expect us to cover the costs.
9. That's wrong.
10. We want a bigger rebate.
11. We must finalise the deal today.
12. You obviously don't understand.

a. Unfortunately, we would be unable to accept that.
b. With respect, that's not quite correct.
c. I'm sure we don't need to remind you of your contractual obligations.
d. We're rather surprised you expect us to cover the costs.
e. We would find this somewhat difficult to agree to.
f. We were rather hoping to finalise the deal today.
g. I'm sorry but we're not very happy with this offer.
h. Actually, we were hoping for a slightly more substantial rebate.
i. I'm afraid you don't seem to understand.
j. We understood there would be a discount.
k. We would need some sort of guarantee.
l. We're not completely satisfied.

Language Focus

Business Grammar 2

Now look at these language points from Business Grammar 1 which help to make your language more diplomatic.

1. What is the purpose of expressions like *unfortunately* and *I'm afraid*?

2. What is the difference between *unhappy* and *not very happy*, *dissatisfied* and *not completely satisfied*?

   Notice the pattern. How would you change: *bad, unprofitable, unpopular, false*?

3. What is the effect of using *would* in sentences *a, e,* and *k*? What is the difference between *that's a problem*, and *that would be a problem*?

   Notice we use *we would be unable to* instead of *we can't* . . .

4. How do words like *quite, rather, slightly,* and *somewhat* change the effect of what you say?

   Do you know any other words like these?

5. What is the difference between *You said* and *We understood* in *4-j*?

6. What is the effect of using *seem* in sentence *i*? Write another sentence using *seem* in a similar way.

Business Grammar 3

Now change the following rather direct remarks into ones which are more diplomatic. The words in brackets will help you.

1. You said the goods were on their way. (understood)

2. We're unhappy about it. (sorry but / not very)

3. That's a bad idea. (might / not very)

4. This is most inconvenient. (afraid / might / not very)

5. We can't accept your offer. (unfortunately / unable)

6. We want a bigger discount. (hoping / slightly)

7. Your products are very expensive. (seem / rather)

8. We must reach agreement today. (actually / rather hoping)

9. It'll be unmarketable. (unfortunately / would / not very)

10. There will be a delay. (afraid / might / slight)

11. You must give us more time. (actually / appreciate / a little more)

12. You don't understand how important this is. (respect / don't seem / quite how)

13. Don't forget the terms of the contract! (sure / don't need / remind)

14. We're getting nowhere! (afraid / don't seem / very far)

Discuss

- Do you take part in meetings in English with native speakers? Do you find the native speakers tend to dominate or do they make allowances for the fact that some participants are speaking a foreign language?

- Is it different when you do business in English when only non-native speakers are present? Which do you prefer?

Fluency Work

The Cultural Awareness Game

You work for a multinational company which produces computer peripherals: printers, monitors, disk and CD drives, etc. But, although these are competitively-priced at the budget end of the market, sales have, in fact, plunged by twenty per cent over the last eighteen months. Naturally, you are keen to reverse this trend before the situation becomes critical.

Step 1

Divide into two groups, each representing a different national division of your company. Work with your group to brainstorm as many possible solutions to the problem as you can. Things you might consider include: bigger discounts, price cuts, special offers, extended guarantees, regular upgrades.

Step 2

If you are in Group A, read the notes on this page; if you are in Group B, your notes are on the next page. The notes contain cultural background information about the fictional country your group represents and instructions on how to behave in the meeting with the other group. Make sure you are familiar with these before you meet up with them.

Step 3

When you are ready, come together with the other group to hold a problem-solving session at which you will discuss your ideas for boosting sales. If you consider it important, draw up an action plan before you wind up the meeting.

Step 4

Hold a debriefing session to report back on the result of your meeting and on your observations of the other group. What did you notice about the way they conducted the meeting? How well did you adapt to any obvious cultural differences? Were there any serious communication breakdowns? Were you at any point offended, confused, or amused by the other group's behaviour? How did this affect the outcome of the meeting? How would you approach such a meeting a second time? Are there any general lessons to be learnt about doing business cross-culturally?

Cultural Background Notes

Group A

1. Appoint a leader. The leader's job is to present their ideas at length, respond favourably to any ideas from other people which do not conflict with their own, and then take the final decision.

2. In your country business meetings are only held when important decisions have to be taken. It is considered vital to draw up an action plan before the end of the meeting.

3. Greet people you don't know at a meeting by shaking their hand vigorously.

4. Don't waste a lot of time on 'small talk' at the beginning of the meeting. A brief enquiry about the family is sufficient before getting down to business. Families are important in your culture. Single people and those who are secretive about their families are regarded with suspicion. Politics are a taboo subject, since the political situation in your country is so unstable, but sport and weather are safe topics.

5. Always address people at a meeting as Mr ... or Ms ..., even if you know them well. Using first names is considered over-familiar except in private conversations. An important part of protocol is to find out everybody's family name at the beginning of the meeting and then use it as much as possible to build rapport. If people forget to use your family name, politely remind them of it.

6. In your country ambition and competitiveness are regarded as the essential qualities of a good manager. In order to impress your colleagues and superiors you will not hesitate to attack any ideas which are different from your own. Excessive diplomacy is seen as a sign of weakness, except when dealing with the boss, with whom you will always appear to agree.

7. This meeting is scheduled to last a maximum of twenty-five minutes, but if it doesn't seem productive, your leader may suggest breaking it off sooner.

Fluency Work

Group B

1. Appoint a leader. The leader's job is to encourage everyone to contribute to the meeting. Protocol demands that everyone be given the chance to voice an opinion on every point under discussion before the meeting can move on.

2. In your country business meetings are seen as a valuable opportunity to network and exchange ideas, but important decisions are always taken at a later stage and never in the meeting itself.

3. Greet people you don't know at a meeting by nodding to them and smiling.

4. Before a meeting can begin, it is customary to spend up to ten minutes in 'small talk'. Getting straight down to business is considered very uncivilised. Conversation topics usually include recent political events, sport perhaps, and especially the weather, which is so changeable in your country. The family, however, is a taboo subject and is never discussed in public. Enquiries about one's family are therefore either dealt with very quickly or even completely ignored.

5. Meetings are generally informal and people try to get on first name terms with each other as quickly as possible. You certainly always insist on everyone else using your first name. Of course, It's OK to address older or more senior colleagues as Mr ... or Ms ..., but you would never speak that way to your peers, younger people or subordinates.

6. In your country courtesy and consensus are valued. People who try to dominate meetings or become argumentative are strongly disapproved of. The way to deal with such people is to interrupt them politely but firmly, thank them and invite someone else to speak. Conflict is avoided at all costs. When arguments arise, it is common for the leader to ask for a two-minute break to give everyone a chance to calm down. Problem people may be asked to leave the meeting.

7. There is no fixed time limit for this meeting, but you think you'll probably need at least forty-five minutes.

Presentation Skills

Language of Presentations

Read this statistic.

According to research, people rank these items as their top fears in life, in this order:

1. speaking in public
2. fear of dying
3. financial ruin
4. spiders
5. snakes

- Do you also fear speaking in public? Discuss this with the class.
- What are some situations in which people have to speak in public? Are there any in non-business settings? Which are the scariest?

Listening

 Listen to the speaker talking about 'tweens'.

1. **What is her definition of a 'tween'?**
2. **Decide if each statement is true or false.**

1. The audience of this presentation is probably business people.
2. The purpose of the presentation is to sell.
3. Audience members are encouraged to ask questions during the presentation.
4. The speaker will use visual aids in the talk.
5. There are handouts.

Key Language

1. These are some expressions used in the presentation you heard. In pairs, put them in a logical order. (The first one has been done for you.)

   1 Good morning, Everyone.
   2 I will then look at some of the challenges
   3 I'm here to talk about the 'tweens' market.
   4 I'll finish by looking at some case studies.
   5 I will begin by outlining an overall profile.
   6 To start off, let me ask you: ...
   7 There will be time at the end for questions.
   8 I guess the best way to answer that question is ...
   9 If you look at this graph, you'll notice ...
   10 My name is Janet Wilkins.

2. **Listen again and check your answers.**

3. **Look at this sentence from the presentation:**
   "I'm here to talk about the growing 'tweens' market."

It is important to put the right verb + preposition together. Fill in the blanks with the correct verbs from the box.

> **talk look go (x2) begin finish start**

1. I'm unprepared. I don't know what I'm going to ... about.
2. Let's ... at some examples, shall we?
3. I think it's best not to ... into that matter just yet.
4. Before I begin, I'd like to ... over some figures with you.
5. To ... off, let's analyse this chart.
6. I'll ... by examining the market potential, and then talk about specific opportunities.
7. I'll summarise and then ... by inviting questions and comments.

Presentation Skills

Case Study

1. Look at the graph below of flight trends and fill in the gaps in the text with the words in the box.

> growth   rise   change   steep
> decline   sharply

What we see here is a (1) ... -trend in the number of hours people are flying. We see a steady (2) ... in 1970, and then a (3) ... rise in 2000, followed by a sudden (4) ... in 2001 – due to the political climate of that year. Since then, we have seen steady growth and then, just this year, the numbers are up (5) ... again, nearly 15 hours per flight average.

Global Flight Trends (in number of hours)

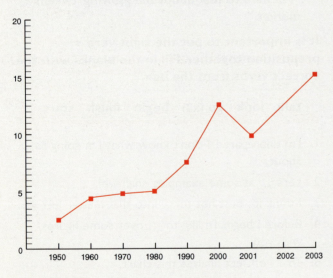

Demographic breakdown of travelers
women 42%   men 56%   children 2%

Travelers who wear some makeup
women 81%   men 11%

Travelers who use other types of cosmetics
(moisturisers, hair treatments, etc.)
women 94%   men 54%

Average international flight length
9.4 hours

Average domestic flight length
2.1 hours

Average cabin space availability (during flight)
First class – 7 seats
Business class – 9 seats
Economy – 2 seats

2. You work for the marketing department of New Image, a beauty products company. Considering these flight trends data on the graph, your company sees an opportunity for in-flight services such as make-up applications, massages and even haircuts. You need to develop a sales presentation to be delivered to major airlines, appealing especially to their business and first class cabin passengers.

Prepare a SWOT analysis.

NEW IMAGE IN-FLIGHT BEAUTY SERVICES		
SWOT	Arguments for	Arguments against
Strengths	...	...
Weaknesses	...	...
Opportunities	...	...
Threats	...	...

Deliver your presentations following these guidelines:

The presentation should be done in teams of 2-3.
- Each speaker will have 5 minutes.
- Prepare handouts (if relevant).
- Prepare visual aids.
- Prepare what you will say.

3. Following the presentation, the audience will give feedback on organisation, clarity, interest and usefulness

Follow Up

1. Which sounds better?
   Good morning, ladies and gentlemen. It is my pleasure to be here today.
   or
   Hi, everyone. Thanks for coming.
   Are they both all right? What's the difference?

2. This is the way one man ended his presentation:
   OK, that's all. Thank you.
   Do you think this is a good way to end a presentation? If not, do you know a better way?

3. Is it useful to memorise a presentation?
4. Should you read a presentation? Why/why not?
5. Is it important to prepare a presentation? If so, how thoroughly should you prepare?

The Persuaders

Look at the advertisement on this page. Do you remember any famous advertising campaigns? Which do you like best?

According to the advertising guru David Ogilvy, *"A good advertisement is one which sells the product without drawing attention to itself,"* and *"Bad advertising can unsell a product."*

Have you seen an advertisement recently which you particularly liked or disliked?
Did it actually persuade you to buy or put you off buying what it was advertising?

Are you familiar with the term 'global advertising'?
A global ad needs to appeal to the greatest number of consumers from many different cultural backgrounds.
Which of the following must a good global ad be?

- simple
- informative
- entertaining
- amusing
- visual
- clever
- cool
- sexy
- timeless
- controversial

Is there anything it should not be?
In your opinion, is the advert on this page global?
Why/Why not?

Now read the article, *Going Global.*

Think different.

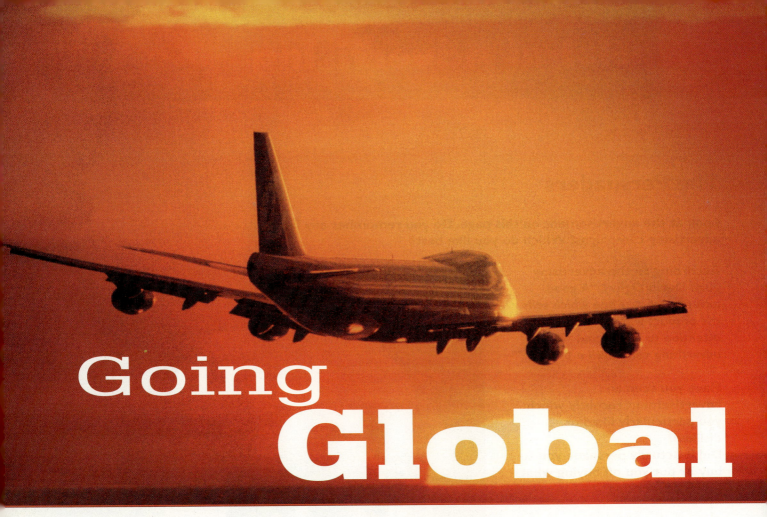

Going Global

Perhaps the biggest challenge now facing the international advertising industry is that of promoting 'world brands', for growing opposition to globalisation has not stopped the market getting more global by the day. And whilst there will always be national and niche markets which require specific marketing strategies, global operations call for global campaigns. Professor Theodore Levitt of Harvard Business School first put forward the theory of 'the globalisation of markets', but the idea that there are more similarities between cultures than differences goes back to the popular image of the 'global village'.

The Best in the Business

It was Marlboro in the 50s who invited us to "come to where the flavor is," Coca-Cola who sang in the 70s "I'd like to buy the world a Coke," and British Airways who announced in the 80s that they were "the world's favourite airline". Their universally recognised TV and cinema advertisements were among the first of a new breed of glamorous global ads, and the agencies who created their award-winning commercials are today widely regarded as the best in the business.

An Advertising Sensation

The very first global commercial Saatchi & Saatchi ran for BA featured Manhattan Island being flown across the Atlantic. The ad was ninety seconds long with no voice-over at all for the first forty. As BA's in-flight magazine put it, "The effect was breathtaking; words were barely needed; the pictures said it all." When the voice-over finally cut in, the message was devastatingly simple: "Every year, we fly more people across the Atlantic than the entire population of Manhattan." The commercial was screened in twenty-nine countries and caused a sensation in the industry.

Ads as Art

Only a handful of worldwide advertising networks have the capacity to take on the world's biggest brands. In fact, this small group of top agencies has been responsible for some of the most successful advertising slogans of the last thirty years – slogans like Coke's "Just for the taste of it' and Nike's "Just do it," IBM's "Think" and Apple's "Think different". It was the Canadian communications theorist Marshall McLuhan who claimed that "advertising is the greatest art form of the 20th century" and in the case of one product, this is almost literally true. Designed by the founder of Pop Art Andy Warhol, the Absolut vodka bottle is as much of a 21st century icon as the Nike swoosh.

Minimalist Approach

So what is it that makes global advertising so compelling and memorable? The answer lies partly in reducing the message to an absolute minimum, in letting pictures, music and a strong, simply-worded concept take the place of product description. Indeed, brand image is often reinforced independently of any real consideration of the product at all. It needs to be. When low-cost no-frills airlines will get you from A to B as quickly as the major carriers, and cheap PC-compatibles offer almost as many features as top-of-the-range IBMs, your image is all you have left to compete on. So Singapore Airlines promises us "a great way to fly" and IBM offers "solutions for a small planet".

Think Big

The beauty of a good global advertising campaign is that it can be used to great effect over a period of many years and still seem fresh. Global image-making, however, is a lengthy, costly and, to some extent, risky business. Bringing together the best creative talent in the advertising industry usually ends up costing the earth. These days there is growing opposition to the power of the world's biggest brand names. And industry critics of global ads point out that for the majority of brands, global advertising is not the answer. Though the world is getting smaller by the day, few companies, even multinationals, have true global status and most 'mass-marketed' products actually sell to fewer than five per cent of the masses. But those five per cent can be spread right across the planet and to reach them you've sometimes no option but to 'think big'.

Crosschecking

Which of the following viewpoints support the opinions expressed in the article?

1. Global advertising is just a current trend.

2. Global ads are generally believed to be superior to other commercials.

3. If global advertising became more widespread, only the top three or four agencies would be left in business.

4. Showing the same commercial in several countries cuts down production costs and saves time.

5. As companies compete more fiercely on price, branding becomes more important.

6. Good global ads often rely on their non-verbal impact.

7. Global commercials have more mileage.

8. Mass marketing is actually a contradiction in terms.

Find the Expressions

Look back at the article. Find the expressions which mean:

1. small, specialised markets (paragraph 1)

2. a new type (paragraph 2)

3. considered by many (paragraph 2)

4. the voice of an unseen speaker in a commercial (paragraph 3)

5. extremely impressive or beautiful (paragraph 3)

6. created a lot of interest and excitement (paragraph 3)

7. a small number (paragraph 4)

8. a famous symbol (paragraph 4)

9. extremely interesting (paragraph 5)

10. basic, offering no extra features (paragraph 5)

11. with excellent results (paragraph 6)

12. costing a lot of money (paragraph 6)

Language Focus

Word Partnerships 1

The following verbs both form strong word partnerships with the word *commercial*. Find three more in the article you have just read.

1. produce

2. devise

A COMMERCIAL

What is the difference between a commercial and an advertisement?

Word Partnerships 2

All the nouns in each list below form strong word partnerships with the words in capitals. Three nouns are in the wrong list. Which three? Which list should they be in?

MARKETING	ADVERTISING	MARKET
plan	budget	leader
strategy	agency	trend
expenditure	forces	share
slogan	costs	segmentation
mix	campaign	drive

Word Partnerships 3

Now complete the three paragraphs below using the words from the following list.

> segmentation   expenditure   mix   slogans   costs   shown   run
> drive   agencies   trends   campaign   produce   leaders

The total marketing (1) . . . includes service or product range, pricing policy, promotional methods and distribution channels, but for 'world brands' who aim to be market (2) . . ., a large part of marketing (3) . . . goes on television advertising. When global companies organise a marketing (4) . . ., a concerted effort is made to promote and sell more of their products, and this will often involve an expensive advertising (5) . . . .

Marketers generally tend to divide markets up into separate groups according to geographical area, income bracket and so on. This is known as market (6) . . . . But a global marketing policy will obviously take much less account of local market (7) . . . and concentrate instead on what different markets have in common.

As global commercials are (8) . . . on TV in many different countries, the advertising (9) . . . tend to be high and obviously only the biggest advertising (10) . . . can (11) . . . commercials on such a global scale. Fortunately, global commercials like those for Marlboro cigarettes and BA can be (12) . . . for many years without looking out of date, and advertising (13) . . ., such as "the world's favourite airline" and "Just do it", will always be universally recognised.

How many word partnerships can you find in the paragraphs above?

Word Partnerships 4

Complete the presentation extract below by matching the two halves of each sentence. Referring back to the article will help you.

1. First of all, let me say that we look forward to facing . . .

2. But first we have to firmly establish . . .

3. However, as you know, in global terms Britain is little more than a niche . . .

4. So the question really is: how are we going to make sure we appeal to . . .

5. Well, I think what the whole campaign requires is . . .

6. We need to be running . . .

7. What I'm saying is that we have to get . . .

8. In other words, the commercial itself should be reinforcing . . .

9. Remember, image outsells . . .

10. Now, obviously, this will mean bringing in . . .

a. the consumer in our home market without making the product too British for European tastes?

b. our brand in the minds of the British consumer.

c. product every time.

d. our brand-image with strong visuals and background music and the minimum of product information.

e. a global marketing strategy.

f. our message across directly and simply and in a way that will cross cultural boundaries.

g. the challenge of breaking into foreign markets with this product.

h. market for our kind of product and demand is always going to be much greater overseas.

i. creative talent from outside, but in the long term creating a Euro-ad will actually save us money.

j. commercials that will work well in Britain but which we can use again at a later stage in Europe.

Quotes

Complete the following quotations on advertising:

1. Never mind the gap in the . . ., is there a market in the . . .?

2. I know half the money I spend on advertising is wasted. The trouble is I don't know . . . .

3. The best . . . is a good product.

4. You can tell the ideals of a nation by its . . . .

5. All publicity is . . . publicity.

Do you agree? Do you have a favourite quote of your own?

Discuss

Think of a well-known market leader. To what do you attribute its market leadership?

- a better brand-image
- superior marketing
- superior production methods
- technological superiority
- innovative research
- something else

Who is the market leader in your particular industry?

Language Focus

Word Partnerships 5

Find the one word in each sentence which does not fit. Some of the words appeared in the article.

1. It is a **reasonably / fairly / quite / highly** cost-effective strategy.

2. It is **comprehensively / widely / universally / generally** regarded as the best TV commercial ever.

3. It is a(n) **well / lavishly / superbly / exceptionally** produced commercial.

4. The message is **powerfully / highly / clearly / vividly** expressed.

Funny Business

What eight-letter word will complete all the following expressions? Two possible words appeared in the article.

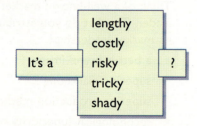

Which of the above expressions refers to:

1. something expensive?

2. something difficult or delicate?

3. something uncertain or dangerous?

4. something illegal?

5. something that takes a long time?

Word Grammar

One way of forming verbs meaning to *make like this* is to add *-ize* (or *-ise*) to the end of the noun or adjective. You can make a lot of verbs in this way from words you probably already know. Complete the following. The first one has been done for you as an example.

1. to make your activities more global
    ➤ globalise

2. to make your activities more international
    ➤ ...

3. to make a private company national
    ➤ ...

4. to make a national company private
    ➤ ...

5. to make something more sensational
    ➤ ...

6. to make something more standard
    ➤ ...

7. to make something more popular
    ➤ ...

8. to be (too) intellectual about something
    ➤ ...

9. to put something into a category
    ➤ ...

10. to introduce computers
    ➤ ...

11. to make something legal
    ➤ ...

12. to make a (too) general statement
    ➤ ...

13. to make something more commercial
    ➤ ...

14. to make something more modern
    ➤ ...

15. to put something on television
    ➤ ...

Brand Names

Read the text below and discuss the questions with a partner.

One of the quickest ways of destroying your brand image is to give your product an unattractive name – or one that, though attractive in your language, does not translate well.

When it comes to embarrassing translations, no-one has made as many costly mistakes as the car industry. Ford, for example, has repeatedly got it wrong in Central and South America with its *Ford Pinto* and Ford Fiera truck. '*Pinto*' means 'small male organ' in Brazilian Portuguese, and '*fiera*' can mean a fierce '*dragon lady*' in Spanish. Latin American customers were understandably reluctant to test-drive these particular models until the names were changed to something more acceptable.

In Germany even the refined Rolls-Royce motor company blundered with the exotic-sounding *Silver Mist*. '*Mist*' literally means '*excrement*' in German or more idiomatically '*rubbish*' – either way not a winner in marketing terms!

Of course, the problem works both ways. Supermarket products that sound fine in their original language may not sound so good in English. Finnish *Koff* beer met some consumer resistance initially, as did Spanish *Bum* crisps. And when a successful product in one market enters another, it has to be ensured that there isn't another product with the same name. The Australian lager *Castlemaine XXXX* (pronounced four ex) had difficulties in America where *Fourex* is a condom manufacturer. Ironically, the condom manufacturer *Durex* had exactly the same problem in Australia where *Durex* is the name of a brand of sellotape!

Do you know of any foreign products that have strange-sounding names in your language?
What alternative names would you suggest for Ford's vehicles?
Can you rename the Finnish beer and Spanish crisps to make them sound more appropriate to an English-speaking market?

Discuss

Here are some well-known brand names you could find in any large British supermarket. What do you think the products are? What image does each name convey?

up-market	glamorous
humorous	trendy
teenage	sporty
hi-tech	classic
exotic	comforting
macho	feminine
middle-of-the-road	scientifically proven
natural and cruelty-free	

1.	Gold Blend	16.	Shreddies
2.	Organics	17.	Blue Nun
3.	Black Magic	18.	Mates
4.	Bold	19.	Eternity
5.	Imperial Leather	20.	Special Brew
6.	Galaxy	21.	Biactol
7.	Hamlet	22.	Flash
8.	Lynx	23.	Dairylea
9.	Reach	24.	Sure
10.	Quality Street	25.	Uncle Ben's
11.	Old Spice	26.	Sensodyne
12.	Taboo	27.	Blue Dragon
13.	Butterkist	28.	Timotei
14.	Pampers	29.	Babycham
15.	Kleenex	30.	Sensor

Would these names work in your country?
Would any cause offence?

Fluency Work

Case Study

Step back in time to consider the branding decisions of one of Britain's best-known companies.

British Airways: Tailfins

In a brave attempt to get away from an image of old-fashioned Britishness, BA decided in the 90s to replace the distinctive red, white and blue tailfin on its fleet of 290 passenger jets with a series of multi-ethnic designs to reflect its global status as 'the world's favourite airline'. The cost of the changeover was £60 million.

The designs, influenced by Chinese calligraphy, Delft pottery, Polish high-rise flats and images from the Kalahari desert, were immediately criticised by BA's customers, who felt the company had abandoned its core values as a world-beating British company. After just four years, and relentless ridicule in the press, the designs were finally painted over with the Union Jack flag.

Look at some of the BA tailfin designs. Do you agree with the majority of BA's customers that the Union Jack is preferable to the ethnic designs? Could there have been a compromise?

Client Pitch

Work in groups. You are advertising agencies competing for the BA account. Produce a short presentation for the potential client on how you would promote awareness of their company into the second decade of the 21st century.

Consider:

1. What are the company's core values?
2. What should be the advertising campaign's key message?
3. What new slogan would reflect this key message?
4. What new logo/tailfin design would reinforce brand image?
5. What kind of global TV commercial would be most successful? (Describe what it would be like including visuals, background music and voice-over. Draw a simple storyboard if you like to illustrate your pitch.)

Give your pitches to the rest of your class (the clients). Decide who gets the account by voting for the best ideas after your own!

UNIT 11

Management Styles

The Same or Different?

Do men and women bring different qualities to business or is it nonsense to talk about male and female management styles?

Decide whether you think the following management qualities are more typical of men, more typical of women or shared by both.

1. Being able to take the initiative.
2. Being a good listener.
3. Staying calm under pressure.
4. Being prepared to take risks.
5. Being conscientious and thorough.
6. Having good communication skills.
7. Being energetic and assertive.
8. Getting the best out of people.
9. Being independent and authoritative.
10. Being supportive towards colleagues.
11. Being able to delegate.
12. Motivating by example.
13. Having a co-operative approach.
14. Being single-minded and determined.
15. Being a good time-manager.

Now select what you consider to be the five most important qualities in any manager and prioritise them in order of importance.

Discuss

- Does your choice indicate a male or female-oriented view of management ability?
- Is it a fairly balanced view or rather biased?
- Which of these qualities do you think you possess yourself?
- How do your views compare with those expressed in the article, *She's the Boss?*

BODY
BY VICTORIA™

 Business has traditionally been and to a certain extent still is 'a boy's game'. Less than six per cent of executive management positions in American and European companies are held by women, and of the Fortune 500 only four have a female CEO!

Yet in Britain one in three new businesses are started up by women, and according to John Naisbitt and Patricia Auburdene, authors of 'Megatrends', since 1980 the number of self-employed women has increased twice as fast as the number of self-employed men.

The Glass Ceiling Syndrome

Is it just a case of women whose career progress has been blocked by their male colleagues - the so-called 'glass ceiling syndrome' - being forced to set up their own businesses? Or do women share specific management qualities which somehow serve them better in self-employment? As many as forty per cent of start-ups fold within their first two years, but the failure rate of those run by women is substantially lower than that. It's hardly surprising, therefore, that though male bosses tend to be reluctant to promote women, male bank managers seem only too happy to finance their businesses.

The Roddick Phenomenon

Anita Roddick, founder of the Body Shop empire, is the perfect example of the female entrepreneur, with her company growing from zero to £470 million in its first fifteen years. Perhaps the secret of her success was caution. Rather than push ahead with the purchasing of new shops, Roddick got herself into franchising - the cheapest way to expand a business whilst keeping overheads down. Caution, forward planning and tight budgeting seem to be more female characteristics than male. They are also the blueprint for success when launching a new company. The recent internet boom allowed women like Martha Lane Fox to set up the massively successful web travel agency lastminute.com. In cyberspace nobody cares what sex you are.

She's the
Boss

More Sensitive

When women join an existing company, it's a different story. Less ruthlessly individualistic in their approach to business, women are more sensitive to the feelings of the group or team in which they work. They are generally more cooperative than competitive, less assertive, less prepared to lead from the front. Though they usually manage their time better than men and may even work harder, they are much less likely than their male counterparts to take risks. And, above all, it is risk-taking that makes corporate high fliers. As one male director put it: "I'm not paid to make the right decisions. I'm just paid to make decisions."

Better Communicators

It's an overgeneralisation, of course, but it remains true that men will more readily take the initiative than women. The female style of management leans towards consensus and conciliation. Women seem to be better communicators than men – both more articulate and better listeners. And perhaps it is women's capacity to listen which makes them particularly effective in people-oriented areas of business. In any mixed group of business people the ones doing most of the talking will almost certainly be the men. But perhaps only the women will really be listening.

The New Achievers

It was predominantly men who led the hierarchical corporations of the nineties. But it may be women who achieve the most in the more democratic, people-centred years to come.

Crosschecking

Which of the following points support the opinions expressed in the article?

1. Women are at least as entrepreneurial as men.

2. Most female managers prefer task-based jobs to people-centred ones.

3. Women tend to be more conscientious than men.

4. Women who do succeed in business have to become even more ruthless than men.

5. Men aren't as financially aware as women.

6. Women are more likely to be the managers of the future than men are.

Find the Expressions

Look back at the article. Find the expressions which mean:

1. the difficulty women face getting promoted to senior positions (paragraph 2)

2. new businesses fail (paragraph 2)

3. a method of selling by which the brand owner permits another to sell their goods exclusively in return for a fee (paragraph 3)

4. make independent decisions (paragraph 5)

5. agreement among all people involved (paragraph 5)

6. the process of ending arguments, bringing the two sides together (paragraph 5)

Response

1. Do you think the article is stereotypical in its view of men and women in management?

2. Are you typical of the male or female management type described in the article?

3. What do you think could be done to change the extreme gender imbalance in middle and senior management?

Language Focus

Word Partnerships 1

Match each of the words in the first column with a word from the second column to make nine word partnerships from the article. There are some alternative partnerships, but there's only one way to match all nine.

1.	senior	a.	budgeting
2.	career	b.	structures
3.	forward	c.	taking
4.	tight	d.	progress
5.	risk-	e.	organisations
6.	high	f.	positions
7.	hierarchical	g.	skills
8.	flexible	h.	planning
9.	communication	i.	fliers

Discuss

- Is the organisation you work for hierarchical or flexible?
- Are the high-fliers the individualistic risk-takers or the group-oriented communicators?
- How about the people in senior positions?
- What kind of staff appraisal and development programme does your company have?
- Does your company generally prefer to fill posts internally or to bring people in from outside?
- Are top people headhunted?

Word Partnerships 2

All the words below form strong word partnerships with the word *company*. But the vowels are missing from each word. How many can you work out? Referring back to the article will help you with some of them. Can you add some more words?

1. r _ n
2. l _ _ n c h
3. s _ t   _ p
4. f _ r m
5. j _ _ n
6. l _ _ _ v _
7. s _ l l   _ f f
8. w _ n d   _ p
9. f l _ _ t
10. h _ l d _ n g
11. p _ r _ n t
12. s _ b s _ d _ _ _ r y

a company

Which of the above verbs mean:

1. to start up a company

2. to close down a company

3. Which of the two adjectives mean the same thing? What is the connection with the third?

Word Partnerships 3

One of the words in each list below will not form a strong word partnership with the word *staff.* Which one?

Verbs

recruit   train   develop   take on   take off
lay off   dismiss   poach   headhunt

Adjectives

full-time   part-time   half-time   permanent
temporary   extra   administrative

1. Which of the verbs mean:
   a. to hire
   b. to fire

2. Two of the verbs mean *to hire another company's best people*. Which two?

3. Which is the less offensive term?

Word Grammar 1

The adjectives listed below describe some of the positive qualities of good managers. Change each adjective into its opposite by adding:
un-, in-, im-, ir- or *dis-*:

co-operative	decisive	responsible	competitive
sincere	practical	communicative	sensitive
supportive	assertive	articulate	discreet
skilled	intelligent	patient	loyal
creative	reliable	consistent	rational
committed	approachable	honest	

Are there any patterns to help you decide which prefix to use? Which adjectives do not follow the main patterns?

Word Grammar 2

Find at least one adjective from the list above to describe the following managers.

1. She always means what she says.
   She's totally ...

2. He always voices his opinions and needs.
   He's very ...

3. She's very good at expressing herself.
   She's extremely ...

4. You can depend on him.
   He's very ...

5. Her door is always open if you've got a problem.
   She's very ...

6. His job comes first.
   He's totally ...

7. She is quick to help colleagues and subordinates.
   She's extremely ...

8. He doesn't go around gossiping behind people's backs.
   He's very ...

9. She doesn't let her emotions interfere with her work.
   She's very ...

10. He always works to the same high standard.
    He's extremely ...

Discuss

- What's the ratio of male to female employees in your company?
  Is it different at management level? Is your boss male or female?

- Do you generally prefer to work for a man or a woman, or does it not make any difference?

Language Focus

Business Grammar

🎧 **Complete the following dialogue by adding the missing prepositions.**

Then listen and check your answers.

over	between	out	from
round	with	of	to
in	about	for	up on

John: David?

David: Yeah?

John: I wonder if I could have a word (1) ... you (2) ... that job in R&D?

David: Er, sure. What's (3) ... your mind?

John: Well, you know that Deborah Norman's applied (4) ... it, I suppose?

David: Naturally. I interviewed her. In fact, she and Robert Fry both came (5) ... extremely well, I thought. To tell you the truth, we're going to find it pretty difficult to choose (6) ... them.

John: That's what I thought. Only I think I should warn you (7) ... Deborah.

David: Oh, really?

John: Yeah. I mean, I don't want to interfere (8) ... your selection procedure, or anything. It's (9) ... to you to make (10) ... your own mind (11) ... the sort of person you want for the post.

David: John, will you just get (12) ... the point? What's Deborah been (13) ... to?

John: Oh, it's nothing like that.

David: Because I know she's got a reputation (14) ... being a bit over-assertive at times.

John: Yeah, but it's not that I object (15) ... so much. I reckon she believes (16) ... what she's doing – even if nobody else does. No, it's just that I know you want to make our internal training more cost-effective and I really don't think you can rely (17) ... someone like Deborah Norman to carry (18) ... your programme of economy measures, that's all.

David: I see. And what makes you think that, John?

John: Well, for one thing, she's always insisting (19) ... bringing (20) ... outsiders to run most of the seminars. You know how expensive that can be. And for another, she's all (21) ... setting (22) ... some joint venture with MP Associates – more outsiders! I've been opposed (23) ... this all along, as you know. And so has Robert. He's quite capable (24) ... running things himself.

David: Ah hah. That's what this is all (25) ..., is it? You don't like the idea (26) ... Deborah taking control away (27) ... you and Robert. Well, I'm glad we've had this little chat, John. I'll certainly bear it all (28) ... mind when we make our final decision (29) ... who gets the post.

John: Thanks, David. I knew you'd come (30) ... to our way of thinking on this. I mean Deborah's very talented. I'd be the first to admit it. And I'd hate to think anything I'd said had spoilt things (31) ... her.

David: Oh, don't worry John. It hasn't. You can bet (32) ... that.

Identify any fixed expressions from the dialogue which you think you could use yourself.

Discuss

- How are people appointed in your company?
- Are there clear guidelines on how to come to a decision about who to recruit?
- How were you yourself recruited?

Fluency Work

Discrimination

In each of the following situations, decide if you would give the applicant the job or not. Make a note of whether you would:

- accept the candidate.
- reject the candidate.
- call the candidate for a second interview.

Be prepare to justify your decisions in each case by noting down your reasons.
Then listen to a short extract from their job interviews.
Do you want to change your mind about any of them?

1. SYSTEMS ANALYST

The applicant is a 36-year-old woman returning to work after giving up her previous job to start a family three years ago. She is well-qualified for the post and much more experienced than any of the other applicants. She is, however, a little out of touch with the latest developments in the industry you work in and would require some retraining. Most of the other applicants are younger men.

2. MARKETING DIRECTOR

The applicant is a 29-year-old woman. On paper she looks impressive and at interview she came across very well indeed. In terms of experience and expertise, she is clearly the best person for the post. There's only one problem: the job is in a country where women do not have equal status with men and where very few women hold management positions at all, let alone senior ones such as this.

3. PRODUCTION MANAGER

The applicant is a 44-year-old woman. You have recently interviewed twenty people for a very responsible post within your company and she is one of the two on your final shortlist. The other most promising candidate is a 29-year-old man. On balance, you think the man would probably be the better choice but, at present, your company has only appointed three female managers out of a total of thirty two and you are under a lot of pressure from the personnel department to exercise 'positive discrimination' in favour of women.

4. MANAGEMENT TRAINER

The applicant is a 31-year-old man. The company you represent runs assertiveness training courses for women in management and at the moment you have an all-female staff. Whilst the applicant has an excellent track record in management training with mixed groups, you have some doubts about his credibility running seminars exclusively for women, some of whom tend to see male managers more as an obstacle than an aid to their progress. You're also concerned about how the rest of the staff will react to him.

Have you ever found yourself in a similar position to one of those above?
What did you do?

Fluency Work

Follow-up Letter

Choose one of the situations on the previous page where you decided to reject the applicant, and write a letter to the person concerned explaining your decision. You may find the notes below helpful.

NOTES

Dear

                        re: [details of post here]

Thank / application / this post.

Whilst / impressed / qualifications and experience / and / performance / interview / regret / inform / this occasion / not successful.

As you know / large number / applications / this post / and / standard / applicants / extremely high. Should not feel / non-selection / due / failings / on your part.

I wish you every success / future career. We / put / details on file / shall consider you / suitable vacancies / may arise / our company.

Yours sincerely

                   UNIT 11 • Management Styles

Mergers and Acquisitions

UNIT 12

Let's Stick Together

"Why anybody thinks they will produce a gazelle by mating two dinosaurs is beyond me."
Tom Peters, management guru and best selling author

What do you think are the advantages and disadvantages of transnational mergers and acquisitions in terms of the following:

- market share?
- trade barriers?
- scale of operations?
- shareholder value?
- healthy competition?
- culture clash?

Look at the companies below. Which have merged with or been taken over by which in the last ten years or so? What commercial sector are they in?

VODAPHONE	CHRYSLER	PHARMACEUTICALS
DAIMLER	AOL	TELECOMS
BP	SMITH KLINE BEECHAM	FOOD & BREWING
COMMERCIAL UNION	GUINNESS	OIL & PETROLEUM
GLAXO	MANNESMANN	INSURANCE
GRAND METROPOLITAN	GENERAL ACCIDENT	MEDIA
TIME WARNER	AMOCO	AUTOMOTIVE

Has your company, or a company you know, been involved in a recent transnational merger or takeover? How has it affected the company? In general, is increasing globalisation a good thing or a bad thing?

Are you familiar with the following terms and acronyms? Compare with a partner.

LBO   junk bonds   WTO   corporate raiding   IMF   hostile takeover
FDI   high-yield   OECD   green field investment

Now read the article, *Greed is Good*.

Greed *is* Good

Drowning in Debt

Most business people would say too much debt is a dangerous thing. But that has not always been the case. Some years ago senior executives began to look at debt in a totally different way. A company could be drowning in debt and still succeed. Debt became 'leverage' and you could build a very profitable business on acquiring companies through debt.

Hostile Takeovers

A classic case is the New York investment banking firm, Kohlberg, Kravis, Roberts & Co. In 1989 KKR shocked the corporate world when it acquired food and cigarette giant, RJR-Nabisco, for what was then a record purchase price of $24.7 billion. At the time, the real controversy centred not so much on the hostility of KKR's takeover or on the huge sum of money involved, as on KKR's method of financing the deal – a leveraged buyout.

A Load of Junk

In a leveraged buyout, or LBO, the target company's own assets and earnings are used to raise capital for the takeover. The buyer simply offers these assets as security to lenders in the form of high-risk, high-yield bonds – or 'junk bonds', as they came to be known. Of course, if the bid is successful, the newly acquired firm starts off on day one with a vast amount of debt. So the buyers (or corporate raiders, depending on your point of view) sell off parts of the new company to bring this under control. Sometimes called asset stripping, the results for the average worker or shareholder can be disastrous.

The Decade of Greed

LBOs and asset stripping cast a dark shadow over the 1980s and early 90s. Takeover specialists like Michael Milken, Ivan Boesky and Sir James Goldsmith, made fortunes buying and selling off companies in what became known as the "Decade of Greed". In Hollywood, films based on their spectacular deals, like *Wall Street* and *Barbarians at the Gate*, made almost as much money as the raiders themselves. Eventually the bubble burst. Boesky ended up getting three years in prison. Milken got ten.

Cross-Border Trade

But the latest wave of mergers and acquisitions is different. Between 1990 and 1998, the value of worldwide M&As rose nearly fivefold to $2.5 trillion. Most of that merger activity was within the US, but the number of cross-border mergers and takeovers rose dramatically, too, with the increasing integration of world financial markets. The objective is no longer quick profit. It's total global domination.

Mega-Mergers

There are many reasons why companies merge. A merger gives them the chance to increase market share and gain access to new markets; to combine operational synergies and reduce costs; to diversify their business, acquire new technologies and, of course, valuable assets. But, above all, they achieve scale and according to analysts Watson Wyatt, increased scale is why we are now seeing 200 billion-dollar mergers. The more globalised and liberalised world markets get, the bigger companies need to be just to stay in the 'game'.

Anti-Globalisation

Predictably, globalisation has its opponents. The famous demonstration outside the World Trade Organization at the 'Battle in Seattle' in 1999 and similar protests outside the International Monetary Fund headquarters in Washington and elsewhere have been extremely successful – even forcing the Organization for Economic Cooperation and Development to abandon its planned Multilateral Agreement on Investment. The protesters have a point. Foreign direct investment, or FDI, by big firms in developing countries nearly always takes the form of acquisition these days, rather than green field investment in new businesses. National economies may benefit, but national cultures and institutions are bound to suffer.

Chasing Profit

But globalisation is not about spreading wealth and democracy. It is about allowing capital to chase profit around the world. Asked why he spent his life buying up mismanaged companies, Sir James Goldsmith once said: "Takeovers are for the public good, but that's not why I do it. I do it to make money."

Response

What's your immediate reaction to the article you just read? Complete one or more of the following.

1. I'm amazed that ...
2. I don't agree that ...
3. I'm not so sure that ...
4. I already knew that ...
5. I can hardly believe that ...
6. I tend to agree that ...

Find the Expressions

Look back at the article. Find the expressions which mean:

1. owe a fortune (paragraph 1)
2. a typical example (paragraph 2)
3. had a negative effect on ...; a period of success came to an end (paragraph 4)
4. the most recent increase in activity (paragraph 5)
5. the ways two companies function more effectively than one; remain competitive (paragraph 6)
6. are sure to (paragraph 7)

Crosschecking

Which of the following viewpoints support the opinions expressed in the article?

1. "The greatest motivator known to man is greed, and there's nothing wrong with greed as long as it's harnessed properly."
   Peter Wood, chief executive of Direct Line Insurance

2. "It is better to take over and build upon an existing business than to start a new one."
   Harold Geneen, business consultant and chairman of ITT

3. "There will be two kinds of CEOs who will exist in the next five years: those who think globally and those who are unemployed."
   Peter Drucker, management theorist and writer

4. "If a company gets too large, break it into smaller parts. Once people start not knowing the people in the building and it starts to become impersonal, it's time to break up the company."
   Richard Branson, head of Virgin Group

Language Focus

Word Partnerships 1

How many word partnerships can you make by combining the verbs in the left hand box with the nouns on the right? There were some in the article you read.

build	gain access to
acquire	diversify
finance	buy up
reduce	sell off
increase	achieve
combine	raise

+

a business	costs
a company	new technologies
capital	assets
scale	a deal
market share	synergies
new markets	

Use some of the word partnerships you made above to complete the following TV interview with the new CEO of a recently acquired company. Then listen and check your answers.

Reporter: Now, Mr Gutenberg. This was, by any standards, a hostile takeover. How did you raise the (1) ... to acquire the (2) ... ?

CEO: Well, I wouldn't call our acquisition of Standlake Hydraulics hostile, Alana. Certainly there was some opposition from the board, but we had the support of the majority of the shareholders. To answer your question, we financed the (3) ... by issuing bonds to our lenders.

Reporter: Junk bonds?

CEO: That's a term I don't like. Let's just say the bonds offer a very high return.

Reporter: And carry a very high risk?

CEO: Well, there's always a risk. But let me make one thing absolutely clear. We have no intention of selling off the company's (4) ... . We plan to build the (5) ... and get it back into profit as quickly as possible. We believe that by combining the (6) ... of the two firms we can both reduce (7) ... and increase (8) ... .

Reporter: I see. So, how would you answer the charge that you're only interested in buying up foreign (9) ... in order to gain access to (10) ... that you'd otherwise be excluded from?

CEO: Well, now, you know that's just nonsense. We all operate in a global market these days. Trade tariffs are down to 5%. The real reason for this takeover was threefold. First, we wanted to diversify our (11) ... . And you know acquisition is the quickest way to do that. Secondly, our own research and development has been a weak point in recent years - we needed to acquire (12) ... . Standlake has a very strong technological lead in this field.

Reporter: And thirdly, you wanted to achieve (13) ... ?

CEO: Exactly. Apart from economies of scale, increased size gives us the kind of market coverage we simply had to have to remain competitive.

Reporter: To stay in the game.

CEO: As you say, to stay in the game.

Reporter: Well, thank you for talking to us, Mr Gutenberg.

CEO: My pleasure.

Word Partnerships 2

All of the verbs below can be used to talk about the running of a company. Match each diagram with the appropriate verb. Some of the verbs were in the article you read.

> globalise   merge   expand   take over
> restructure   break up   centralise
> diversify   de-layer

1.

2.

3.

4.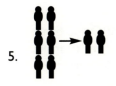

5.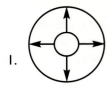

6.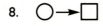

7.

8.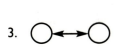

9.

Turn the verbs in the box above into nouns. Then use either the verb or noun to complete the following text.

In the corporate world trends change fast. The 70s, for example, were the age of the conglomerate. Everybody was into (1) … in those days - making companies as big as possible, but (2) … , with authority coming from head office. Then along came the corporate raiders of the money-grabbing 80s, and (3) … any company that looked like it had got too big and vulnerable. Most of their acquisitions were later (4) … by selling off their assets to make a quick profit.

But the raiders taught big business a useful lesson, and in the mid-90s a lot of companies decided just to concentrate on their core businesses instead of (5) … . Many realised, too, that to remain competitive they needed to get rid of a large part of their middle management by (6) … or downsizing the workforce. Some firms went too far and laid off half their workers!

Now with the rise in cross-border trade and increased (7) … , many corporate giants are (8) … or forming strategic alliances to achieve even greater scale and market penetration, as well as (9) … their operations to take advantage of the Internet.

Language Focus

Word Grammar 1

The article *Greed is Good* on page 104 talks about cross-border trade, mega-mergers and anti-globalisation. Many prefixes in English have a specific meaning. Match the following with their meanings:

1.	anti-	a.	big
2.	pro-	b.	many
3.	mega-	c.	against
4.	mini-	d.	one
5.	multi-	e.	small
6.	uni-	f.	in favour of
7.	cross-	g.	all
8.	pre-	h.	after
9.	post-	i.	not
10.	ex-	j.	between
11.	non-	k.	former
12.	pan-	l.	before

Which of the prefixes above often precede the following words?

1. national
2. president
3. industrial
4. standard
5. lateral
6. participant
7. bar
8. tax
9. European
10. democracy
11. media
12. payment
13. purpose
14. wife/husband
15. specialist
16. cultural
17. functional
18. millionaire
19. communist
20. crisis
21. bucks

Discuss

- How important is cross-border trade to your national economy?
- Do you think people in your country are generally pro or anti-globalisation?
- Have there been any demonstrations there like the ones in Seattle, London, Prague and Quebec?

Word Grammar 2

The words in capitals can be used to form other words which will fit in the spaces. Complete each sentence in this way.

1. FINANCE
   … speaking, the company is in very good shape.

2. FINANCE
   Ivan Boesky was the most notorious … of the 80s.

3. INVEST
   SBC is the main … in the project.

4. INVEST
   In an management buyout, or MBO, the banks usually like the managers themselves to make some kind of … in the target company.

5. CAPITAL
   A company that is short of money may need to … some of its assets to raise cash.

6. CAPITAL
   Asset stripping was one of the ugliest examples of … gone mad.

7. NEGOTIATE
   The new management and the trade unions hope to reach a … agreement soon.

8. NEGOTIATE
   We can discuss how the merger will affect the management structure in the two companies, but the question of overall control is not … .

Fluency Work

"Without competitors, there would be no need for strategy."
Kenichi Ohmae, management consultant and business author, *The Mind of the Strategist*

Simulation: Takeover Battle

The global media are increasingly dominated by a small number of all-powerful, transnational corporations. Many of these achieved their scale through an aggressive programme of acquisition, merger and strategic alliance. But it's a never-ending battle to stay ahead of the competition.

1. **Read the company profile below and discuss the questions.**

VIACOM
WWW.VIACOM.COM

From the 52nd floor of 1515 Broadway in the middle of Times Square, Manhattan, Sumner Redstone rules a media empire that includes MTV, Nickelodeon, Paramount Pictures, CBS News and Blockbuster Video. This is the headquarters of Viacom, perhaps the largest diversified entertainment company on the planet.

"I've always had that obsessive will to win," says Redstone. Raised in a tiny apartment with no bathroom by an entrepreneurial father, who went on to open America's first drive-in movie theatre, Redstone entered Harvard at 17, became fluent in Japanese, graduated at 19, and eventually gave up a partnership in a Boston law firm "to risk it all," as he puts it, "to bet my life."

The bet paid off. MTV is now beamed into over 100 different countries—pop culture brands like Levi's, Nintendo and Pepsi all eager to advertise on the phenomenally successful rock music channel. Nickelodeon children's channel attracts more viewers than anything else on cable. Blockbuster, in trouble before Redstone took it over, is now the biggest video rental store on earth.

With 13 US television stations, publishing interests in Simon & Schuster, Scribners and Macmillan, no less than five theme parks and a 50% stake in United Cinemas International, Viacom is now seeking to build on its success with MTV Asia, Europe and Latino. It's also planning to develop new-generation computer games through Viacom Interactive Media. By his own admission, Redstone is a risk-taker, but not on the scale of his friend and rival Rupert Murdoch of News Corporation. "I wouldn't take the risks he does," he says. "The one thing I wouldn't do is risk Viacom. I'm not going back to where I was."

- What would you say is Viacom's core business (choose one): music, movies, news, entertainment, sport, publishing, software, Internet, communications?

- What kind of businessman do you think Sumner Redstone is: a cautious decision-maker, a calculated risk-taker, a maverick?

- The MTV brand is obviously incredibly strong in youth markets. What other services or products could the brand be 'stretched' to include?

- Blockbuster stores currently rent videos and music CDs, as well as retailing confectionery, soft drinks and ice-cream. What else could they sell?

- Do you think Viacom should be consolidating its position in music, movies and television or venturing further into new electronic media?

- What sort of companies might be on Viacom's 'hit list' of possible acquisition targets?

Fluency Work

2. **Work in groups. You are high-level decision-makers in the M&A department of Viacom and are about to take part in a strategy meeting. Turn to page 174 to see profiles of ten possible acquisition targets. You have a total six billion dollars allocated to new aquisitions. Discuss each target company with your group and decide which you are going to take over.**

Here is a suggested agenda for the meeting:

Acquisition Strategy Meeting

AGENDA

1. Introductions

Outline of objectives (Chairperson).

2. Analysis of each target company:

Does it complement our current businesses?
How risky is the business the target company is in?
Does the company sound like it's well-managed?
Could there be cultural problems?
Should we buy it just to keep it out of the hands of our competitors?

 3. Prioritise six companies and decide bids.

A year has passed. Listen to a business news report to find out what happened to the companies you took over twelve months ago. How many of your acquisitions paid off?

Which group would have done the best job for Viacom?

Negotiating Skills

Language of Negotiating

Language Focus

1. **These are some tips from negotiation experts. Fill in the gaps.**

1. You should ... more than you ... . (speak/listen)
2. Remember: never ... but always ... . (ask questions/interrupt)
3. He who talks figures ... will finish ... . (first/last)
4. Don't be ... wise and ... foolish. (penny/pound)
5. Being ... is a powerful tool. Being ... is only destructive. (assertive/aggressive)
6. Sellers should ask for ... than they expect to receive, and buyers should offer ... than they are prepared to pay. (more/less)

2. **Now compare your answers with the rest of the class. Does everyone agree?**

Listening

🎧 **Amanda is a sales manager at a British computer parts supplier and George is the owner of a large chain of electronic stores in the United States. Listen to the opening of the negotiation. Does George seem happy with the proposal?**

Now listen to the rest of the negotiation and circle the correct information.

1. What is Amanda initially asking for?
   a. $180,000   b. $178,000   c. $177,000

2. What is her *bottom line* (minimum she will accept)?
   a. $180,000   b. $178,000   c. $177,000

3. What is her compromise settlement?
   a. $177,000 + 5% discount
   b. $178,000 + 10% discount
   c. $177,000 + 10% discount

Who came out winning: Amanda or George or both? Why?

Key Language

1. **These are some expressions for negotiating you heard in the recording. First unscramble them. The first word is in the correct place.**

showing flexibility

1. It's / discussion / to / open
2. I / fair / think / that's
3. I'm / to / suggestions / open

showing hesitation/caution

4. I'll / writing / see / it / need / to / in
5. We / some / need / think / over / it / time / to
6. We're / prepared / that / much / pay / not / to
7. That's / exactly / mind / in / what / not / had / we

asking questions to open dialogue

8. And / is / why / that
9. How / sound / does / that
10. Are / you / with / that / happy
11. What / see / happen / like / you / would / to

pushing to a close/closing

12. Then / settled / it's
13. You / hard / a / bargain / drive
14. That's / best / do / the / can / we
15. You've / deal / got / a / yourself
16. So / on / we're / agreed / that / all
17. What / an / agreement / will / take / it / to / reach

Now listen again and check your answers.

3. **These are useful sentence starters for negotiating. Choose the correct ending for each (A or B).**

   a. reduce the price
   b. reducing the price

1. We're not prepared to ... .
2. I don't feel comfortable with ... .
3. I see no problem in ... .
4. In return, we'd like to ... .
5. There's still the matter of ... .
6. We would be willing to ... .
7. If we ... , will, you ...?
8. Are you happy with ...?
9. Would you be happier with ...?
10. Would you be willing to ...?
11. How would you feel about ...?

Negotiating Skills

Case Study

1. **Look at the case below to prepare for negotiations between an employee and his/her boss.**

Student A

You are:
a tired administrative assistant.

The Demand:
1. more pay
2. a four week vacation
3. a new office with a view: plus a new computer, new phones and a coffee machine.
4. next Monday off to go to your son's football match
5. a complete health benefits package to include dental and vision

Your bottom line
1. I won't take less than ...
2. I will settle for ...
3. I will be happy if I get just ...
4. I will settle for ...
5. I just ... is enough

Your reasoning
1. ...   4. ...
2. ...   5. ...
3. ...

Student B

You are:
One mean boss.

You will say no because ...
1. It's not in the budget.
2. This is the busiest time of the year.
3. There just isn't the space.
4. Monday is going to be incredibly busy.
5. Why should I? No other employee has such benefits!

If they insist, your compromise will be ...
1. ...
2. ...
3. ...
4. ...
5. ...

2. **Now choose one item from above to negotiate. When you finish, negotiate with another classmate, and choose another item. Take turns being employee and boss.**

Follow Up

- Do you think you are a good negotiator? Why or why not?
- Do you know someone who is a good negotiator? What makes him/her such a good negotiator?
- Have you ever negotiated for something and got what you wanted? What was it? How did you do it?
- Some experts believe that reacting to an offer or a price with an expression like "*What!*", or "*How much?*", or even "*You're joking!*" is a good negotiation technique. What do you think?

"*That's our final offer – take it or leave it!*" Do you think this is an effective way to close a deal?

Ed Brodow, American negotiation guru, says the best advice to a negotiator is, "*Always be willing to walk away.*" What do you think this means? Do you agree?

Can Business be Green?

Where do you stand on green issues? And how important, would you say, is the role of business in protecting or destroying the environment? Does the international business community really have a responsibility to sustain the natural resources it commercially exploits? Or is that a matter for the world's politicians to sort out?

The Worst Dangers

What, in your view, are the four major industrially created dangers facing the environment?

- nuclear reactors
- industrial emissions
- the destruction of the rainforest
- industrial waste
- nuclear waste
- carbon monoxide fumes from vehicles
- oil spills at sea
- chemical effluent
- the greenhouse effect
- the consumption of non-renewable energy
- the use of non-biodegradable materials
- nuclear and chemical weapons build-up

Ecology and Business

To what extent is ecology an economic issue? And to what extent is economics an ecological one? How environmentally sound is your company?
What do you know about the following? See what your colleagues know.

- Chernobyl
- The Union Carbide Company
- The Exxon Valdez
- The Shell Brent Spar oil platform
- The Kyoto Agreement

Work in pairs. List the ways in which business harms the environment and discuss what measures can be taken to help.
Now read the article *Managing the Planet*.

Nowadays, most of us are more or less aware of environmental issues. How many of us conscientiously deposit our empty bottles at the bottle bank, save electricity by switching off lights, or make a big thing of using recycled paper – all in the belief that we are 'doing our bit' for the environment? But what impression are we actually making on the environment by doing so?

Tragically, the answer is almost none. For even if every household in the world recycled everything it used, solid waste would be reduced by a mere two per cent. In global terms, that would make absolutely no difference whatsoever, because the real problem lies, not with the private individual, but with big business and the $35 trillion world economy.

Managing *the* Planet

No Solutions Yet

Business, just like everything else, depends upon the survival of the eco-system, and it can only be in the interests of commerce and industry to learn how to manage Corporation Earth. But the fact is that though business is the only mechanism powerful enough to reverse the current global trend towards ecological disaster, it has yet to come up with a practical plan to halt the destruction of the planet. In 2002 the USA, by far the world's biggest producer of greenhouse gases, refused to sign the Kyoto Agreement on global warming. Many think they were pressured into rejecting it by giant corporations who simply had too much to lose.

Poor Track Record

Certainly, the track record of the world's companies is poor. Whereas the Chernobyl disaster can perhaps be attributed to lack of funds and the antiquated technology of a crumbling Soviet regime, no such excuse can be offered in the case of Union Carbide. When the full horror of the chemical accident at Bhopal in India became apparent, the company, quite legally, liquidated a large portion of its assets in the form of shareholders' dividends, thereby reducing the company's compensatory liability to its 200,000 victims. And when the Exxon Valdez tanker ran aground, the Exxon company seemed more concerned to reassure the stock markets that its financial strength was undiminished than to console the Alaskans, whose livelihoods were wrecked by the catastrophic oil spill. Over the last 100 years some 200 oil tankers have sunk, many, like the one that broke up off the north-west Spanish coast in 2002, causing irreversible environmental damage.

Large Scale Pollution

The mighty General Electric, consistently amongst the world's five richest companies, has taken what some people call 'corporate crime' to even greater extremes. So much so, that it actually had its contracts suspended by the Pentagon. It stood accused, amongst other things, of bribery and insider trading, and being one of America's greatest toxic polluters. One of its nuclear operations in Washington State alone has created sufficient radioactive pollution to charge fifty atom bombs of the kind dropped on Nagasaki during World War Two.

Making Conservation Profitable

The situation seems hopeless. But, as ecological expert Paul Hawken, points out if business is not only about making money, but also about sustaining life, then perhaps it really can make conservation profitable, productive and possible. And some say that if they wanted to, the commercial powers could actually halt environmental degradation within as little as twenty years. For why must what is good for business always be bad for nature?

Short-term Goals

The simple answer to that is that big business is by definition, antagonistic to nature. True, some companies like Royal Dutch Shell have very publicly 'gone green', introducing all kinds of environmental initiatives and renewable energy programmes. But cynics point out that it was only after Shell's clash with Greenpeace over the disposal of the Brent Spar oil platform in 1995, that the company found its corporate conscience.

Appearing green may indeed be good for business, but Hawken reminds us that ultimately 'business is designed to break through limits, not to respect them'. It is about exploring, discovering, mining, extracting, and exploiting. It is quite definitely not about putting things back. Although, in the long term, a living rain forest is more profitable than a dead one, the goals of big business are notoriously short-term. And, contrary to popular belief, big business is not in decline. The largest one thousand companies in the United States still account for over sixty per cent of GNP. With modern telecommunications, their global reach is almost complete. And what can the environmentalists do when our planet's greatest enemy turns out to be the only force strong enough to save it?

Crosschecking

Which of the following viewpoints support those expressed in the article?

1. Environmental awareness is greater now than it used to be.
2. People are still largely unaware of the scale of the environmental problem.
3. Domestic recycling is a waste of time.
4. Without government support, the business community can do little to protect the environment.
5. The corporations of the world only step in to put things right after the disasters have already happened.
6. Green politics need not be a hopeless cause.
7. Commercial gain and ecological balance are incompatible.
8. As our business culture changes, the environment will be given a higher priority.

Response

Do you find yourself mostly agreeing or disagreeing with the article?

Compare your views with those of your colleagues.

Find the Expressions

Look back at the article. Find the words and expressions which mean:

1. making our contribution (paragraph 1)
2. past performance (paragraph 4)
3. destroy jobs, means of living (paragraph 4)
4. persuading people to do what you want by illegal payment (paragraph 5)
5. illegal manipulation of share price (paragraph 6)
6. opposed, hostile to (paragraph 7)

Language Focus

Word Partnerships 1

In his book, *The Ecology of Commerce*, Paul Hawken outlines practical ways in which we might work our way back towards a sustainable economy. Complete the checklist below by selecting from the lists of words:

> technology   consumption
> resources   hemisphere

Reduce (1) ... of energy and natural (2) ... in the northern (3) ... by 75%. This is not as difficult as it sounds. We already have the (4) ... to make things last twice as long with half the resources.

> war   inequality
> employment   security

Provide secure (5) ... for the whole populace. A sustainable economy without job (6) ... would only lead to social (7) ... and civil (8) ... .

> goods   quality   dynamics   nature

Honour market principles. Since you cannot change the (9) ... of the market, you have to operate within it. Taxing morality by charging higher prices for environmentally-friendly (10) ... doesn't work. It is basic human (11) ... to shop around for the cheapest goods of comparable (12) ... .

> earth   restoration
> systems   programme

Extensive (13) ... will be needed as it is simply too late to sustain what we have. As part of our overall economic (14) ..., we shall need to redesign all industrial, residential and transport (15) ... so that everything we use comes from the (16) ... and returns to it.

> acts   circumstances
> society   users

Governments alone cannot create a sustainable (17) ... . Everything largely depends on the daily (18) ... of billions of ordinary people. Humans are not naturally wasteful and predatory, but intelligent (19) ..., who adapt to fit in with their (20) ... . In a sustainable culture people would naturally conserve.

Word Partnerships 2

The following business words appeared in the article in the order in which they are listed. How many of their words partners can you find in just five minutes?

BUSINESS WORD PARTNERS		
1. environmental ...	7. ecological ...	13. corporate ...
2. solid ...	8. greenhouse ...	14. insider ...
3. private ...	9. giant ...	15. commercial ...
4. big ...	10. track ...	16. environmental ...
5. eco- ...	11. antiquated ...	17. environmental ...
6. global ...	12. irreversible ...	18. renewable ...

Discuss

- What environmental problems does your country face? What are their causes? How do you think they could be resolved?

- Does Hawken's blueprint for a better planet strike you as plausible or idealistic? Where would the motivation come from for the business community to change its attitude to ecology and commerce?

Word Partnerships 3

Choose one noun to form a strong word partnership with all the verbs in each example.

resources	power	a promise	an issue
the environment	a goal	pollution	a policy

1. protect / harm / threaten
2. control / create / cut
3. develop / exploit / tap
4. address / face / settle

5. make / break / keep
6. adopt / implement / abandon
7. set / achieve / reach
8. exercise / wield / seize

Business Grammar 1

Form project teams. Appoint a project team leader to co-ordinate teamwork and implement decisions.

This project is designed to help you use Attitude verbs more effectively. Attitude verbs (*must, may, might, will, would, can, could, shall, should, have to, need, etc.*) are essential when you want to express doubt, certainty, degrees of ability and feasibility. They are also useful when you want to give advice or make suggestions.

You have just 10 minutes to solve as many of the following language problems as you can. At the end of the project you will be asked to report your findings.

1. In which of the following is spending more money an option?
   We mustn't spend any more money on this.
   We don't have to spend any more money on this.
   Which of the two sentences means almost the same as *We don't need to spend any more money on this?*

2. Which of the following is more likely to be my opinion?
   We must cut down on waste.
   We have to cut down on waste.

3. In which of the following are you sure I finished the report?
   I didn't need to finish the report today.
   I needn't have finished the report today.

4. Which of the following is more diplomatic?
   That isn't enough.
   That wouldn't be enough.

5. What is the opposite of *That can't be right?*
   That can be right.
   That must be right.

6. What is the opposite of *We should have known what would happen?*
   We shouldn't have known what would happen.
   We couldn't have known what would happen.

7. Which of the following seems more certain?
   We could do it if we tried.
   We might be able to do it if we tried.

8. Which of the following seems more certain?
   If he calls, tell him I'm out.
   If he should call, tell him I'm out.

9. Do either or both of the following refer to future time?
   You could ask her but she won't know yet.
   You could ask her but she won't help you.

Language Focus

Business Grammar 2

Now match up the rather unnatural sentences on the left with their natural equivalents on the right:

1.	It's necessary to take action.	a.	We should take action.
2.	It's not necessary to take action.	b.	We could've taken action.
3.	It would be a good idea to take action.	c.	We should've taken action.
4.	It's not possible for us to take action.	d.	We must take action.
5.	It's possible we will take action.	e.	We needn't have taken action.
6.	It would have been a good idea to take action.	f.	We can't take action.
7.	It wasn't a good idea to take action, but we did.	g.	We didn't need to take action.
8.	It was possible for us to take action but we didn't.	h.	We may take action.
9.	It wasn't necessary to take action, so we didn't.	i.	We shouldn't've taken action.
10.	It wasn't necessary to take action but we did.	j.	We don't have to take action.

Have you ever been in the position at work where you should have taken some kind of action but didn't? Or where you needn't have taken the action you did?

Business Grammar 3

🎧 **Match up the words and phrases below to make 16 common expressions. Then listen to short extracts from two different crisis meetings and check your answers. The expressions are listed in the order you'll hear them.**

1.

You can't …	… have a point there.
I can …	… be wrong, of course.
There must …	… agree more.
I could …	… be serious!
I couldn't …	… be any point.
You must …	… be a way round this.
You may …	… be joking!
There wouldn't …	… understand how you feel.

2.

You can …	… think so.
I might …	… be certain.
We can't …	… be time.
We'll have …	… have known!
I shouldn't …	… to wait and see.
There wouldn't …	… to tell me.
You don't have …	… be a problem.
That shouldn't …	… say that again!

Fluency Work

Business Ethics

Procedure

Work in 'think-tanks'. Each think-tank should look at one of the situations below and on the next page and decide how to deal with the dilemma. Make sure you reach a consensus before you make your final decision. Remember you are accountable both to the general public and to your shareholders. So try to avoid being either too ruthless or too idealistic.

When you are ready, report the dilemma and your decision to the other groups in your class and be prepared to defend your views. The other groups should vote on whether they think you made the right decision.

The Tobacco Company

You work for a multinational tobacco company. In spite of the restrictions on tobacco advertising throughout Europe and the USA and a strong anti-smoking lobby, your company continues to gross in excess of $30 billion every year. You are, of course, aware of all the arguments against smoking, but you also firmly believe in freedom of choice and realise the huge social and financial benefits the tobacco industry has to offer, particularly in poorer countries.

The World Health Organization is proposing to put a substantial 'green tax' on cigarettes to offset the $60 billion a year tobacco use costs society in terms of medical bills, lost income and reduced productivity. This is bound to affect your sales and may result in widespread layoffs in the Latin American countries where most of your cigarettes are manufactured. You understand, however, that a major political figure in the United States has promised to plead your case with the W.H.O. in return for sponsorship in his forthcoming election campaign.

Decide your course of action.
What reasons lie behind your decision?

The Chemical Company

You work for the chemicals division of an American multinational. A recent explosion at one of your plants in India has resulted in millions of tonnes of toxic gases being released into the atmosphere. Hundreds of local workers employed at the plant were killed in the accident with thousands more suffering from severe chemical burns. But, with such high levels of contamination, the threat to the local community is even more serious. Over the next five to ten years, the fatalities could run into tens of thousands.

Obviously, a massive clean-up programme has already been put into effect, but there is still the matter of compensation for the victims and their families to be settled. Although you are well aware of the scale of the tragedy, you also have your shareholders to think of. As your Indian plant was inadequately insured, compensation claims could bite deep into company funds. You might even have to pull out of Asia altogether, which would mean thousands of job losses. Your lawyers inform you that there is a perfectly legal way of liquidating a large part of your assets and significantly reducing your liability.

Decide your course of action.
What reasons lie behind your decision?

Fluency Work

The Steel Company

You work for a large steel company in Germany which is currently planning to set up a new processing plant, and have been informed that a suitable site in Portugal has become available at very reasonable rates. You are also well aware that local labour costs would be far lower than in Germany, especially as unemployment in the region is extremely high.

Unfortunately, however, the site is one of great scenic beauty and environmental importance. It is the natural habitat of many rare species of wildlife, which would almost certainly be harmed, if not totally destroyed, by the building of your plant. You would, in fact, meet very little opposition if you went ahead with your plans to build, for job creation is much higher on the agenda of the local government that conservation. Times are hard and your firm badly needs to cut costs wherever it can. But company image may be affected by any adverse publicity in the German press.

Decide your course of action.
What reasons lie behind your decision?

The Fast-Food Company

You work for the European Division of one of the world's biggest fast-food chains. In recent months you have found yourself the target of a vicious campaign by environmental groups concerning the amount of waste your company generates. In fact, your environmental record is no worse than that of any of your major competitors, but your international profile makes you easy to attack. Your marketing department is particularly concerned – the vast majority of both your customers and staff are teenagers and young adults who tend to be the most environmentally aware members of society. Clearly, action must be taken before the protests get out of hand.

One problem is that the polystyrene containers your company packages its meals in may be cheap and insulate the food well, but they take thousands of years to biodegrade. Although recyclable, they are frequently taken away by your customers and discarded elsewhere. The Environmental Defence Fund or EDF, has become so interested in your case that the story looks set to hit the news-stands any day now.

Decide your course of action.
What reasons lie behind your decision?

The Drinks Company

You work for a mineral water company based in France. Chemists working in your research labs have recently discovered minute traces of benzene in samples routinely taken from your bottles. You know benzene has been found to have carcinogenic properties, but frankly the amount of benzene in your mineral water is so minute that it presents no health hazard whatsoever.

Nevertheless, if the story gets out, it could ruin you, especially as you have no idea how the water was contaminated in the first place. You could go public and try to limit the damage to your business or you could keep the whole thing quiet and continue to sell your mineral water until you've sorted out the problem yourself.

Decide your course of action.
What reasons lie behind your decision?

Finance and Credit

Urgent Action

Work with a partner. Read the problem below and outline four possible courses of action.

It's an increasingly familiar scenario. You billed a client company for £250,000 three months ago but although you have sent them one polite, and one less polite, reminder, the money has not yet been paid. Their excuse is that current cashflow difficulties are causing the delay, but the non-payment of such a large sum is now creating serious cashflow problems for you as well. You could, of course, take legal action against your bad debtor, but since they are promising you half a million pounds worth of business next year, you are naturally reluctant to upset them unnecessarily. What can you do?

Discuss

Who in your experience are the worst debtors?

the British
the Germans
the Italians
another nationality
small companies
big multinationals
government departments

Who would you give the highest credit rating to? Compare your views with those expressed in the article, *Credit Out of Control*.

Credit
Out of Control

Regulation is taboo to the business community, but do we need more control over credit?

They say money makes the world go round. But it isn't money: it's credit. For when the corporations of the world buy, they buy on credit. And if your credit's good, no one asks to see the colour of your money. Indeed, if everyone were to demand immediate payment in cash, the world would literally go bust. But as Trevor Sykes points out in his book, *Two Centuries of Panic*. "There are few faster ways of going broke than by buying goods and then passing them on to customers who cannot pay for them." As if getting orders wasn't tough enough, these days getting paid is even tougher. And with the amount of cross-border trade increasing every year, credit is rapidly going out of control.

Companies on Brink of Collapse

In Germany, Denmark and Sweden, whose governments strictly regulate business-to-business relations, companies pay on time. They have to. Late payers may actually be billed by their creditors for the services of a professional debt collector. But in Britain, companies regularly keep you waiting a month past the agreed deadline for your bill to be paid. That's why a Swedish leasing agreement can be drafted on a single page, but a British one is more like a telephone directory. The French and Italians, too, will sit on invoices almost indefinitely and push creditor companies to the brink of bankruptcy.

Money Management the Key

But bad debt does not necessarily mean bad business. Ninety years ago the legendary Tokushichi Nomura was racing round the streets of Osaka in a rickshaw to escape angry creditors. They are not angry now, for today, Nomura is the biggest securities company in Japan. Nomura knew what all good financial directors know: that what distinguishes the effectively managed commercial operation from the poorly managed one is the way it manages its money. And, increasingly, a key feature of successful money management is the skill with which a company can stall its creditors and at the same time put pressure on its debtors.

Minimising the Risk

So how can the risk of bad debt be minimised? From the supplier's point of view, pre-payment would be the ideal solution: make the customer pay up front. But it is a confident supplier indeed, who would risk damaging customer relations by insisting on money in advance. For the goodwill of your biggest customers – those who by definition owe you the most money – is vital to securing their business in future. And the prospect of a bigger order next time puts you in a difficult position when payment is late again this time.

Instant Access

We might expect modern technological advances to have eased this cashflow situation, but they haven't—quite the reverse. In the past it was common for companies to employ credit controllers who carefully processed letters of credit and bank guarantees. Now you get a telephone call, the computer runs a simple credit check and you deliver straightaway. Buyers have almost instant access to goods ... and to credit.

Be Prepared for Losses

For more and more companies, it's a no-win situation. Charge interest on outstanding debts, and you risk alienating customers with genuine cashflow problems. But cut your losses by selling those debts on to a factoring agency, and it'll be you, not your debtor, who ends up paying the factor's commission. In order to recover what you're owed, you'll effectively have to write some of it off. Such is the delicate balance of power between debtor and creditor. For though debtors do, of course, show up in a company's current assets, it is hard cash, not promises to pay, that finances new projects. People forget their promises, and creditors have better memories than debtors.

Information Check

Which of the following topics does the article discuss?

1. European attitudes to credit
2. the credit-worthiness of Japanese companies
3. risk limitation
4. national debt
5. information technology

Interviews

In pairs, spend 10 minutes preparing a set of questions about the article to ask other pairs. Use the 'question starters' below:

1. What would be the result of ...?
2. What exactly ...?
3. In what way ...?
4. What's the main reason why ...?
5. According to the article ...?
6. What practical measures could be taken to ...?
7. How might ...?
8. Why is it that ...?
9. Why can't ...?
10. What do you think is meant by ...

Find the Expressions

Look back at the article. Find the expressions which mean:

1. see proof that you have the necessary capital (paragraph 2)
2. go bankrupt [two expressions](paragraph 2)
3. be sent an invoice (paragraph 3)
4. nearly go bankrupt (paragraph 3)
5. delay payment to the people you owe money to (paragraph 4)
6. force the people who owe you money to pay up (paragraph 4)
7. pay in advance (paragraph 5)
8. making customers dissatisfied or angry (paragraph 7)
9. accept a small loss in order to prevent a big one (paragraph 7)
10. agree to lose money (paragraph 7)

Language Focus

Word Partnerships I

Re-arrange these 'word dominoes' so that each makes a strong word partnership with the one after it. Make a list of the word pairs you create. The first and last 'dominoes' are half-blank. All the word partnerships are taken from the article.

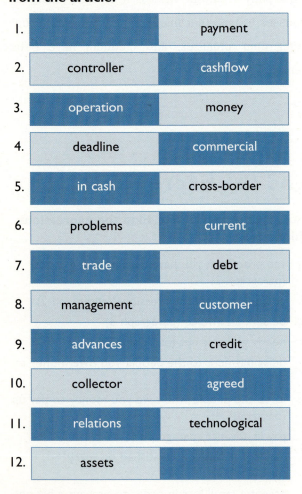

1.		payment
2.	controller	cashflow
3.	operation	money
4.	deadline	commercial
5.	in cash	cross-border
6.	problems	current
7.	trade	debt
8.	management	customer
9.	advances	credit
10.	collector	agreed
11.	relations	technological
12.	assets	

Going Bankrupt

Have you ever thrown good money after bad on a project that turned out to be a non-starter?

All of the following expressions mean **go bankrupt**, except for one. Which one?

1. go bust
2. go like a bomb
3. go to the wall
4. go down the tubes
5. go under
6. go broke
7. go down the pan

How many companies do you know of where you live which have gone under recently? How much confidence is there amongst the business community in your country at the moment?

Expressions with *money*

Complete the following dialogues using the words below. What do the money expressions mean?
Now listen and check your answers.

> tight   waste   throw   channelling
> tied   liquid   bad   made

1. What do you think of the plan to install an executive gym?
   ➤ To be honest, I think it's a complete . . . of money.

2. Why don't we just inject some more cash into the project if it's still underfunded?
   ➤ Because there's no point throwing good money after . . . .

3. Can't we pay off the loan with the money that's coming in from our subsidiaries in the Gulf?
   ➤ Well, most of that money's . . . up, I'm afraid.

4. So why aren't we investing in a new plant?
   ➤ Because I'm afraid money's a bit . . . at the moment.

5. How much of that money's . . . ?
   ➤ Very little. In fact, hardly any of it can be turned into cash for over a year.

6. Look, we can't just . . . money at the problem.
   ➤ No, but it wouldn't hurt to spend a bit more on advertising, would it?

7. We've made a pretty good profit for the last three years running.
   ➤ In that case, shouldn't we be . . . some of that money into R&D?

8. I don't suppose you could lend me a couple of hundred pounds, could you?
   ➤ What do you think I am: . . . of money?

Discuss

Is it really more difficult to work with foreign suppliers and / or customers than it is to deal with people in your own country? How much cross-border trade does your company do?

Word Partnerships 2

Now match the following words and phrases to make complete expressions from the article. You will generally find it easier if you match columns 2 and 3 first. The first one has been done for you as an example.

1.	to demand	business-to-business	on debtors
2.	to regulate	pressure	payment
3.	to put	immediate	relations
4.	to minimise	customer	in advance
5.	to damage	money	relations
6.	to insist on	the risk	of bad debt
7.	to ease	a credit	situation
8.	to process	letters	check
9.	to run	the cashflow	of credit
10.	to charge	new	customers
11.	to risk	interest	projects
12.	to finance	alienating	on outstanding debts

Word Partnerships 3

All the words below form strong partnerships with the word *order*. The vowels are missing in each word. How many can you work out?

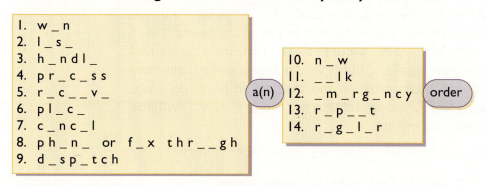

1. w _ n
2. l _ s _
3. h _ n d l _
4. p r _ c _ s s
5. r _ c _ _ v _
6. p l _ c _
7. c _ n c _ l
8. p h _ n _   or   f _ x   t h r _ _ g h
9. d _ s p _ t c h

a(n)

10. n _ w
11. _ _ l k
12. _ m _ r g _ n c y
13. r _ p _ _ t
14. r _ g _ l _ r

order

Use these words to complete the following:

15. Well, we were expecting you to . . . your order last month, but, since we only . . . it yesterday, it will now need to be . . . before we can . . . it.

16. Although we managed to . . . another new order from Holland three weeks ago, we've . . . this one rather badly, and if they end up . . . it and going back to their previous supplier, I'm worried that we may just . . . all our Dutch orders before very long.

Language Focus

Business Grammar

Complete the following summary of the article by writing in the correct prepositions:

> **by (x2)**   **on (x5)**   **in (x4)**   **up (x2)**   **off**   **behind**   **with**

Referring back to the article will help you with some of them.

Most people pay for everyday items (1) … their credit card or (2) … cash and pay their domestic bills (3) … cheque or direct debit. In business, buying (4) … credit is common practice. But allowing customers to buy large amounts of stock (5) … 90 or 120 days credit is not without its problems. It is extremely difficult to ask a valued customer for payment (6) … advance because it may look as if you don't trust them. You can't really charge them interest (7) … the outstanding sum either, even if they miss the agreed deadline for settlement, or they might get upset and withdraw their business altogether.

To make matters worse, many companies these days will deliberately sit (8) … your invoice and wait to see how long it is before you actually put pressure (9) … them to pay (10) … . Of course, you can ease both your cashflow situation and theirs by offering them the facility to pay (11) … what they owe you (12) … regular instalments. But that doesn't mean to say they won't fall (13) … with their repayments whenever they're short of cash. And you may end up writing (14) … half the debt altogether.

Things would probably be a lot simpler if everyone paid (15) … front for the goods they bought, and in theory a customer should be able to pay straightaway (16) … direct bank transfer. This, of course, would mean customers remained (17) … constant credit with their suppliers, but it would also prevent them from playing the waiting game with their creditors, and that would never do. Since most companies cannot pay you your money till they get theirs, they will continue to conserve cash until the very last minute.

How many word partnerships can you find in the summary above?

Discuss

It was recently reported in the British press that a private individual earning just £12,000 a year had applied for, and been given, so many credit cards he had a combined credit limit of one and a half million pounds! By the time they caught up with him he was already £120,000 in debt.

How many credit cards do you have? How many do you actually use? What would you do if they took away your cards?

Fluency Work

Getting Tough

Thanks to slow payers and a lot of bad debt recently, your company, Halliday Electronics, is experiencing serious cashflow difficulties and cannot meet several payments of its own. The situation has become so serious that you are now forced to get tough with at least one of your debtors, even if it means losing their business in the future. The question is: Who is it going to be? Who can't pay and who won't pay?

Listed below are the four companies who owe you the most money. An immediate settlement by any one of them of their outstanding debt would be enough to solve your current problems.

Work in groups. Group A, read about Pineapple Computers and Bonnetti Processors. Group B, read about Schaudi- Meyer and Jensen and Jensen on page 128. Tell the other group about the two debtors you have read about. Discuss which company you are going to ask to pay up now. You must reach a consensus before you make your final decision.

Pineapple Computers owe you £275,000 and are four months late in settling their bill. You have been doing business with Pineapple for over 15 years. They were, in fact, your first major client and are currently your second biggest customer. You know the owner of the company socially and wonder how long he can continue to compete in a market dominated by the big multinationals. Pineapple probably have the funds to pay you if you press them, but it may seriously damage their business. On the other hand, what will happen to your money if they go bust?

Bonnetti Processors are six months late with the £190,000 they owe you. Bonnetti is a relatively new customer and it has taken nearly eighteen months of ongoing negotiations to win their business. Financially, Bonnetti is in extremely good shape with its share price more than doubling in the last two years. You believe that late payment is simply regarded as a money-saving policy in their finance department. And apparently they used to enjoy a fairly flexible arrangement with their previous suppliers from whom you won their business.

Fluency Work

Schaudi-Meyer is by far your biggest client, accounting last year for 1.9 million pounds worth of business. At the moment they owe you £285,000 and are two months behind with the payment. They have contacted you about this and explained that it is the result of the temporary cashflow difficulties caused by their recent expansion and, therefore, nothing to worry about. They would like to treble their credit limit and are promising you considerably more business in the future if you can be patient with them now. You feel quite confident that SM will keep their word, but you see no way of offering them the huge amount of credit they're asking for.

Jensen & Jensen are six weeks late paying you the £210,000 they owe. Normally this would not worry you unduly, but, since this is the first time they haven't paid on time in 11 years, you are a bit concerned. When you phoned them about the problem three days ago, they were unable to offer a satisfactory explanation but promised to get back to you. So far you've heard nothing. A business contact in Scandinavia has told you the company is rumoured to be on the verge of bankruptcy and that you are unlikely to get your money even if you call the debt in. However, there was a similar scare four years ago, which the company survived.

Follow-up Letter

Write a polite but forceful letter to the company you have selected, explaining the situation, setting out your demands and detailing the course of action you will take if those demands are not met. These notes may help you:

Notes:

I / again / writing / you / regard / outstanding sum of £.... / owed by your company / goods / supplied / Halliday Electronics. As I / written / you / this matter / two previous occasions / you must / aware / account / now ... months in arrears / and so far / received no payment whatsoever.

Perhaps / inform us / reason / this delay. If / merely the result / administrative error / we / appreciate / prompt resolution / whatever problems / you may be having.

We sincerely hope / your company / not experiencing / difficulties / more serious nature / and whilst we / always / enjoyed / excellent relationship with ... / afraid / we must now insist / immediate settlement. Otherwise / no alternative / refer the matter / legal department.

I trust / you / give this matter / urgent attention.

Economic Issues

An Uncertain Future

We live in uncertain times, both politically and economically. In your view, what are the greatest threats to the world economy?

- political instability
- mass unemployment
- massive trade deficits
- poverty in the Third World
- the North-South divide
- the collapse of communism
- a population explosion
- under-employment
- arms build-up
- international terrorism

- racial tension
- hyperinflation
- cheap labour markets
- the debt crisis
- the East-West divide
- environmental damage
- an ageing population
- trade wars
- oil supplies
- the collapse of communism

Which of these do you consider to be the key global issues? Are there others that you believe to be even more important? What do you think their economic implications might be?

Which countries or geographic areas do you think will have the most direct or indirect impact on the global economy over the next five to ten years. Can you justify your view?

Compare your views with your colleagues and those expressed in the article, *The Death of Economics*.

The Death of Economics

 The world economy is falling apart. And no one has a clue what's going wrong – least of all the economists.

Whereas in the past, supply and demand had a way of evening themselves out, we now swing from hyperinflation to soaring unemployment as slump follows boom. The once predictable business cycles which drive the market economy have gone out of control. The economic statistics issued by governments seem more unreliable than ever. And, for the first time, politicians have started talking about 'the death of economics'.

Speculative Greed

A major cause of the crisis has been the business sector's ruthless pursuit of capital. It was largely corrupt property speculators and poorly managed financial institutions that caused the collapse of the Japanese economy in the 90s and the subsequent 'Asian meltdown'. The dotcom boom at the beginning of the 21st century was also motivated by short-term speculative greed. More money actually changes hands in four and a half days on the global currency markets than is exchanged annually through trade in merchandise and services. Business, it seems, is a very slow way to make money. The fastest way to make money is money.

Merger-mania

Two decades of bigger and bigger mergers and acquisitions have compounded the problem. In 1997 alone $1.6 trillion were spent on M&As. For the board members and shareholders of the companies concerned, there were huge windfall profits to be made, but for the companies themselves it was not always good news. Nor was it good news for the thousands laid off as a result of bringing ex-competitors together. In the new globalised economy, the need to grow at all costs has also led companies like Enron and WorldCom to become increasingly creative in their accounting methods. In some companies, hiding debts to finance acquisitions has become common practice.

Different Worlds

But the real long-term crisis is the widening gap between rich and poor. Thirty per cent of the world's population represents ninety per cent of the world's GDP, whilst the other seventy per cent have to survive on the remaining ten per cent. The income ratio between the richest and poorest countries went from 30:1 in 1960 to 74:1 in 1997 – and it's getting worse. So it isn't trade deficits, post-communist chaos or the global arms build-up that pose the greatest threat to the world economy. Nor is it political instability in Africa and the Middle East, international terrorism or the Latin American debt crisis. It is the emergence throughout both the developed and developing world of a vast and permanent underclass of seriously poor.

Cheap Labour from the East

In some cities in Central and Eastern Europe, unemployment is running as high as eighty per cent. Wages have fallen so far behind escalating inflation that immigration controls in the West have had to be tightened to prevent an influx of workers from the East. But, of course, this hasn't stopped some Western companies exploiting cheap labour in both Eastern Europe and South-East Asia, and putting their own employees out of work.

The Working Poor

In the USA, where unemployment benefit is cut after six months and staying out of work is not an option, they are creating jobs at the cost of decreased incomes. For in many of the inner cities of the USA they have something approaching a Third World economy. According to the latest figures, 12.7% of Americans currently live below the poverty-line. The problem is not so much unemployment as under-employment, with millions of people in low-paid, dead-end, so-called 'McJobs' that have zero prospects.

Corporate Rule

The result of all this is that corporations now exercise an unprecedented influence on the global economy and the distribution of wealth, as the world's governments, powerless to regulate them, become increasingly irrelevant. Near-monopolies like Microsoft are hard to fight and in industries like telecoms, the top ten companies control eighty-six per cent of the market. In fact, half the world's richest institutions are not countries but companies. No wonder then that both countries and companies try to conceal the real figures. As the famous saying goes, 'It's often easier to be economical with the truth than truthful about the economy'.

Information Check

Which of the following topics does the article discuss?

1. the boom-bust economy
2. political extremism
3. the money markets
4. social inequality
5. retraining the unemployed
6. corporate fraud
7. the black economy
8. government cover-ups

Interviews

What are your personal reactions to the article?

I totally agree that ... .
I think the point about ... is probably true.
I don't agree with the point about ... at all.
I already knew ... , but I didn't realise ... .
I'm not sure I can believe ... .
What shocks me most is ... .

Find the Expressions

Find the words and expressions in the article which mean:

1. no one has any idea (Introduction)
2. a period when the economy is weak (paragraph 1)
3. a period when the economy is strong (paragraph 1)
4. sudden and complete economic failure (two words) (paragraph 2)
5. is exchanged (paragraph 2)
6. made things worse (paragraph 3)
7. large amounts of money you get unexpectedly (paragraph 3)
8. rising rapidly (paragraph 5)
9. to be made stricter (paragraph 5)
10. the arrival a large number of people (paragraph 5)
11. never having happened before (paragraph 7)
12. it's not surprising (paragraph 7)

Language Focus

Word Partnerships 1

Without referring to the text, complete the following notes on the article using the pairs of words in the boxes.

> profits + employees
> institutions + collapse
> boom + greed
> hyperinflation + unemployment
> markets + money
> supply + demand
> debts + acquisitions
> increase + acquisitions

1. In the past ... and ... used to even themselves out.
2. We now swing from ... to soaring ... .
3. Poorly managed financial ... caused the ... of the Japanese economy.
4. The dotcom ... was motivated by short-term ... .
5. The currency ... are where the real ... is made.
6. The ... in the number of mergers and ... has compounded the problem.
7. Shareholders made huge ... but thousands of ... were laid off.
8. Many companies now hide ... to finance ... .

> unemployment + inflation
> population + GDP
> jobs + poverty
> threat + underclass
> power + institutions
> truth + economy
> crisis + gap
> controls + influx

1. The real ... is the widening ... between rich and poor.
2. Seventy per cent of the world's ... has to survive on just ten per cent of its ... .
3. The greatest ... to the world economy is a new ... of seriously poor.
4. ... is running high and wages have fallen behind ... .
5. Immigration ... have been tightened to prevent an ... of workers from the East.
6. In the USA many have low-paid, dead-end ... and live below the ... -line.
7. Companies now have more ... than countries and comprise fifty per cent of the world's richest ... .
8. It is easier to be economical with the ... than truthful about the ... .

Discuss

How strong is the economy in your country? Would you say it was about to enter a period of growth or decline?

Word Partnerships 2

Complete these words by adding the vowels. Each word can follow the adjective *economic*.

1. g r _ w t h
2. _ n d _ c _ t _ r s
3. c r _ s _ s
4. f _ r _ c _ s t
5. f _ r c _ s
6. t h _ _ r y
7. p _ l _ c y
8. _ _ t l _ _ k
9. r _ c _ s s _ _ n
10. m _ _ s _ r _ s
11. d _ v _ l _ p m _ n t
12. r _ _ n
13. r _ f _ r m
14. s t r _ t _ g y
15. r _ c _ v _ r y
16. _ n _ _ n
17. s _ n c t _ _ n s
18. _ _ d

Word Partnerships 3

Now complete the following using some of the word partners above:

1. Economic ..., such as the rate of inflation and the level of unemployment, are the signs that economists look for to help them produce their economic ... .

2. Economic ... is what a country faces if it builds up too great a national debt.

3. The prospects for a country's economic future might be called its economic ... .

4. During a period of economic ... the government is forced to take strong economic ... to revitalise the economy.

5. Despite all the talk of political and economic ..., Europe seems more divided than ever.

Current Affairs 1

Here are some of the most common expressions you will need when reading or listening to business news. You probably know most of the nouns already, but do you know the verbs that go with them? Whenever you learn a new expression, try to learn its opposite as well. Choose verbs from the boxes which are the opposite of those on the left.

| close impede scrap cut improve |
| relax break off come out of harm privatise |

1. nationalise   INDUSTRY
2. increase   SOCIAL BENEFITS
3. go into   RECESSION
4. damage   INTERNATIONAL RELATIONS
5. tighten   IMMIGRATION CONTROLS
6. set up   AN INVESTMENT PROGRAMME
7. widen   THE TRADE GAP
8. enter into   NEGOTIATIONS / TALKS
9. promote   OUR IMAGE ABROAD
10. bring about   ECONOMIC RECOVERY

| help adopt put off divide push up |
| neglect launch reduce pay off resist |

11. raise   TAXATION
12. unite   PUBLIC OPINION
13. bring down   UNEMPLOYMENT
14. hit   THE UNEMPLOYED
15. give in to   PRESSURE
16. attract   FOREIGN INVESTORS
17. come under   AN ATTACK
18. accumulate   DEBTS
19. abandon   A POLICY
20. invest in   EDUCATION

Language Focus

Current Affairs 2

Now complete the following newspaper headlines using words and phrases from the previous exercise.

1. Signs that Europe may be coming out of ... .
2. Widening ... must be closed, says Trade Minister.
3. Unions furious as government cuts ... for out of work.
4. Quebec relaxes ... for French-speakers.
5. Row over scrapping of 'Investing in People' ... .
6. Football hooligans can only harm our ... warns Home Secretary.
7. EU resists ... to intervene in Middle East crisis.
8. Brussels bureaucrats come under ... in corruption scandal.
9. ... united on Northern Ireland peace accord.
10. New Brazilian government prioritises bringing down ... .
11. Washington breaks off ... with North Korea.
12. How India attracts ... in IT sector.

Abbreviations & Acronyms

🎧 **How do you say the following? Which are pronounced as words and which are pronounced letter by letter? When pronounced letter by letter, which letter is always stressed? Now listen and check your answers.**

1. UN
2. NATO
3. IMF
4. GNP
5. GDP
6. GATT
7. VAT
8. NAFTA

Do you know what all the above stand for?

Word Grammar

In each example, use another form of the word in capitals to complete the sentence.

ECONOMICS

1. She's a leading ... .
2. You can call it being ... with the truth, if you like. I call it lying!
3. We need to think of practical ways in which we can ... .

POLITICS

4. Politics is too serious a matter to be left to the ... .
5. The whole thing is ... motivated.
6. They've ... the issue by involving the government.

Discuss

Do you have strong political views? Is there anything you're strongly in favour of or violently opposed to?

Business Grammar

Using the statistics below, complete these sentences describing a country's economic situation:

	1985	1995	Now	3yrs from Now
GDP	$61bn	$130bn	$98	$80
Inflation	21%	16%	18%	23%
Unemployment	6%	12%	15%	20%
Population	34m	32m	36m	39m

1. Since 1985 GDP ... .
2. Between 1985 and 1995 GDP more than ... .
3. But for the last ... years GDP ... .
4. Over the next 3 years GDP ... .
5. There's been a 2% rise ... .
6. Inflation is expected ... .
7. Compared with 1985, the 1995 inflation figure ... .
8. Unemployment has been ... .
9. The most dramatic rise in unemployment ... .
10. Over the next 3 years unemployment ... .
11. Compared with ... years ago, the unemployment situation ... .
12. In terms of population, the overall trend ... .
13. In spite of a fall of 2m ... .
14. The rise in population is expected ... .
15. Overall, the country is in a worse economic ... situation than ... .
16. The outlook for the next ... .

Word Partnerships 4

Which words don't fit in the following quotes from a political speech?

1. honestly
    I thoroughly   believe that I was right.
    genuinely

2. totally
    I utterly   refuse to accept that.
    sincerely

3. deeply
    I completely   regret having to do that.
    profoundly

4. distinctly
    I clearly   remember the occasion.
    firmly

5. categorically
    I freely   admit I was to blame.
    openly

If you have done the previous exercise correctly, you should have found five words which will fit into the quotes below.

6. I ... agree with what they say.
7. I ... deny having said that.
8. I ... hope that we can reach some sort of agreement.
9. I ... approve of what they're trying to do.
10. I ... maintain that we did the best we could.

Discuss

Think of a strong belief, hope, memory or regret of your own which you don't mind sharing with your colleagues.

Fluency Work

Election Campaign

Country Profile

Study the map below, which depicts the fictitious state of Ambrosia and its neighbouring countries. Using the economic statistics from the previous exercise and the information shown here, draw up a profile of the country. What do you think are its economic and political prospects?

Things you might consider include:

- the country's principal industries
- its transport system and infrastructure
- the location of industrial and commercial centres
- natural resources
- environmental hazards
- demographics
- the threat of war from a hostile foreign power
- political unrest at home
- the Northwest-Southeast divide

Outlining Proposals

We are committed to ...
Above all, we must ...
Unless we ...
Provided that we ...
Basically, what we're proposing is ...
In no circumstances must we allow ...
If elected, we aim to ... by ...
We need to be thinking in terms of ...
We see no alternative but to ...
A vote for us will mean ...

Political Strategies

In two weeks' time the troubled country of Ambrosia is to hold a general election. What political parties do you imagine would exist in such a country? A right wing or nationalist party? A left wing socialist or communist party? A liberal democratic party? A green party?

Work in groups, each representing a different political party. First, hold a strategy meeting to decide on your general policies. Then, in note form, put together a manifesto. Finally, give a five-minute election broadcast to the nation outlining what measures you intend to take to rebuild your country, if elected.

The General Election

Hold the election. You should vote for the party whose policies (apart from those of your own party) you most strongly support. Announce the winning party and interview them on their election victory.

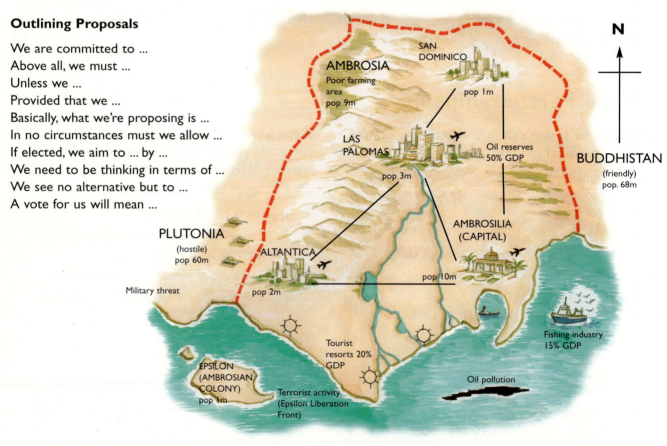

| Climate: Sub-tropical | —— Road & rail links | ✈ Airport |
| Mountain range | Rivers | Lakes |

New Business Matters

CNN Worksheets

You are going to watch a report about women working on Wall Street.

1. When do you think women first started to work on Wall Street?
2. What do you think it is like working on Wall Street today?
3. *"Don't get mad, get even."* What do you think this could refer to in the context of Wall Street?

Before You Watch

Read the sentences.

Can you work out what the words in bold mean?

Many women want to **work their way to the top** of their chosen profession, but in some sectors they still hit **a glass ceiling** and find it impossible to progress further, finding that there are **barriers** in their way.

In senior management roles, men still greatly **outnumber** the women and the **old boy's network** is alive and well. But some women *have* made it to the top, a huge **achievement**, and have paved the way for others to follow. They have shown that while it is **a struggle** to **balance a career and family** life, it is not impossible. And they have also created their own strong **support network**.

While You Watch

Read questions one and two. Then watch and choose the correct answer(s).

1. The report suggests:
   a. Opportunities for men and women are the same.
   b. Women have come a very long way, but there is still
   c. further to go.
   d. Things haven't changed very much in the last 75 years.

2. What is or was special about:
   A. Muriel Siebert?
      a. She was the first woman to work on Wall Street.
      b. She is the head of the New York Stock Exchange.
      c. She bought a seat on the New York Stock Exchange in 1967.
   B. Sayra Lebenthal?
      a. She and her husband founded Lebenthal & Co. in
      b. the 1920s.
      c. She worked until she was 93.
      d. She had a family.

Read the question below and watch the first part of the report again and answer.

3. Decide if the following are true or false.
   a. Muriel Siebert was the only woman on Wall Street for nearly 10 years.
   b. Sayra Lebenthal had an important influence on her grand-daughter.
   c. Alexandra Lebenthal has a company called Diamonds.
   d. Muriel Siebert experienced considerable discrimination.
   e. Muriel Siebert was not allowed to attend meetings.
   f. Muriel Siebert accepted the discrimination.

Read questions four to eight. Watch the second part of the report and answer the questions.

4. What is 85 Broad?
5. Who started it?
6. What is still difficult for women today?
7. What does Patricia Chadwick think about women's career opportunities?
8. Does Alexandra Lebenthal think that women have the same opportunities as men?

After You Watch

Work in pairs.

You are recruiting for an executive post. There are two front-runners, one male one female.
Student A: argue in favour of the female candidate.
Student B: argue in favour of the male candidate.

You are going to watch a report about Leslie Wexner, entrepreneur and the founder of The Limited, a retail empire.

1. What do you think motivates an entrepreneur?
2. What qualities do you think are needed to be an entrepreneur?
3. Do you think these are evident early in life?

Before You Watch

The words and phrases a – h appear in the video. They all relate to money. Match them to the definitions 1–8.

a. to peddle
b. to eke out a living
c. lucrative
d. to turn a profit
e. bankruptcy
f. a gamble
g. to earn a buck
h. pocket change

1. a small amount of money
2. an action or plan that involves taking risks
3. something which makes a lot of money is described in this way
4. to earn a small amount of money
5. to earn just enough money to live on
6. to make money
7. to sell
8. You are in this situation when a court of law judges that you are unable to pay your debts and so all your assets are shared out among the people and businesses you owe money to.

While You Watch

Read the questions, then watch and answer.

1. When did Leslie Wexner's entrepreneurial spirit develop?
2. The interviewer says, "*All work and no play did not make Les Wexner a dull boy – it made him rich.*"
   a. Can you give some examples of his work?
   b. What did he think of his parents' work?

Read tasks 3–6 below. Watch the report again and do the tasks.

3. Which brands are part of The Limited?
   a. Victoria's Secret
   b. Express
   c. Body and Bath Works
   d. The White Barn Candle Co.
   e. Leslie's

4. Which of the following things has Leslie Wexner done in his life?
   a. shovel snow
   b. cut grass for free
   c. wash cars
   d. run a day camp
   e. sell T-shirts and stationery
   f. do landscaping
   g. become a landscape architect
   h. get a business degree
   i. get a law degree
   j. work in his parents' store
   k. open the Limited, focussing on women's sportswear
   l. turn a small women's store into a $9 billion retail empire
   m. go bankrupt
   n. work with his parents in his business

5. Why does the example of running a day camp show particularly good business sense?

6. Decide whether the statements are true or false.
   a. His father wanted him to get a business degree.
   b. He joined his parents' business to prove his value to his father.
   c. His father was enthusiastic about Leslie's idea for The Limited.
   d. Leslie borrowed $50,000 from his aunt to get started.

After You Watch

Work in pairs and discuss the following.
1. Do you think he is happy with what he has done?
2. What do you think was his main motivation?

Work in pairs and role-play.
Student A: You are Leslie Wexner. Tell your father about your idea for opening a store focussing on women's sportswear.
Remember – it is the best-selling item at Leslie's, the family store.
Coats and dresses are not turning a profit at Leslie's.

Student B: You are Leslie Wexner's father. You are very sceptical about your son's idea.

Unit 3 — E-tombs

You are going to watch a report about an unusual use of the Internet in China. E-tombs are web sites where you can remember the people who have died.

1. What do you think of this idea?
2. In what other areas has the Internet changed the way we live?

Before You Watch

Watch part 1 of the report.

1. Which of these objects and actions can you identify?
   - a burial site/a graveyard /cemetery
   - a grave
   - a ritual
   - a web page
   - to clean
   - to bow
   - to burn incense
   - to light a candle people commemorating or remembering their loved
   - ones/people paying their respects to the dead

2. Look at the list of words below. Do you connect them with the Internet or with the dead? Decide which words should go under which heading: **the Internet   the dead**

to attract visitors, to bury, a click of the mouse, cyberspace, to feature, a graveyard, in memory of   to commemorate, a memorial a message board   modernization, a subscriber, technology, a web page

While You Watch

Read the questions, then watch and answer.

1. What does Netor.com offer?
2. Why have e-tombs become popular?
3. What can you do on an e-tomb?

Read tasks 4-5 below. Watch the report again and do the tasks.

4. Decide which sentences refer to an e-tomb and which to a traditional grave. Some sentences refer to both.
   1. It can cost around $3,000.
   2. Some people find it a lot of trouble.
   3. It contains a biography of the dead person.
   4. It features photos, essays and a message board.
   5. People can pay their respects and show their love whenever they want to.
   6. It is very convenient to visit.
   7. You can light candles, burn incense, offer flowers and songs.
   8. Thousands of people can easily visit.

5. Match the quotes to the speakers. Then say who you agree with.
   1. Jaime Florcruz, Reporter
   2. Liu Yi, CEO Netor.com
   3. Yang Tuan, online grave-sweeper

   a. "*The Internet offers a better way to commemorate [the dead].*"
   b. "*E-cemeteries will not replace traditional graveyards, but they offer a convenient alternative.*"
   c. "*Now on the Internet the buried may be remembered well.*"

6. Watch one more time and complete the sentences with the correct numbers.
   a. The Chinese give … deep bows in memory of the dead.
   b. The family visiting the grave visit … times a year.
   c. His wife's burial site cost … to build.
   d. Netor.com set up … years ago and now has … subscribers.
   e. Yang Tuan only spent … to open an e-tomb for her mother.
   f. In the … months since Yang opened her mother's e-tomb, it has attracted more than … visitors, and … of them are strangers.

After You Watch

Work in pairs and discuss the following.

1. Would you want to remember your loved ones in this way?
2. Do you think it will become popular in your country? Is it already popular in your country?
3. What do you think about the use of such a web site to commemorate:
   a. September 11th, the World Trade Center tragedy.
   b. the death of Princess Diana.
   c. Major air disasters.

Work in pairs and role-play.

Decide on a product or service you are both interested in.
Student A: You are a web site designer.
Student B: You want to have a web site for your business.
You meet to discuss:
1. What your web site should look like.
2. What features it needs to include.

Draw the web site home page including an index.

You are going to watch a report about the Ford motor company and the brands it owns.

1. Do you know which brands are owned by Ford?
2. What do you think of when you think of Ford?

Before You Watch

1. Read sentences a–g and match the meaning of the words and expressions in bold with the definitions 1–7 below.

a. You can buy everything **under one roof**.
b. They want to **lure** customers away from their competitors.
c. Many models of cars look so similar, it's hard to **distinguish** one from another.
d. They would not do anything that would **harm** the brand's **integrity**.
e. A poor advertising campaign can **degrade** the brand's character.
f. He **has** cars **in his blood**.
g. He's a **hot-shot** executive, the youngest President of the company.

1. to make something less valuable, less desirable
2. very successful and confident
3. to damage or hurt the character and strength of something
4. to form an important part of someone's character
5. to attract
6. to see a difference between things
7. in the same place

2. Decide whether the following words refer to:
a. the automotive industry.
b. the automobiles themselves.

> automaker component dealership
> high-end brand luxury market parts safety
> systems suspension vehicle retail

3. The report talks about brand DNA. What do you think this means?

While You Watch

Read, and then watch and answer.

1. What brands does Ford own?
2. What does Ford do to advertise the fact that they own these high-end brands?

Read task 3, then watch again and answer.

3. Choose the best answer. There may be more than one correct answer in each case.

1. The little blue oval is:
   a. Ford's badge.
   b. Volvo's badge.
   c. Aston Martin's badge.

2. PAG stands for:
   a. Premier Automotive Group.
   b. Personality Automobile Group.
   c. Premium Automobile Group.

3. The little blue oval appears:
   a. on all PAG vehicles.
   b. not on any of the PAG vehicles.
   c. only on Land Rovers.

4. Brand DNA means:
   a. the essence of a brand, its most recognisable characteristics.
   b. a brand's development.
   c. the person behind the brand.

5. Ford PAG brands are sold:
   a. in the same showroom.
   b. in different showrooms, but often in the same building.
   c. always in completely different locations.

6. PAG and the rest of Ford share:
   a. back offices, sales, marketing, repair shops.
   b. safety and navigational systems.
   c. both *a* and *b*.

7. Fields says cost-cutting will not harm the brand's integrity. What does he mean?
   a. They won't cost-cut.
   b. They don't cost-cut because it would have a negative effect on the character of the brand.
   c. They will cost-cut if it doesn't affect the character of the brand.

After You Watch

Work in pairs. Choose one of the brands above and 'sell' it to your partner.

You are going to watch a report about a luxury product, truffles. Have you ever bought them?

Do you think that the price of truffles is:
1. what the market will stand?
2. too expensive?
3. a refection of their worth and rarity?

Before You Watch

Match the words in the two columns to make word partnerships.

a.	create	1.	value
b.	have a market	2.	developed
c.	undermine	3.	test
d.	highly	4.	controversy
e.	switch	5.	the genetic code
f.	gourmet	6.	food
g.	crack	7.	allegiance
h.	sense of	8.	products
i.	scientific	9.	smell
j.	put something	10.	to the test
k.	competing	11.	business

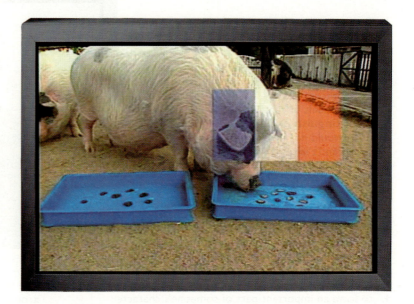

While You Watch

Read questions 1 and 2. Then watch the report and answer.

1. What is the problem that the report describes?
2. Does the pig get it right?

Now read questions 3–6 below. Then watch again and answer.

3. Put the words under the correct heading:

   French truffles   Chinese truffles

   Cheap, exported from France, $30/kg, high-priced $600/kg, gourmet food, imported to France

4. Choose the correct words in italics to complete the sentences.
   a. Truffles grow *underground / on the ground*.
   b. Pigs are used to *find / finding* truffles.
   c. Dogs *can / can't* be trained to find truffles.
   d. Truffles grow in Périgord in *southwestern / southeastern* France.
   e. *French / Chinese* truffles have more natural flavor than *French / Chinese* truffles.
   f. French truffle oil is added to Chinese truffles to give them *flavor / color*.

5. Choose the correct answer.
   1. Who is trying to crack the genetic code of the Périgord truffle?
      a. Chinese exporters
      b. French scientists
      c. French importers

2. They are doing this so they can:
   a. taste food and identify where it comes from.
   b. test food and identify where it comes from.

6. Put the following expressions in order of the pig's movements and the commentary you hear.
   investigates thoroughly
   rejects Chinese truffles
   returns to the French truffles
   switches allegiance
   favors the French truffles

After You Watch

Work in pairs and discuss the following.

1. How aware do you think consumers usually are of exactly what they are buying?
2. What measures could be introduced to remedy this?

Work in pairs and role-play.

Think of a commodity or a product. Decide on a price for it. This price should be much higher than its actual price. Persuade your partner that it is worth this high price.

You are going to watch a report about the Earth summit in Johannesburg.

1. How much do you think it costs the UN to host an Earth Summit?
2. How many people do you think attend?
3. What do you think most of the money is spent on?

Before You Watch

1. Check you understand the meaning of these expressions. Which of these things do you think you will *see* in the report?

- wining and dining
- up-market hotel
- bonanza
- fresh oysters
- extravagance
- sandwiches
- high living
- frugality
- lavish dinners
- disparities between rich and poor
- heads of state
- delegates
- no frills restaurant

2. Which words in the list above have a similar meaning to the words below?
   a. extravanganza
   b. summit-goer
   c. to live a high life

3. Complete the sentences with words from the box below.

> **host a function flock affluent seedy**

   a. Hundreds of world leaders ... to Johannesburg for this large-scale summit.
   b. Johannesburg is a city of contrasts with ... neighborhoods and ... slums.
   c. At the conference, our company will ... for all new delegates and their partners.

While You Watch

Read the questions. Then watch the report and answer.

1. Is the Earth Summit a UN extravaganza?
2. What are the positive effects for Johannesburg of holding a summit there?
3. How does the cost compare to the Rio Earth Summit ten years before this?

Read the questions below. Then watch the first part of the report again and answer.

4. Put these points in the order you hear them. Note the words are not exactly the same as the report.
   a. All parts of the accommodation and catering industry welcome the summit.
   b. Delegates pay for their own meals.
   c. Most importantly the Earth Summit provides employment opportunities.
   d. Tens of thousands of delegates attend the summit.

Read the questions. Then watch the second part of the report and answer.

5. Choose the correct answer/s.
   1. Delegates go to:
      a. up-market areas.
      b. areas like Soweto.
      c. both 1 and 2.
   2. Delegates go to *Wandies* which is:
      a. an up-market restaurant.
      b. a no-frills restaurant.
      c. a good restaurant.
   3. The UN encouraged frugality by:
      a. not hosting any functions.
      b. living on sandwiches.
      c. having lavish dinners.
   4. The Johannesburg Earth Summit cost:
      a. $1 million.
      b. $10 million.
      c. half a million dollars.

After You Watch

Work in groups A and B.

Group A
You are each head of a small department. You have received a call from your superior saying that you have to cut down on the number of people who can attend the annual conference for your industry.
You each decide to inform your department at a meeting. Prepare what you are going to say.

Group B
Your boss is going to tell you that the number of people who can attend your industry's annual conference will have to be reduced. Think of arguments against this.

Now divide into groups of one A and a few Bs. Hold the meeting. Student A, explain the situation to your staff. Students B, ask your boss questions and put forward your point of view disagreeing with the decision.

You are going to watch a report about tracking service developed for the Hong Kong market.
Can you think of useful applications for a tracking device?

Before You Watch

Read the following sentences. Can you guess the meaning of the words in bold?

a. The employee's phone is linked to a computer that **tracks his movements** so that his employer knows exactly where he is.

b. Watson's Water has hundred of suppliers **out in the field**, delivering supplies and fixing water coolers.

c. Companies want to **keep tabs on** their employees, to make sure they are doing what they say they are and where they are. Some employees may find this very **intrusive**.

While You Watch

1. Watch the report, then choose the statement that gives the best summary.
   a. It's about the use of satellite technology to track people's movements.
   b. It's about a tracking device which does not use satellite technology.
   c. It's about a water supplier.

2. Do you think the company name, The Pinpoint Company, is a good name for the company? Why/not?

3. Read the questions below, then watch again and answer. Decide whether the statements are true or false.
   a. As Jo walks around Hong Kong, people at his company can see where he is on a computer screen.
   b. There is a time delay of ten minutes.
   c. The information is accurate to within 200 meters.
   d. The tracking system uses mobile phones.
   e. The people who are being tracked can receive messages from their employers on their mobile.
   f. The tracking system increases productivity.
   g. Before this tracking system, employees might call from a bar called 'The Office' to say they were at the office.

After You Watch

Work in pairs and discuss the following.

1. Do you think this technology is too intrusive?

2. Imagine you work for a company like the Pinpoint company. You can develop a tracking service for ONE of the following. Choose which one you think would be best for business and discuss why.
   a. To show the location of an elderly relative or a child.
   b. To show the location of people's cars.
   c. For the emergency services.
   d. For transport and equipment.

3. Look at this list of benefits of using a tracking devices from the Pinpoint website. In your business, which of the following are the most important?
   a. Increase ability to track people and objects.
   b. Reduce theft of vehicles and equipment, and increase recovery rate of stolen items.
   c. Lower insurance costs.
   d. Improve employee safety and security.

You are going to watch a report about the press and the fashion world.
How important do you think the media is to a fashion designer?

Before You Watch

1. Match the words and phrases a–j to the definitions 1–10.

   a. acidic article
   b. negative review
   c. a nod from someone
   d. to clamour to do something
   e. to ban someone from something
   f. glossy magazines
   g. the power of the pen
   h. to feed each other
   i. to pull ads from a magazine
   j. to make or break someone

   1. a bad review
   2. attention and approval
   3. a very critical review
   4. remove or withdraw advertisements
   5. the influence a written article, etc. can have
   6. to be interdependent
   7. to have a very important positive or negative impact
   8. to stop someone from doing something
   9. to try very hard to do something and be very enthusiastic
   10. up-market publications usually for women, e.g. *Vogue.*

2. Match the following to make word partnerships.

   1. media   a. stunt
   2. two-page   b. content
   3. editorial   c. spread
   4. publicity   d. critic
   5. fashion   e. revenue
   6. fashion   f. attention
   7. to promote   g. a designer
   8. advertising   h. media

3. How many of these headlines reflect the content of the report?

   a. **designer ignores media**

   b. **huge press presence at Paris fashion show**

   c. journalists banned from show

   d. ***Vogue* bans Armani from advertising**

   e. *Vogue* loses thousands in advertising revenue

   f. movie star Malkovitch *at* fashion show

   g. *Vogue* backs avant-garde designers

   h. *Vogue* supports designers with realistic dress sense

   i. they can't live without each other

While You Watch

Read questions 1 and 2. Then watch the report and answer.

1. Does the presenter answer this question?
   "The real question is whether or not the power of the pen can make or break a designer."

2. The relationship between the fashion and the media is described as a love-hate relationship.
   What examples are there in the report?

Now read question 3. Then watch again and answer.

After You Watch

Work in pairs and discuss the following.

1. Imagine you are a designer. Decide which famous people you would like to attend your fashion show.

2. You receive a very critical review from a top fashion magazine. What would you do to limit the damage?

Unit 9 | The Britishness Test

You are going to watch a report which looks at Britishness and the test that immigrants will have to pass before being granted citizenship. When you think of Britain, what do you think of?

Before You Watch

These words and phrases appear in the report.
Match them with the correct definitions.

a. immigrant
b. ethnic community
c. multicultural
d. to be granted citizenship
e. to punch
f. isolation
g. to prescribe
h. curriculum
i. to institute
j. habits and customs

1. things people do in a particular society
2. subjects that are taught
3. to hit someone with your fist
4. someone who comes to live in a country from another country
5. to say what someone has to do
6. groups of people usually of non-western origin
7. made up of many races and cultures
8. when someone is alone or separated from others
9. to start, to establish
10. to be given legally recognised membership of a country

While You Watch

Read questions 1 and 2. Watch the report and answer.

1. How does modern Britain differ from the traditional stereotype?

2. What does the government want to introduce? Why?

Read questions 3 to 8. Watch again. Choose the correct answer/s.

3. Which of these things mentioned are typically British:
    a. the Union Jack (UK flag)?
    b. changing of the guards at Buckingham Palace?
    c. red telephone boxes?
    d. red letter boxes?
    e. double-decker buses?
    f. black cabs?
    g. rain?
    h. a cup of tea and scones?
    i. multi-cultural society?
    j. warm beer on a cold day?

4. What will the government do if immigrants cannot pass the test?
    a. Deport them.
    b. Give them free lessons.
    c. Give the three lessons.

5. Which of the following features of the test are mentioned?
    a. It will be in English.
    b. It will deal with British customs and habits.
    c. It will include reading, writing, listening and speaking.

6. What is one of the difficulties mentioned in setting the test?
    a. Traditions vary from one part of the country to another.
    b. Immigrants do not want to take it.
    c. It will be expensive.

7. Is the test universally welcomed?
    a. Yes.
    b. No.

8. Which of these definitions of being British is mentioned in the report?
    a. Not being European.
    b. Sense of feeling united, but individual at the same time.
    c. Being part of a young and dynamic culture.

After You Watch

One of the people interviewed says this:
 "*The whole idea of compulsion and setting rules and so on is a terrible mistake and it's against what I regard as British traditions.*"

Work in pairs and discuss the following.

1. What is the situation in your country? Do immigrants have to take any tests to gain citizenship? What do you think of this idea?

2. Work in pairs and think of five questions that you would include in a citizenship test for your country. You can then ask other people in your group.

You are going to watch a report about the marketing of Hollywood films. What Hollywood films are currently being marketed in your country?

Before You Watch

1. Read and answer these questions.
   a. What factors do you think Hollywood takes into account when marketing films in different countries?
   b. How do they market films?
   c. What are the threats that Hollywood faces?

2. All the words and phrases appear in the report. Match them with the definitions.
   a. a campaign
   b. a territory
   c. box office
   d. counterfeiting
   e. marketing machine
   f. overseas markets
   g. piracy
   h. promotion
   i. release date
   j. revenues
   k. to customise

   1. money that a business receives from its activities
   2. all the elements a business uses to market its product
   3. markets abroad – opposite of domestic market
   4. the advertising for a film
   5. to make changes for a specific market
   6. the time when a film is first shown
   7. advertising and marketing
   8. a geographical area, often the responsibility of a particular sales team
   9. ticket sales for a film
   10. illegal copying (of films etc.) (2 expressions)

While You Watch

Now watch and compare your answers in Preview question 1.

Read the questions below. Then watch the first part of the report again.

1. Choose the correct answer.
   1. How much of a film's revenue usually comes from international sales?
      a. 50%
      b. 80%
   2. Occasionally the international market can make:
      a. twice as much as the domestic market.
      b. half as much as the domestic market.
   3. What types of film does the reporter say are internationally successful?
      a. Films with big stars and action movies.
      b. Films with romantic themes.
   4. When it comes to international marketing, there's no such thing as 'one size fits all'. This means:
      a. The studios have to run different campaigns for their films in different countries.
      b. Studios market their films in exactly the same way around the world.

5. What does Dick Cook mean when he says, "You have to check your own ego and really rely on what your people are telling you."
   a. You have to put your own ideas to one side and listen to people with local knowledge.
   b. Our local people have had ideas for campaigns which we didn't like and so we didn't use.

6. You have to schedule a film's release date:
   a. so the film can open all over the world at the same time.
   b. taking into consideration the local calendar.

Now watch the second part of the report again.

2. What is important all over the world for a film's success?

3. Why did Revolution Studios send Vin Diesel to so many countries?

4. How much money has the film XXX taken at the box office?

5. What is the biggest threat to Hollywood's revenue?

After You Watch

1. Complete the summary of the report. Use the words in the box.

> **piracy   campaigns   promotional tours   revenues
> customized   overseas market   marketing machine**

Fifty per cent of Hollywood's (a) ... come from the (b) ... . Hollywood has a huge (c) ... to promote its product. This ranges from (d) ... which are (e) ... for individual markets to (f) ... of the stars. But Hollywood is facing a threat to its global dominance: (g) ... .

Work in pairs. Think of a foreign film you know.

2. Discuss the issues to take into account when marketing this film in your country.

3. Discuss the type of campaign that would be successful and the best release date.

You are going to watch a report about Tote Le Monde, an accessories business. Look at the picture.

1. How much do you think these handbags cost?
2. What materials do you think they are made of?
3. In the US, they are sold in Neiman Marcus, Barneys, Saks Fifth Avenue. What type of stores do you think these are: high-end or low-end?

Before You Watch

Match the expressions to the definitions. Use your dictionary to help you.

1. fine arts graduate
2. flair
3. accessories
4. high-end fashion
5. skeleton-size staff
6. sample
7. signature style
8. niche market

a. bags, shoes, belts, jewellery, scarves, gloves etc.
b. someone who has studied painting and sculpture at university level
c. ability, talent
d. instantly recognisable as certain brand
e. an example of the product shown to potential buyers
f. expensive clothes, shoes, jewellery, etc.
g. the minimum of people needed to run a business
h. product or service that is profitably and carefully targeted at a relatively small number of customers

While You Watch

1. **Watch the report, then read this summary and choose the correct phrases in bold.**

   This is the story of a Tote Le Monde, a very (a) **successful**/struggling (b) **large/small** business. The company designs and manufactures (c) **accessories/clothes** and sells its collections into (d) **major/small** stores at very (e) **reasonable/high** prices alongside much more (f) **expensive/ inexpensive** brands.
   The company's founder (g) **Tia Wou/Carmen Borgonovo** started off by going from store to store, asking to speak to the buyers. Barneys were interested and things took off from there.
   The brand has captured a (h) **niche/mass** market and is profitable because, with its (i) **medium-size/ skeleton-size** staff, it is able to keep its overhead (j) **low/high** and returns (k) **high low**

2. **Look at the table. Watch again and complete.**

company name	_____
products	_____
some products made from	_____
price tag on a Tote Le Monde bag	_____
annual sales figures	_____
country of design	_____
country of manufacture	_____
designer	_____
number of full-time staff	_____
retail outlets where sold	_____

After You Watch

1. Tia Wou says, 'I think it's a very strong concept. I think it's a very strong product.'
   a. Do you agree?
   b. Which of these factors do you think is particularly important in the brand's appeal to consumers: look?   price?   made in Bolivia from recycled plastic?
2. Tote Le Monde was set up by two childhood friends.
   a. What advantages and disadvantages can you think of in going into business with a friend?
   b. What effect do you think this can have on the style of management?

Unit 12 PCCW's Acquisitions

You are going to watch a report about PCCW, Hong Kong's dominant telecoms company.

1. What do you know about the telecoms industry?
2. Do you know of any mergers and acquisitions that have taken place within this sector?
3. What do you know about the Hong Kong economy?

Before You Watch

Match the words on the left to the words on the right to make word partnerships.

a. to scotch	1.	money
b. a bold	2.	offer
c. to borrow	3.	rumours
d. a mountain	4.	of debt
e. credit	5.	assets
f. a buying	6.	an acquisition
g. to make an informal	7.	market
h. a mature	8.	spree
i. to buy	9.	move
j. to undertake	10.	rating

While You Watch

Read the questions below. Then watch the report and answer.

1. Has PCCW acquired any other companies? If so, which?
2. Is it trying to acquire any companies? If so, which?
3. What is PCCW's position with Moody's, credit rating agency?

Read the questions. Then watch again and answer.

4. Choose the correct answer.
   1. PCCW stands for:
      a. Pacific Century CyberWorks Limited.
      b. Pan Credit CyberWorks.
   2. PCCW acquired Hong Kong Telecom by:
      a. borrowing a large amount of money from banks.
      b. issuing bonds.
   3. PCCW was left with considerable debts:
      a. when the Internet and telecoms markets collapsed.
      b. when it acquired Cable & Wireless.
   4. Richard Li is:
      a. PCCW's chairman.
      b. Moody's chairman.

5. Moody's is concerned that an acquisition by PCCW at this stage, will:
   a. adversely affect PCCW's credit rating.
   b. positively affect PCCW's credit rating.
6. What do Cable & Wireless and Japan Telecom have in common?
   a. Richard Li has bought both of them.
   b. It would relatively inexpensive to acquire them.
7. According to the analyst, the sale of Cyberport will:
   a. mean PCCW loses a valuable asset.
   b. give PCCW a much-needed injection of cash

After You Watch

Work in pairs and discuss the following.

1. PCCW had been growing organically, but has switched to growth by acquisition.
2. Which type of growth do you think is best and why?

You are going to watch a report about the construction of a pipeline in Central Africa. What effects do you think the construction of such a pipeline could have on:

a. the economy?
b. the environment?

Before You Watch

1. **Look at this list of vocabulary. Watch the first part of the report without sound and identify these items and activities.**

    gruelling (*adjective*) work
    laying a pipeline
    welding
    digging a trench
    rainforests
    logging

2. **Now complete these expressions with words from the box.**

    > crops   a project   standards
    > the environment   oil companies
    > group   of line   need of

    a. a consortium of …
    b. to undertake …
    c. to threaten or harm …
    d. to replant …
    e. to comply with …
    f. an advisory …
    g. to step out …
    h. in dire …

While You Watch

Read the question, then watch and answer.

1. Do you think the reporter is in favour of this project? Why? Why not?
2. Which companies and organisations are involved in the project?

Read exercise 3. Then watch again and answer.

3. Decide which topics are discussed to make a point in favour of the project and which are to make a point against the project?
    Be ready to explain your answers.

    a. providing Chad with a market for its crude oil
    b. future of Cameroon's rainforests
    c. ensuring compliance with environmental standards
    d. future of farmers' land
    e. lack of development of towns along the pipeline route
    f. creation of jobs
    g. growth of Chad's GDP

4. What do these figures refer to? Watch again to check your answers.

    a. 7:00 a.m.
    b. 5km
    c. $4 billion
    d. October 2000
    e. 25–30 years
    f. 85%
    g. 1%
    h. 9%

After You Watch

Work in pairs. Use the information you have learnt from the report.

Student A: Argue in favour of the project.
Student B: Argue against the project.

You are going to watch a report about **UMU**, a microfinance organization operating in Uganda which gives loans to people on low incomes.

1. What do you think of this idea?
2. What do you think of possible problems and their solutions are for both creditors and debtors?

Before You Watch

Look at the list of words. Which four words or phrases do not specifically relate to money and finance?

- a loan
- Master's students
- to conceive of
- funding
- a mission
- a misconception
- an asset
- financial services
- household income
- repayment
- a borrower
- to repay a loan
- a guarantor
- to guarantee

While You Watch

1. Read the questions, watch all the report and answer. Decide whether the statements are true or false.

   a. UMU lends money to people all over the world.
   b. UMU stands for Ugandan Microfinance Union.
   c. UMU has made a big difference to Regia Kokkures' life.
   d. A micro entrepreneur is someone who has a small business.
   e. UMU has a system which minimizes the risk of bad debt.

Read the questions. Watch the first part of the report again and answer.

2. Choose the correct phrase in italics.

   a. Charles Nayalli and Rodney Schuster came up with the idea of UMU while they were *studying / working*.
   b. The first UMU bank opened in *1996 / 1997*.
   c. They used money from *the Bank of Uganda and USAID / their own money* to start UMU.
   d. *UMU / Large commercial banks* tend to think that poor people will not repay a loan.
   e. Thanks to UMU, many people's lives have been *made easier / more complicated*.

3. Which of these examples are given about the improvement in people's lives?

   a. Increase household incomes.
   b. Send children to school.
   c. Send children to better schools.
   d. Improve the quality of meals.
   e. Improve quality of accommodation.
   f. Give political freedom.
   g. Allow them to borrow money.

Read the questions. Watch the second part of the report again and answer.

4. Complete the following with figures.

   a. average loan size
   b. typical business
   c. repayment on time
   d. overall repayment
   e. monthly interest rate
   f. number of people in group
   g. role of people in group
   h. why is the interest rate so high?
   i. why is the repayment rate so high?

After You Watch

Work in pairs and discuss the following.

1. What do you think about:
   a. the idea of UMU?
   b. the interest rate they offer?
   c. the system they have set up to minimise risk of debt?

Work in pairs and role-play.

Student A: You are a representative of UMU.
Explain the terms and conditions of borrowing to your client.

Student B: You want to borrow money from UMU. Decide how much you want to borrow and what for.

You are going to watch a report about MCIWorldCom.
This company was very much in the news in 2002. Can you remember why?

Before You Watch

These words and expressions appear in the report.

1. Match them to the correct definitions.

    a. a bid
    b. to go on a buying binge
    c. alleged fraud
    d. an investigation
    e. bankruptcy
    f. on his watch
    g. reckless ambition
    h. to block an attempt to do something
    i. to dip your toes in the (dot.com) ocean
    j. to throw bags of money at something

    1. an official attempt to find out the truth
    2. determination to get something, but with no regard to others
    3. price offered to buy something
    4. situation when you are unable to pay your debts (as judged by court of law)
    5. to buy a lot of things in a short time
    6. to fund generously
    7. to have a small amount of involvement in something, as a first test
    8. to stop someone from trying to do something
    9. when it is said, but not proved, that money has illegally been taken, e.g. from a company
    10. while he was in charge

2. Three of the expressions are informal. Which three do you think they are?

Read the questions. Then watch again and answer.

2. What sector was WorldCom in?
3. What did the telecoms companies do in the 1990s?
4. What was Ebbers' ambition for WorldCom?
5. What is Ebber's background?
6. Which company did Ebbers buy in 1998? Which company was he blocked from buying?
8. Why is Ebbers under investigation?

After You Watch

Based on the information in the report and any other information you may know about Ebbers and WorldCom, give a presentation of the company to your group.

While You Watch

Read the question. Then watch and answer.

1. The WorldCom story exemplifies some of the features of the 21st century economy. Decide which ones.
    a. merger and acquisition mania
    b. the gap between rich and poor
    c. unemployment
    d. creative accounting
    e. unpredictable business cycles

Answer Key

Unit 1 Career Management

Page 9 High Flier or Wage Slave?
If you answered yes:
five to six times:
you're a career opportunist, always ready to take a risk or make a career move to climb the corporate ladder. You should go far, but be careful you don't get a reputation for disloyalty, lack of commitment and over-ambition!

three to four times:
you're a calculated risk-taker, always on the lookout for a good career opportunity but cautious about doing anything too drastic. This is a sensible strategy, but are you sure you're giving yourself enough of a career challenge?

zero to two times
you're the better-safe-than-sorry type, reluctant to try something new if it means risking what you've already got. This might have been a good attitude 50 years ago when there was still a certain amount of job security, but these days there's no such thing as a safe job unless it's in the family business – and not always then!

Page 11 Crosschecking
1, 2, 4

Page 11 Against the Clock
1. temporary 2. contract 3. disbanded 4. prospects 5. life
6. wage 7. kicked out 8. opportunities 9. shortages
10. priorities

Page 12 The Appointments Pages
1. company 2. atmosphere 3. overtime 4. CV 5. leadership
6. career 7. skills 8. pressure 9. experience 10. salary

Page 12 Reading between the Lines
a.10 b.4 c.9 d.6 e.1 f.2 g.3 h.7 i.5 j.8

Page 13 Quotes
William Raduchel: boss, factor, success, opportunities;
Lisa Gansky: options, economy, standard, team;
Simon Roy: detour, experiences, skills, connections;
Esther Dyson: thing, trouble, adventure, work

Page 14 Recruitment
2. Draw up a job description.
4. Place a job advertisement.
6. Invite applicants to a first interview.
8. Compile a shortlist of the best candidates.
10. Conduct in-depth interviews.
12. Offer the post to the successful applicant subject to satisfactory references.
14. Send out rejection letters.

Page 14 Interview Skills
1. c 2. a 3. b 4. i 5. f 6. h 7. d 8. j 9. e 10. g

Page 14 Phrase-building
1. put + ease
2. do + company
3. ask + questions
4. conduct + presentation
5. build + humour
6. don't + ex-employers
7. give + examples
8. make + references
9. don't + CV
10. dare + chances

Page 15 Who said it?
Interviewer: 1, 2, 8, 10, 12, 13, 14, 15
Interviewee: 3, 4, 5, 6, 7, 9, 11, 16

Page 15 Phrases and Expressions
1. managerial 2. challenge 3. pressure 4. thrive 5. budget
6. contribution 7. package 8. insurance 9. pension 10. clash

Unit 2 Entrepreneurs

Page 19 Information Check
1, 3, 4

Page 19 Find the Expressions
1. is in 2. in retrospect 3. crackpot 4. made it
5. losing money hand over fist
6. brought back from the dead 7. took on
8. a 20th century icon 9. rise through the ranks
10. budding entrepreneur 11. flair 12. corporate raider

Page 20 Word Grammar
a. driven b. intuitive c. determined d. ingenious e. dynamic
g. dedicated h. gutsy i. faithful

1. a/e 2. h 3. f 4. j 5. i

Page 20 Word Partnerships 1
a, c, m, k, i, o, l, g, d, h, b, f, n, j, e, p

Page 21 Word Partnerships 2
1. make 2. starter 3. reliant 4. thrive 5. adapting 6. plan
7. building 8. dealing 9. handle 10. cope 11. stamina
12. minded 13. taking 14. open, suggestions
15. sacrifices, goals

Page 21 Entrepreneurial Indicator Score
If you scored:
51-75:	You are in no doubt already of your entrepreneurial flair. If you don't already work for yourself, you could almost certainly do so.
26-50:	You have some, but not all the skills needed to become an entrepreneur. You should consider your position carefully before launching into a business of your own.
0-25:	No doubt, you are an excellent team-member and you would do well to stay where you are. The risks and demands of individual enterprise are not for you.

Page 21 Quotes
1. wanting, get 2. busy 3. percent, percent 4. unless

Page 22 Business Grammar 1
1. b 2. e 3. a 4. f 5. d 6. c 7. i 8. k 9. l 10. h 11. j 12. g

Page 22 Business Grammar 2
1. The Managing Director stressed the importance of forming a strategic alliance with the Japanese.
2. The Finance Director demanded to know how the project was going to be financed.
3. The Managing Director questioned the need for extra capital.
4. The Finance Director conceded that it was going to take an injection of cash at the outset.
5. The Managing Director reaffirmed his position on the importance of teaming up with the Japanese.
6. The Managing Director recapped on the main points.

Answer Key

Page 23 Business Grammar 3
1. to take 2. losing 3. involving 4. you concentrate / concentrating 5. to agree 6. to work 7. to taking 8. to get 9. drawing 10. meet 11. to have 12. sending 13. to do 14. meeting

Page 23 Business Grammar 4
1. of leaving 2. for agreeing 3. in meeting 4. in taking 5. on doing 6. for starting 7. from going 8. about taking 9. on being

Unit 3 E-business

Page 27 Recall
Refer to article

Page 27 Crosschecking
1, 3

Page 28 Abbreviations
IT = information technology
SME = small and medium-sized enterprises
B2C = business to customer
B2B = business to business

Page 28 Computer Speak
1. fix
2. website names
3. changed
4. the material part of a business (factories, offices, inventory, etc.)
5. the virtual part of a business (websites, online payment systems, etc.)
6. involving the minimum number of people/departments

Page 28 Find the Words
1. tendency 2. frenzy 3. flood 4. bust 5. prestigious 6. phenomenon 7. potential 8. virtual 9. retailers 10. transactions

Page 28 Prepositions
1. out 2. in 3. to 4. up 5. up 6. through 7. for 8. in 9. on 10. in 11. through 12. out 13. between 14. on

Page 29 Word Partnerships 1
1. is registered 2. is linked 3. is managed 4. is able to receive 5. ensures 6. monitors 7. recognises and welcomes 8. manages

Page 31 Word Partnerships 2
a. exchange data b. publish a website c. enable customers to communicate d. place orders via a Website e. engage in e-commerce f. trade 24 hours a day g. deliver service and support h. reduce operating costs

Page 31 Find the Expressions
1. an immediate boost 2. serving as a shop window 3. the world at large 4. a global presence 5. on line 6. tumbles 7. Intranets 8. Extranets 9. remote workers 10. businesses at the leading edge 11. key 12. logistics 13. automated 14. seamless 15. unprecedented

Page 31 Which stage?
stage 1: j, c; **stage 2**: e, g, i; **stage 3**: a, b, h; **stage 4**: d, f, k

Meeting Skills

Page 33
1. c 2. g 3. d 4. a 5. f 6. e 7. b 8. n 9. l 10. i 11. m 12. h 13. j 14. k

a. 11 b. 12 c. 1 d. 7 e. 6 f. 13/3 g. 14 h. 5

Unit 4 Brand Management

Page 37 Recall
Refer to the article

Page 37 Response
1. **brand loyalty**: what makes the customer continue to buy a well-known brand
2. **bandstretching**: putting a well-known brand on secondary products to promote the name
3. **me-tooism**: the copying by competitor companies of a successful product
4. **lookalike products**; cheap imitations of well-known products
5. **brand-awareness**: how well the customer knows the name of a brand
6. **own label products**: products sold under the retail outlet's own name
7. **subliminal advertising**: an indirect method of advertising to the customer on a sub-conscious level.
8. **market saturation**: when the number of products competing in a market exceeds demand

Page 37 Find the Expressions
1. has now reached fever pitch 2. slash 3. cut-throat 4. knocked 40c off 5. went to the wall 6. corporate heavyweights 7. turnover 8. mark-up 9. spent a fortune 10. the book value 11. additional revenue 12. a crackdown

Page 38 Word Partnerships 1
1. c 2. a 3. d 4. b 5. h 6. g 7. e 8. f 9. k 10. i 11. l 12. j

Page 38 Word Partnerships 2
leaders, domination, value, share, saturation

Page 38 Word Partnerships 3
wars, loyalty, awareness

Page 38 Word Partnerships 4
consumer 1. consumer advertising 2. consumer non-durables 3. consumer goods 4. consumer durables 5. consumer protection 6. consumer research 7. consumer profile

Page 39 Word Partnerships 5
1. brands 2. advertising 3. pouring 4. market, their prices 5. brand 6. consumers, label 7. label, account 8. fight 9. City 10. value 11. names 12. names 13. revenue 14. raised 15. advertising 16. products 17. crackdown 18. saturation 19. consumerism 20. Product 21. fail

Page 40 Business Metaphors
War: 1, 4, 14, 15, 16 **Sport & Games**: 2, 7, 12, 18, 20
Water: 3, 6, 9, 13, 17 **Health**: 8, 11, 19 **Flight**: 5, 10

Page 40 Use the Expressions

1. stalemate situation 2. The company really took off
3. a strategic alliance 4. playing for high stakes
5. takeover battle 6. shoot down someone's idea
7. pour money into advertising 8. Sales have soared
9. the market has completely dried up 10. take a time-out
11. be an easy target 12. the company is suffering 13. the flow
of capital 14. backing a winner 15. A few orders are trickling
in 16. make a recovery 17. A flood of new products
18. the company is in good shape 19. defend our market share
20. the economy is in freefall.

Page 41 Business Grammar

1. ever 2. to 3. may 4. will 5. not. 6 yourself 7. of
8. a 9. clearly 10. of 11. which 12. a 13. the 14. should
15. more 16. to 17 other 18. as 19. Send 20. According
21. are 22. looking 23. with 24. to 25. make 26. can
27. need 28. got 29. instead 30. makes 31. all 32. like
33. all 34. you 35. could 36. be 37. sound 38. such
39. if/since/as because 40. way

Unit 5 Prices and Commodities

Page 45 Recall
Refer to the article

Page 45 Find the Expressions
1. strictly speaking 2. pay over the odds 3. money talks

Page 46 Word Partnerships 1
1. goods 2. margins 3. pricing 4. volume 5. profits 6. position
7. profile 8. forces 9. Europe 10. currency 11. trade
12. barriers 13. goods 14. market 15. market

Page 46 Cheap or Expensive?
cheap: 3, 4, 6, 8; expensive: 1, 2, 5, 7, 9

Page 46 Word Grammar
1. Tradeable 2. trading 3. profitable 4. profitability 5. profited
6. competitive 7. competitors 8. competition 9. pricing, price
10. pricey

Page 47 Word Partnerships 2
1. cut 2. fix 3. slash 4. reduce 5. raise 6. quote 7. freeze
8. equalise 9. fixed 10. competitive 11. reasonable
12. attractive 13. elastic 14. unbeatable 15. cut 16. war
17. rise 18. reduction 19. sensitivity 20. elasticity
21. index 22. hike

Page 47 Word Partnerships 3
1. freeze 2. war 3. competitive, unbeatable 4. slashed
5. elastic 6. rise 7. quoted 8. sensitivity

Page 47 Money Expressions
1. Let's talk figures. 2. Just take a look at the figures. 3. Can
you give us a rough figure? 4. How did you arrive at these
figures? 5. Where did these figures come from? 6. The figures
speak for themselves. 7. The figures are not very
encouraging./There are not very encouraging figures.
8. Can you put a figure on it? a.3 b.7 c.6 d.4, 5 e.8

Page 48 Word Partnerships 4
1. Tradeable goods are exported all over the world.
2. Non-tradeables are consumed where they are produced.
3. Too many customers are prepared to pay over the odds.
4. People pay the price they deserve.
5. Product pricing lies at the heart of the marketing
   process.

6. Its impact is felt in sales volume and profits.
7. Every product occupies a strategic position in the
   marketplace.
8. A high price often raises a product's profile.
9. A high product profile usually commands a higher price.
10. Economic and market forces are also at work.
11. Prices remain elastic.
12. Most commodities are heavily subsidized.
13. Trade barriers compound the problem.
14. Different rates of tax are imposed on homogeneous
    commodities.
15. Governments distort prices even further.

Page 49 Trends 1
1.c 2.f 3.l 4.i 5.a 6.d 7.b 8.e 9.j 10.g 11.k 12.h

Page 49 Trends 2
group 1: soar, escalate, take off, rocket; **group 2**: rise, climb;
group 3: hold steady, stabilize, flatten out; **group4**: drop, fall,
decline, slide, dip; **group 5**: slump, plunge, plummet, crash;
group 6: recover bounce back, pick up, rally;
group 7: fluctuate

Unit 6 Corporate Entertaining

Page 51 What's your price?
a. = totally incorruptible – are you for real?
b. = you have your principles but are not a slave to them.
c. = you see no reason not to take advantage of your good
    fortune.
d. = utterly unscrupulous – you can certainly be bought, but
    few people can afford you

Page 53 Expand
Refer to the article.

Page 54 Summary
1. entertainment 2. luxury 3. contribution 4. marketing
5. scandals 6. extravagant 7. hospitality 8. clients 9. part
10. culture a. major b. overall c. staggering d. crucial

Page 54 Word Partnerships
1, 11, 9, 5, 8, 4, 6, 10, 7, 3, 2, 12

Page 55 Describing Food
1. meal 2. food 3. dish 4. meat 5. steak 6. vegetables
7. salad 8. red wine 9. white wine 10. beer

Page 55 Expressions with *deal*
we reached a deal: 1, 2, 4, 5; we failed to reach a deal: 3, 6, 7, 8

Page 56 The Business Lunch
1. There's a nice new Italian restaurant just round the
   corner.
2. There's a pretty good Thai restaurant where we usually go.
3. There's a very popular little restaurant which has just
   opened.
4. There's quite a nice fish restaurant which you might like.
5. There's an excellent vegetarian restaurant which does a
   wonderful lasagne.

Page 55 Spoken English
1.g 2.a 3.j 4.d 5.h 6.k 7.c 8.e 9.b 10.i 11.f

Answer Key

Telephoning Skills

Page 59 Listening
Call 1: information call
Call 2: appointment call
Call 3: contact call

1. How/help 2. calling/because 3. Let/transfer 4. call/later
5. name/from 6. mine/referred 7. afraid/in 8. put/down
9. sorry/was 10. speak/please 11. this/speaking
12. remember/met 13. wondering/help 14. I'll/message
15. time/reach

Unit 7 Innovation

Page 61 How creative are you?
More than 5 lines = Are you sure you wouldn't be happier in
a less intellectually demanding job, like public relations?
5 lines = No prizes for creativity, I'm afraid. The average six
year old could have come up with this solution.
4 lines = You show promise. You've obviously questioned at
least one wrong assumption about the task.
3 lines = Well done! You've successfully bent the rules without
breaking them, and that's what rules are for.
Fewer than 3 lines = Congratulations! You must be cheating.
Cheating is highly creative.

Page 63 Find the Expressions
1. is tearing his hair out 2. has backfired 3. a blueprint
4. lucky breaks 5. flopped 6. speaks for itself 7. a climate for
creativity 8. it's no coincidence 9. management guru
10. brainstorming session 11. commercial proposition
12. concealing your source

Page 64 Word Partnerships 1
1.f 2.c 3.h 4.j 5.e 6.g 7.b 8.d 9.i 10.a

Page 64 When do you say ...?
1. When you say *We've really done our homework on this one*,
    you mean, *We have found out everything we need to know to
    prepare for this.*
2. When you say, *Let's not make a mountain out of a molehill*,
    you mean, *Let's not make this seem more important/serious
    than it is.*
3. When you say, *We'll just have to make the best out of a bad
    job*, you mean, *It's a bad situation and we can't change it, so
    we must do what we can.*
4. When you say, *We'll just have to make do*, you mean, *Because
    we haven't got what we really want/need, we must manage as
    well as we can with what we've got.*

Page 65 Word Partnerships 2
Research: fund, carry out, put money into, promote,
cut back on
Problems: solve, create, face, develop, tackle, define, have,
come up against, cause
Ideas: implement, generate, develop, brainstorm, promote,
come up with, have

Page 65 Word Partnerships 3
1. put money into 2. come up with 3. cut back on
4. generate 5. developed 6. tackle 7. solve 8. carry it out

Page 66 Word Partnerships 4
MAKE: a decision, money, progress, a breakthrough, a mistake,
an impact, a discovery, a comment, an offer, an effort, a profit, a
loss, a phone call, a proposal, arrangements, recommendations,
an excuse, an improvement, an appointment, a comparison;

DO: business, research, a project, tests, a good job, a rush job,
a feasibility study; **MAKE /DO**: a survey, a deal, a report, a
presentation

Page 66 Word Partnerships 5
1. encouragingly 2. dramatically 3. promisingly 4. slowly

Page 67 Problem Solving
1.e 2.a 3.c 4.g 5.d 6.f 7.b

Page 67 Idea Killers
1. It would cost too much.
2. It would take too long.
3. Our customers would never go for that.
4. We tried that before and it didn't work.
5. I could never get the boss to agree to it.
6. Now isn't the time to be trying anything new.
7. Don't you think we've thought of that already?/Don't you
    think you've already thought of that?
8. It's a nice idea, but we could never get it to work.

Unit 8 Public Relations

Page 69 The Power of the Media
Microsoft on Trial, Nike Sweatshops in Asia, Leeson Brings
Down Barings, Collapse of Sumitomo Bank, Lewinsky Affair
Threatens Clinton, EU Ban on British Beef, Intel Pentium Chip
Defective Claims US Professor

Page 71 Crosschecking
1, 2

Page 71 Recall
Refer to the article.

Page 71 Find the Expressions
1. networking 2. knowledge management
3. a wave of bad publicity 4. being 'on message'

Page 72 Word Partnerships 1
Right, the first thing is not to panic. I suggest we issue a press
release this afternoon stating quite clearly that we carefully
monitor working conditions in all our overseas factories and
that, no matter what these pressure groups are saying, we
simply do not exploit our workers. I recommend we arrange a
television interview as soon as possible to make our position
absolutely clear on that. I've just been on to TV9. We spend
$10 million a year with them on advertising. So, believe me,
our corporate image means as much to them as it does to us!
Now, press and TV coverage are only a partial solution. We
also need to be downloading everything written about us on
the Internet and taking swift action if necessary to counteract
what we expect to be a wave of bad publicity. It may be time
to take a fresh look at our mission statement as well. The one
we have is strong on brand and differentiates us from our
competitors very effectively, but it wouldn't do any harm to
raise public awareness of how we've actually championed
workers' rights in the developing world. Later on, we should
give some thought to sponsoring an appropriate charitable
event. For now, let's just concentrate on getting ourselves
back on message. And, sir – please calm down, there's a group
of reporters outside waiting to see you!

Page 72 Making Recommendations
1. The first thing is not to ... 2. I suggest we ...
3. Let's just concentrate on ...ing 4. We should give some
thought to ...ing. 5. I recommend we ... 6. We also need to be
...ing. 7. It may be time to ... 8. It wouldn't do any harm to ...

Page 73 Word Partnerships 2

1. Serious financial problems – Suppress company accounts while a rescue plan is devised. 2. A hostile takeover bid – Urge shareholders to hang on to their stock. 3. Adverse publicity – Discredit your critics and put the other side of the story. 4. An industrial accident – Call for calm as the situation is brought under control. 5. Corporate restructuring – Explain the greater efficiency of the new system. 6. Insider trading – Promise to thoroughly investigate the allegations. 7. Mass redundancies – Express deep regret and stress there was no option. 8. Product sabotage – Recall all products unconditionally. 9. Product failure – Set up customer helplines and offer refunds. 10. A major court action – Issue an official statement through your lawyers. 11. A top management clear-out – Emphasise the need for new leadership. 12. Loss of investor confidence – Publish a set of favourable end-of-year figures.

Page 74 Mission Statements

Adjectives: 1. successful 2. respected 3. superior 4. innovative 5. growing 6. premier 7. outstanding 8. unique;
Nouns: 1. excellence 2. teamwork 3. quality 4. responsibility 5. profitability 6. goal 7. value 8. vision;
Verbs: 1. satisfy 2. sustain 3. improve 4. serve 5. inspire 6. benefit 7. accomplish 8. achieve

successful, respected, innovative, growing, unique **company**
superior, outstanding, unique **service**
superior, innovative, premier **products**
growing, unique **market**
outstanding, unique **achievement**
sustain, achieve **growth**
improve **quality**
satisfy, serve, benefit **customers**
satisfy, inspire **consumers**
accomplish, achieve **objectives**

Page 74 Do-It-Yourself Vision Maker

world-class, market-leading, cutting-edge, ground-breaking; high-quality, cost-effective, client-oriented, user-friendly; serve the global marketplace, create shareholder value, satisfy our customers, advance the frontiers of technology; rapidly changing, highly competitive, electronically connected, increasingly borderless

Page 75 Word Partnerships 3

create and develop, change and update, preserve and maintain, project and present, harm and damage, strengthen and reinforce
1. harmed/damaged 2. projecting/presenting 3. change/update 4. strengthening/reinforcing 5. create/develop 6. preserve/maintain

Page 75 Word Grammar

1. communications 2. communicative 3. publicity 4. publicized 5. persuasion 6. unpersuasive 7. reputable 8. reputed

Page 76 Case Study: Intel in Trouble

A fault with the Intel microchip.
Consumer expectations were higher.
To more or less ignore it.
Professor Nicely shared their views on the Internet.
It could have started manufacturing its own processors.

Unit 9 Cultural Awareness

Page 79 Crosschecking

1, 3, 5

Page 79 Find the Expressions

1. be convinced 2. proved yourself 3. keep your competitive edge 4. come up with the goods 5. losing face 6. meet disagreement head on 7. doesn't go down too well

Page 80 Word Partnerships 1

1. a meeting 2. a minor point 3. good business relationships 4. superiors 5. a deal 6. a decision 7. team-spirit 8. their business 9. their arguments 10. an opinion 11. tension 12. results 13. new ideas 14. information 15. information

Page 80 Word Partnerships 2

1. profit 2. quality 3. price 4. market 5. client 6. technology 7. cost

Page 81 Business Grammar 1

1. g 2. l 3. a 4. j 5. c 6. k 7. e 8. d 9. b 10. h 11. f 12. i

Page 82 Business Grammar 2

1. *unfortunately* and *I'm afraid* warn the other person that bad news is coming. 2. *Not very / completely / entirely* + a positive adjective sounds friendlier than lots of negative adjectives. Examples: *not very good, not very profitable, not entirely true.* 3. *That would be a problem* in fact means the same as *That's a problem*, but it sounds less direct. Using *would* suggests that the problem might be solved: *That would be a problem … unless we can find a solution.* 4. *Quite, rather, slightly* and *somewhat* are softeners. They make bad news sound better. 5. *You said there would be a discount* makes it sound as if you lied!
We understood there would be a discount means it may just be a misunderstanding. 6. *You don't seem to understand* is strong language, but less offensive than *You don't understand.* It allows the possibility that you might understand.

Page 82 Business Grammar 3

1. We understood the goods were on their way. 2. I'm sorry, but we're not very happy about it. 3. That might not be a good idea. 4. I'm afraid this might not be very convenient. 5. Unfortunately, we're unable to accept your offer. 6. We were hoping for a slightly bigger discount. 7. Your products seem rather expensive 8. Actually, we were rather hoping to reach agreement today. 9. Unfortunately, it would not be very marketable. 10. I'm afraid there might be a slight delay. 11. Actually, we'd appreciate a little more time. 12. With respect, you don't seem to understand quite how important this is. 13. I'm sure I don't need to remind you of the terms of your contract. 14. I'm afraid we don't seem to be getting very far.

Presentation Skills

Page 84 Listening

1
2
a T b F c F d T e T

Key Language

1
Good morning, Everyone
My name is Janet Wilkins.
I'm here to talk about the 'tweens' market
I will begin by outlining an overall profile …
I will then look at some of the challenges …
I'll finish by looking at some case studies.
There will be time at the end for questions.
To start of let me ask you …
I guess that the best way to answer that question is …
If you look at the graph, you'll notice ..

Answer Key

3
1 talk 2 look 3 go 4 go 5 start 6 begin 7 finish

Case Study
1
1 growth 2 rise 3 steep 4 decline 5 sharply

2 sample answers

NEW IMAGE IN-FLIGHT BEAUTY SERVICES

SWOT	Arguments for	Arguments against
Strengths	possibly untapped market	never done before
Weaknesses	available space limited	first and business class always have many available seats
Opportunities	airlines need to boost sales service could be differential	airlines reducing in flight services to reduce costs
Threats	air safety; heightened security	all New Image employees will be thoroughly screened

Unit 10 Global Advertising

Page 89 Crosschecking
2, 3, 6, 7, 8

Page 89 Find the Expressions
1. niche markets 2. a new breed 3. widely regarded
4. voice-over 5. breathtaking 6. caused a sensation
7. a handful 8. icon 9. compelling 10. no-frills
11. to great effect 12. costing the earth

Page 90 Word Partnerships 1
1. create 2. screen 3. run

Page 90 Word Partnerships 2
marketing drive, advertising slogan, market forces

Page 90 Word Partnerships 3
1. mix 2. leaders 3. expenditure 4. drive 5. campaign
6. segmentation 7. trends 8. shown 9. costs 10. agencies
11. produce 12. run. 13. slogans

Page 91 Word Partnerships 4
1.g 2.b 3.h 4.a 5.e 6.j 7.f 8.d 9.c 10.i

Page 91 Quotes
1. market, gap 2. which half 3. advertisement 4. commercials
5. good

Page 92 Word Partnerships 5
1. quite 2. comprehensively 3. exceptionally 4. highly

Page 92 Funny Business
business. 1. costly 2. tricky 3. risky 4. shady 5. lengthy
Page 92 Word Grammar
1. globalise 2. internationalise 3. nationalise 4. privatise
5. sensationalise 6. standardise 7. popularise 8. intellectualise
9. categorise 10. computerise 11. legalise 12. generalize

Page 93 Discuss
1. instant coffee, up-market/glamorous 2. shampoo, natural
and cruelty-fee 3. box of chocolates, exotic 4. washing
powder, macho/sporty 5. soap, up-market 6. bar of chocolate,
exotic 7. cigars, classic/glamorous 8. aftershave, macho
9. toothbrush, sporty 10. tin of chocolates, up-market
11. aftershave, classic/macho 12. alcoholic fruit cocktail, exotic
13. popcorn, teenage 14. babies' nappies, comforting
15. paper tissues, comforting 16. breakfast cereal, sporty
17. white wine, humorous 18. condoms, sporty/macho
19. perfume, glamorous 20. strong lager beer, exotic/up-
market 21. anti-spot skin treatment, scientifically proven
22. household cleaner, trendy/sporty
23. processed cheese slices, middle-of-the-road
24. anti-perspirant, comforting/scientifically proven
25. American rice, comforting 26. toothpaste &brushes,
scientifically proven 27. tinned & packeted Chinese food,
exotic 28. shampoo, exotic/trendy 29. sparkling alcoholic
drink, trendy 30. men's razor, high-tech

Unit 11 Management Styles

Page 97 Crosschecking
1, 3, 5, 6

Page 97 Find the Expressions
1. glass ceiling 2. start-ups fold 3. franchising 4. take the
initiative 5. consensus 6. conciliation

Page 98 Word Partnerships 1
1.f 2.d 3.h 4.a 5.c 6.i 7.b 8.e 9.g

Page 98 Word Partnerships 2
1. run 2. launch 3. set up 4. form 5. join 6. leave 7. sell off
8. wind up 9. float 10. holding 11. parent 12 subsidiary
1: launch, set up, form; 2: sell off, wind up; 3: a holding or
parent company owns more than half the shares in each of its
subsidiaries.
Page 98 Word Partnerships 3
take off 1a. recruit, take on; 1b. lay off, dismiss;
2. poach, headhunt 3. headhunt

Page 99 Word Grammar 1
UN: unco-operative, uncompetitive, uncommunicative,
unsupportive, unassertive, unskilled, unintelligent, uncreative,
unreliable, uncommitted, unapproachable;
IN: indecisive, insincere, insensitive, inarticulate, indiscrete,
inconsistent;
IM: impractical, impatient;
IR: irresponsible, irrational;
DIS: disloyal, dishonest
Patterns: un- is by far the most common negative prefix;
in- is the second most common; im- usually precedes a word
beginning with a 'r' (impossible, improbable, impolite); ir-
usually precedes a word beginning with an 'p' (irregular,
irrelevant, **but** unrealiable)

Page 99 Word Grammar 2
1. sincere 2. assertive 3. articulate 4. reliable 5. approachable
6. committed 7. supportive 8. discrete 9. rational
10. consistent

Page 100 Business Grammar
1. with 2. about 3. on 4. for 5. over 6. between 7. about
8. in/with 9. up 10. up 11. about 12. to 13. up 14. for
15. to 16. in 17. on 18. out 19. on 20. in 21. for 22. up 23. to
24. of 25. about 26. of 27. from 28. in 29. about / on
30. round 31. for 32. on

Page 102 Follow-up Letter

(model letter) Thank you for your application for this post. // Whilst we were impressed with your qualifications and experience, and with your performance at interview, we regret to inform you that on this occasion you have not been successful. // As you know, there were a large number of applications for this post and the standard of applicants was extremely high. So you should not feel that your non-selection was due to any failings on your part. // I wish you every success in your future career. We have put your details on file and shall consider you for any suitable vacancies that may arise in our company.

Unit 12 Mergers and Acquisitions

Page 103 Let's Stick Together

Vodaphone and Mannesmann (telecoms), Daimler and Chrysler (automotive), BP and Amoco (oil & petroleum), Commercial Union and General Accident (insurance), Glaxo and Smith Kline Beecham (pharmaceuticals), Grand Metropolitan and Guinness (food & brewing), Time Warner and AOL (media)
LBO = leveraged buyout (using a company's assets to raise capital to take it over); junk bonds (bonds issued to finance an LBO); WTO = World Trade Organization; corporate raiding (mounting hostile takeovers of companies, often in order to sell off their assets); IMF = International Monetary Fund; hostile takeover (takeover against the wishes of the board); FDI = foreign direct investment; high-yield (high paying investments); OECD = Organization for Economic Cooperation and Development; green field investment (building new businesses, often in newly developed industrial parks, as opposed to taking over existing ones)

Page 105 Find the Expressions

1. drowning in debt 2. a classic case 3. cast a dark shadow over; the bubble burst 4. the latest wave 5. combine operational synergies; stay in the game 6. are bound to

Page 105 Crosschecking

1, 2, 3

Page 106 Word Partnerships 1

build: a business, a company, market share; **acquire**: a business, a company, capital, scale, new technologies, assets; **finance**: a business, a company, new technologies, a deal; **reduce**: scale, market share, costs; **increase**: market share, costs, assets; **combine**: new technologies, synergies; **gain access to**: new markets, new technologies, assets; **diversify**: a business; **buy up**: a business, a company; **sell off**: a business, a company, assets; **achieve**: scale; **raise**: capital, costs
1. capital 2. company 3. deal 4. assets 5. business 6. synergies 7. costs 8. market share 9. companies 10. new markets 11. business 12. new technologies 13. scale

Page 107 Word Partnerships 2

1. expand 2. take over 3. centralise 4. diversify 5. de-layer 6. globalise 7. merge 8. restructure 9. break up
expansion, takeover, break-up, diversification, de-layering, globalization, merger, restructuring
1. expansion 2. centralized 3. took over 4. broken up 5. diversifying 6. de-layering 7. globalization 8. merging 9. restructuring

Page 108 Word Grammar 1

1.c 2.f 3.a 4.e 5.b 6.d 7.j 8.l 9.h 10.k 11.i 12.g
1. multi- 2. ex- 3. pre-, post- 4. non- 5. multi-, uni- 6. ex-, non- 7. mini- 8. pre- 9. anti-, pro-, pan- 10. pro-, anti- 11. multi- 12. pre-, non- 13. multi- 14. ex- 15. non- 16. multi-, cross- 17. multi-, non- 18. ex-, multi- 19. ex-, pre- post- 20. mega- 21. mega-

Page 108 Word Grammar 2

1. Financially 2. financier 3. investor 4. investment 5. capitalise 6. capitalism 7. negotiated 8. negotiable

Negotiating Skills

Page 111 Language Focus

1.
1. listen/speak 2. interrupt/ask questions 3. first/last 4. penny/pound 5. assertive/aggressive 6. more/less

Listening

1. a $180,000 2. c $177,000 3. c $177,000 + 10% discount

Key Language

1.
1. It's open to discussion 2. I think that's fair. 3. I'm open to suggestions. 4. I'll need to see it in writing. 5. We need some time to think it over. 6. We're not prepared to pay that much. 7. That's not exactly what we had in mind. 8. And why is that? How does that sound? 9. Are you happy with that? 10. What would you like to see happen? 11. Then it's settled. 12. You drive a hard bargain. 13. That's the best we can do. 14. You've got yourself a deal. 15. So we're all agreed on that. 16. What will it take to reach an agreement?

2.
1. a 2. b 3. b 4. a 5. b 6. a 7. a 8. b 9. b 10. a 11. b

Unit 13 Business and the Environment

Page 115 Crosschecking

1, 2, 3, 6, 7

Page 115 Find the Expressions

1. doing our bit 2. the track record 3. wreck livelihoods 4. bribery 5. insider trading 6. antagonistic to

Page 116 Word Partnerships 1

1. consumption 2. resources 3. hemisphere 4. technology 5. employment 6. security 7. inequality 8. war 9. dynamics 10. goods 11. nature 12. quality 13. restoration 14. programme 15. systems 16. earth 17. society 18. acts 19. users 20. circumstances

Page 116 Word Partnerships 2

1. issues 2. waste 3. individual 4. business 5. system 6. trend 7. disaster 8. gases 9. corporations 10. record 11. technology 12. damage 13. crime 14. trading 15. powers 16. degradation 17. initiatives 18. energy

Page 117 Word Partnerships 3

1. the environment 2. pollution 3. resources 4. an issue 5. a promise 6. a policy 7. a goal 8. power

Page 117 Business Grammar 1

1. *We don't have to spend money on this* is the answer to both questions (don't have to = it's not necessary)
2. *We must cut down on waste* is more likely to be my opinion (here, must = internal obligation).
3. *I needn't have finished the report,* the use of the present perfect indicates that the report has been completed unnecessarily.

4. *That wouldn't be enough* is more diplomatic.
5. *That must be right.*
6. We couldn't have known what would happen.
7. *We could do it if we tried* (here, could = would be able to).
8. *If he calls, tell him I'm out* (here, if he should call = if he happens to call).
9. *You could ask her, but she won't know yet* is clearly not about future time (here won't know = is certain not to know) *You could ask her, but she won't help you* may be a prediction, but it is probably more a description of how unhelpful 'she' is: she'll refuse to help you because she always refuses to help people (here, she won't help you = she's not 'willing' to help).

Page 118 Business Grammar 2
1.d 2.j 3.a 4.f 5.h 6.c 7.i 8.b 9.g 10.e

Page 118 Business Grammar 3
1. You can't be serious! I can understand how you feel. There must be a way round this. I could be wrong, of course. I couldn't agree more. You must be joking! You may have a point there. There wouldn't be any point.
2. You can say that again! I might have known! We can't be certain. We'll have to wait and see. I shouldn't think so. There wouldn't be time. You don't have to tell me. That shouldn't be a problem.

Unit 14 Finance and Credit

Page 123 Information Check
1, 3, 5

Page 123 Find the Expressions
1. see the colour of your money 2. go bust, go broke
3. be billed 4. the brink of bankruptcy 5. stall creditors
6. put pressure on debtors 7. pre-payment 8. alienating customers 9. cut your losses 10. write it off

Page 124 Word Partnerships 1
1, 5, 7, 10, 4, 3, 8, 11, 9, 2, 6, 12

Page 124 Going bankrupt
2. *To go like a bomb* means to go very fast or to be very successful.

Page 124 Expressions with *money*
1. waste 2. bad 3. tied 4. tight 5. liquid 6. throw
7. channelling 8. made

Page 125 Word Partnerships 2
1. to demand immediate payment 2. to regulate business—to-business relations 3. to put pressure on debtors
4. to minimise the risk of bad debt 5. to damage customer relations 6. to insist on money in advance 7. to ease the cashflow situation 8. to process letters of credit 9. to run a credit check 10. to charge interest on outstanding debts
11. to risk alienating customers 12. to finance new projects

Page 125 Word Partnerships 3
1. win 2. lose 3. handle 4. process 5. receive 6. place
7. cancel 8. phone or fax through 9. dispatch 10. new
11. bulk 12. emergency 13. repeat 14. regular 15. place, received, processed, dispatch 16. win, handled, cancelling, lose

Page 126 Business Grammar
1. with 2. in 3. by 4. on 5. on 6. in 7. on 8. on 9. on 10. up
11. off 12. in 13. behind 14. off 15. up 16. by 17. in

Unit 15 Economic Issues

Page 131 Information Check
1, 3, 6, 8

Page 131 Find the Expressions
1. no one has a clue 2. slump 3. boom 4. collapse, meltdown
5. changes hands 6. compounded the problem 7. windfall profits 8. escalating 9. to be tightened 10. an influx of workers 11. unprecedented 12. no wonder

Page 132 Word Partnerships 1
1. supply + demand 2. hyperinflation + unemployment
3. institutions + collapse 4. boom + greed 5. markets + money 6. increase + acquisitions 7. profits + employees
8. debts + acquisitions

1. crisis + gap 2. population + GDP 3. threat + underclass
4. Unemployment + inflation 5. controls + influx
6. jobs + poverty 7. power + institutions 8. truth + economy

Page 132 Word Partnerships 2
1. growth 2. indicators 3. crisis 4. forecast 5. forces
6. theory 7. policy 8. outlook 9. recession 10. measures
11. developments 12. ruin 13. reform 14. strategy
15. recovery 16. union 17. sanctions

Page 132 Word Partnerships 3
1. indicators, forecasts 2. ruin 3. outlook
4. recession, measures 5. union

Page 133 Current Affairs 1
1. privatise 2. cut 3. come out of 4. improve 5. relax
6. scrap 7. close 8. break off 9. harm 10. impede 11. reduce
12. divide 13. push up 14. help 15. resist 16. put off
17. launch 18. pay off 19. adopt 20. neglect

Page 134 Current Affairs 2
1. recession 2. trade gap 3. benefits 4. immigration controls
5. programme 6. image abroad 7. pressure 8. attack
9. Public opinion 10. unemployment 11. negotiations/talks
12. investment

Page 134 Abbreviations & Acronyms
1. United Nations 2. North Atlantic Treaty Organization
3. International Monetary Fund 4. Gross National Product
5. Gross Domestic Product 6. General Agreement on Trade and Tariffs 7. value added tax 8. North American Free Trade Area

Page 134 Word Grammar
1. economist 2. economical 3. economise 4. politicians
5. politically 6. politicized

Page 135 Business Grammar
(model answers) 1. has increased by over 50% 2. doubled
3. has fallen 4. is expected to fall by a further $12bn 5. in inflation 6. to rise 7. was relatively encouraging 8. steadily increasing 9. was between 1980 and 1990 10. is likely to be pushed up by a further 5% 11. is considerably worse 12. is upward 13. between 1980 and 19990, the population is now growing rapidly 14. to continue over the next three years
15 it was in 1990 16. three years is not encouraging

Page 135 Word Partnerships 4
1. thoroughly 2. sincerely 3. completely 4. firmly
5. categorically 6. completely 7. categorically 8. sincerely
9. thoroughly 10. firmly

Tapescript

Unit 1 Page 14 Interview Skills

OK, tip number one - seems obvious, but the first two minutes really are vital. So stay cool, smile, put the interviewer at ease. Remember, most of them are as worried about choosing the wrong person as you are about not getting the job. Imagine that you're just there to help them make the right decision.

Tip number two - show you've really done your homework on the company you're applying for a job with. Actually, the best way to show this is by asking informed and intelligent questions during the interview. If you simply spout a lot of facts about the company, you'll just look like some creep who's spent the last month memorising the company website.

Number three - with the interviewer's permission, try conducting part of the interview as a short presentation entitled 'Why I want to work for YOU and why YOU should want to employ ME'. This is a great way of selling yourself, but be careful not to look too pushy and over-confident. Remember to build in a bit of humour, especially if you're applying for a job in the UK or the States.

Four – and this really is relevant if you follow tip number three – be careful how you describe yourself to the interviewer. Don't just describe yourself using adjectives - you know, "I'm very conscientious and self-motivated", that kind of thing. It sounds so conceited and phoney. Instead, try to give concrete examples of things you've actually done. For example, "When I worked at O&M we often had to work a 14-hour day to get a project finished on schedule" or "When I was at university I made a point of never handing in an assignment late". Let THEM work out what kind of person you are. That's their job.

Umm, my fifth tip would be: never say negative things about ex-employers however awful they were to work for. They'll wonder if you're going to be as disloyal to them at some point in the future. A lot of interviewers will ask you about your previous jobs. So remember to be tactful when asked about why you left such-and-such a job or fell out with the boss.

OK, as I've said, nobody likes a show-off. But don't be too modest about your achievements either unless you're sure they know how good you really are. Don't assume they'll be able to see through your modesty. They might just think you're an under-achiever who lacks ambition. So my sixth tip is to be proud of what you've achieved in your career so far, tell them what you're good at and make absolutely sure you have great references.

Seven - unfortunately, any negative information about you - for instance, that you left college without taking your degree - will usually attract more follow-up questions than positive information. So, don't be afraid to admit your mistakes, but always balance them with a positive outcome. For example, with the degree problem, you could say: 'In retrospect, a degree would have been nice after all that hard work. But leaving college early enabled me to gain a lot of on-the-job experience and become an account manager before the age of 23.'

Everyone has gaps in their CV. So tip eight - don't try to cover these up or lie about spending a year in the Sudan working for Oxfam when you didn't. Tell them how these transitional periods in your career have helped you focus on what you really want to do. Anyway, your CV or resume may not be quite as important as you think. A lot of employers tell me the cover letter is even more important, provided you meet the basic requirements of the job. And they're quite happy to take on people who've followed an unusual career path.

Tip nine - if you can, visit the building where the interview is to be held a few days before the interview itself. Look at the people going in and out. What kind of clothes, haircuts, jewellery do they have? No-one's saying you have to be a clone, but if they're all in suits, don't turn up in combat trousers and Nikes unless you're very confident!

Finally, though, BE very confident. After all, what have you got to lose? The worst thing that can happen is that you leave the same way you came in - without the job. So, going back to my first tip, dare to take a few chances to create a strong impression.

Unit 3 Page 29
Case Study: Microsoft Under Attack

Microsoft, if not yet the world's biggest company, is probably the one with the highest market valuation. At its height, before the slump in PC sales in the first years of the 21st Century, Microsoft was worth more than 300 nation states! At such a powerful and cutting-edge company one would have expected the security to be airtight. And it was – almost.

But in September 2000 hackers successfully managed to break into the Microsoft system and remain undetected for an amazing five weeks. Fortunately for Microsoft, the hackers didn't corrupt the files they opened, but they did gain access to the 'source code' for a new computer program, which was then still in development and top secret.

Similar incidents have sometimes resulted in companies being blackmailed into paying money to prevent information about their software being published on the Internet, but in this case that didn't happen. The FBI was called in to investigate, but, ironically the technology simply didn't exist to track down the hackers. Nor was there provision in the law to prosecute them unless they actually interfered with the files they hacked into.

The likelihood is that the security breach was just a publicity stunt aimed at embarrassing Microsoft. The company is not popular with those who see the its activities as monopolistic. But it remains popular with the nine out of ten PC users who buy its software, earning co-founder and chairman, Bill Gates, somewhere in the region of a million dollars an hour.

Meeting Skills Page 33 Listening

Chair: OK, can we get started, please.
We have a lot to get through today. First of all, I want to apologise for the delay. I was caught up in another meeting and … so … anyway, let's get started. Does everyone have a copy of the minutes from the last meeting and today's agenda?

All right, um … sorry about that. So, as I'm sure you're all aware we're here to discuss next year's product line. The first item on the agenda is whe—

Marcelo: Sorry, I'd just like to say that we need to have some space on today's agenda to discuss the vacation time issue. I think I speak for everyone in this room when I say that there is a real problem wh—

Chair: Just – sorry – before you continue, I really think that's an issue to be dealt with at another time. Unfortu—

Marcelo: But you said that at the last meeting and –

Paul: I personally agree with Marcelo. My experience with the company's policy on this matter is really awful. I mean –

Chair: OK, OK. All in favour of adding vacation time to the agenda?

Sandra: Well, no. I'm sorry, but I have to disagree. I think we have other priorities right now – I'm sorry.

Chair: OK, so I think those of you who want to discuss the company's paternity leave policy should talk to Susan at HR after the meeting today, and I'll make sure I take time out to be present. As I was saying before, the first order of business is –

Sandra: But there are-

Chair: Sandra?

Sandra: Sorry, I just wanted to say that there are some unresolved issues from the last meeting which I think need, you know, to be dealt with.

Chair: For instance?

Paul: For instance the drop in sales in Singapore. I for one think that we need to deal with that first.

Marcelo: Singapore? What about Mexico? We're losing millions over there.

Chair: OK. Susan, uh, what are your thoughts on the Mexico problem?

Paul: Now, wait a minute. It's not their fault. If they had the support that Brazil has they wouldn't be in the situation they're in now.

Marcelo: I'm sorry, I'm not sure I follow.

Paul: Well, for instance, they had a budget of 25 million for the launch of 'Blue Tree', whereas we had just under 10.

Marcelo: But their market is much smaller. You can't compare wh—

Paul: I'm sorry, but that's where you're wrong. We—

Chair: Hang on, hang on. Just a second, please. Going back to what Paul said about Singapore, I agree that the situation is crucial, but if we don't expand our line, things are just going to get worse. Our competitors are beating us on all levels – price, market share, loyalty…you name it. There's a real problem with piracy at the moment, as I'm sure you're all aware, so we need to get the authorities on board. These and other issues need to be discussed so, if I can just continue …

Marcelo: Sorry, I'm not sure I follow. What do you mean 'piracy'? Where is there piracy going on of our product?

Chair: Well, surely you-realize

Sandra: I have some thoughts on that, actually. I'm not sure if this would work but-

Paul: Sorry to interrupt, but I think I know what you're going to say, and, we've already tried it – believe me, it doesn't work.

Sandra: Well, hang on … I'm not finished!

Chair: People! People! Please! Please!

Unit 5 Page 50
Fluency work. Case study: Sumitomo Bank

Of all the markets in which goods are traded, the most volatile and unpredictable are the commodities markets. In theory, international commodity exchanges exist to set the standards and fix the prices of primary products such as gold, silver, copper, tin, coffee, sugar and crude oil. In practice, the prices of some of these commodities fluctuate wildly, earning and losing speculators' fortunes overnight.

So it's not surprising that even at the Sumitomo Bank, one of Japan's biggest financial powerhouses and for a while the company with the highest turnover in Japan, there could be errors of judgement. But nothing had prepared the bank for the scandal caused by just one of its employees—Yasuo Hamanaka. Hamanaka was Sumitomo's chief copper trader. Known as Mr 5% because of his success in cornering a twentieth of the world copper market, he was a legend in metals trading.

But in 1997 it suddenly became known that during his 10-year career Hamanaka had lost $2.6 billion in unauthorised deals. As scandalous as the enormous loss itself, was the fact that it had gone undetected for so long. At his trial, Hamanaka naturally made excuses, claiming that changes in the rules of trading at the London Metal Exchange, or LME, had forced him to liquidate a million metric tons of copper at the wrong time. But the court wasn't sympathetic and Mr 5% was eventually sentenced to eight years in prison.

Unit 5 Page 50
The commodities Game: Updates

Update 1

| Current Prices: | Gold 400 | Silver 5 | Copper 2,500 |
| Tin 5,000 | Coffee 3,500 | Sugar 300 | Oil 20 |

Forecast: In the short term, a rising price index is likely to push up the price of gold as a hedge against inflation, but long-term prospects are much less attractive. Copper looks promising. We're not predicting much movement in tin, coffee, sugar or oil. Risk-takers should take a chance on silver.

Update 2

Current Prices: Gold up at 450	Silver down at 4.5
Copper down at 2,000	Tin stable at 5,000
Coffee stable at 3,500	Sugar down at 275
Oil down at 19	

Forecast: Gold is still very much in demand and the price will probably continue to climb. Copper looks disappointing. Tin looks set to remain firm at 5,000 but rumours of crop damage may boost the price of coffee and sugar. Oil prices should recover in the short term. Our advice is to go long on silver.

Update 3

Current Prices: Gold up at 525	Silver stable at 4.5
Copper up at 3,000	Tin stable at 5,000
Coffee up at 4,000	Sugar down at 250
Oil up at 20	

Forecast: The bubble must burst soon for gold as inflation rates start to come down. Copper is again a good investment. The tin market is still showing no movement at all and long-term prospects are poor. We remain confident that a reduced world supply of coffee and sugar will escalate prices. Brave speculators will hang on to silver which will eventually come good. Buy oil.

Update 4

Current Prices: Gold down at 450	Silver down at 3.25
Copper down at 2,500	Tin stable at 5,000
Coffee up at 4,500	Sugar down at 200
Oil down at 18	

Forecast: As predicted, the price of gold has slipped back and the indications are that it will continue to slide. Although we've not had much success forecasting the price of copper, we now firmly expect it to fall. Hold coffee and sugar. Oil should bounce back to somewhere in the region of $21 a barrel. Silver must soon turn the corner as industrial demand begins to exceed supply. Sell tin.

Update 5

Current Prices: Gold down at 225	Silver up at 3.5
Copper up at 3,500	Tin down at 2,000
Coffee stable at 4,500	Sugar down at 150
Oil up at 22	

Forecast: If you've been taking our advice you will by now have sold all your gold. Buy it back - it's about to stage a recovery. Also buy tin. Silver has picked up only slightly but get ready for a price explosion here. Copper too will perform well. Coffee may have reached a ceiling at 4,500 but our advice is to hold. Sugar is proving to be a poor investment. Sell oil.

Update 6

Current Prices: Gold up at 300	Silver up at 5.5
Copper down at 2,000	Tin stable at 2,000
Coffee up at 6,000	Sugar up at 200
Oil up at 26	

Forecast: Go short on gold - there's still room for further improvement. Buy silver - it's about to go through the roof! The bottom really has dropped out of the copper market, so get rid of holdings in copper. The clever money's on tin which looks set to double in price. Coffee surely cannot exceed an all-time high of 6,000. Sell sugar. Problems in the Middle East may trigger a rise in the price of oil.

Update 7

Current Prices: Gold up at 350	Silver up at 10
Copper up at 3,500	Tin up at 4,000
Coffee stable at 6,000	Sugar up at 250
Oil up at 38	

Forecast: The trend for gold prices is now downward. Sell all holdings in gold. Take a chance on copper. Sell coffee. Sell sugar. Buy oil - even at this high price, the worsening situation in the Middle East should push it higher. Buy tin - it's about to go sky high. The silver market's going crazy! Buy as much silver as you can afford before it takes off.

Update 8

Current Prices: Gold down at 300	Silver up at 25
Copper down at 2,500	Tin up at 7,000
Coffee stable at 6,000	Sugar up at 300
Oil down at 22	

Forecast: If you have any gold left, sell it. It's going to fall through the floor. Those who like to live dangerously should take a risk on silver. It's ridiculously high now but it could go even higher. Sell copper. Sell tin. Sell sugar. Sell coffee - it's reached its peak and must now fall. Apologies for our previous misinterpretation of the oil market. A surprise peace deal in the Middle East means that oil prices will continue to drop back and may even hit an all-time low. It's time to sell.

Final Update

Current Prices: Gold down at 200	Silver up at 50
Copper up at 3,000	Tin down at 3,500
Coffee up at 8,500	Sugar up at 400
Oil down at 17	

Now calculate your total assets by adding your remaining capital to the current value of your holdings. Have you made a profit or a loss? Who made the most money? Did you notice any clear trends in commodity prices? Did they help you to make your investment decisions?

Telephoning Skills Page 59 Listening

Call 1

Recorded Message: Thank you for calling Organica Pharmaceuticals. Please hold while we transfer your call to one of our representatives.

Operator: Thank you for calling Organica Pharmaceuticals, this is Sheila speaking. How can I help you?

Caller: Good morning, I'm calling because I need some information. I'm interested in importing a few of your products to Chile. Specifically, I would like to know about the—

Operator: Let me transfer you to Sales. One moment, please.

Caller: Thank you.

Tapescript

Recorded Message: Thank you for calling Organica Pharmaceuticals. Your call is extremely important to us. Please hold while we transfer you to our next available representative.

Operator 2: Sales, good morning.

Caller: Good morning, my name is Andy Hague and I represent a drugstore chain in Chile called 'Farmacia Facil', and we would be interested in importing a few of your products. What I need to know first of all is—

Operator 2: Uh, sir, you're going to need to speak to Barbara Gallagher in Foreign Sales, who handles this sort of thing but she's not in right now. Would you like to call back later? Say in, oh, about an hour or so? She should be back by then. Thanks for calling Organica Pharmaceuticals and have a nice day.

Caller: B-but…

Call 2

Operator: Hallston and Associates, how may I help you?

Caller: Good afternoon, I'd like to speak to Jane Adams, please.

Operator: I'm afraid she's not in this week. Is there something I can help you with?

Caller: Well, my name is Chris Robb from York Paper in the UK and I'm calling because a colleague of mine, Liz Peterson, referred me to you. It's regarding some problems with customs clearance.

Operator: Oh, yes, you really need to talk to Jane about that.

Caller: When will she be available?

Operator: Let's see. She's back on Friday next week. I could put you down for Friday afternoon?

Caller: Friday afternoon…er…no, I can't Friday. How about the following Monday morning?

Operator: Yes, Monday's fine. Sorry, your name was?

Caller: Chris Robb.

Operator: Right, then speak to you on Monday.

Caller: Thanks. Bye.

Call 3

Mark: Good morning. Who are you holding for?

Caller: Yes, I'd like to speak to Mark Chin, please.

Mark: This is Mark speaking.

Caller: Hello, Mark, you may not remember me, my name is Diane Washington, we met last year — at the International Food and Beverage conference in Orlando?

Mark: Oh, yes, of course. How's it going?

Caller: Great. Just great, thanks. I'm calling because we're looking for a new bio-engineer here at Cal Foods and I was wondering if could help me.

Mark: You know, to be honest, I'm not really available, but I think I know someone who might be interested.

Caller: Oh, fantastic. And what's their name?

Mark: Ed Stanford – but he's not in right now – would you like to leave a message for him?

Caller: Sure. Could you ask him to call me at 415-555-3005?

Mark: OK, 555-3005. I'll give him the message.

Caller: Thank you.

Mark: And what's a good time to reach you?

Caller: I'm usually in the office most of the day, so …

Unit 8 Language Focus.
Page 72 Word Partnerships 1

Right, the first thing is not to panic. I suggest we issue a press release this afternoon stating quite clearly that we carefully monitor working conditions in all our overseas factories and that, no matter what these pressure groups are saying, we simply do not exploit our workers. I recommend we arrange a television interview as soon as possible to make our position absolutely clear on that. I've just been on to TV9. We spend $10million a year with them on advertising. So, believe me, our corporate image means as much to them as it does to us! Now, press and TV coverage are only a partial solution. We also need to be downloading everything written about us on the Internet and taking swift action if necessary to counteract what we expect to be a wave of bad publicity. It may be time to take a fresh look at our mission statement as well. The one we have is strong on brand and differentiates us from our competitors very effectively, but it wouldn't do any harm to raise public awareness of how we've actually championed worker's rights in the developing world. Later on, we should give some thought to sponsoring an appropriate charitable event. For now, let's just concentrate on getting ourselves back on message. And, Sir - please calm down there's a group of reporters outside waiting to see you!

Unit 8 Fluency Work
Page 76 Case Study: Intel in Trouble

Part 1
In 1993 Intel was the world's most valuable brand after Coke and Marlboro. It was quite an achievement considering the invisibility of the product - a tiny microprocessor powering 90% of the world's computers. But in 1994 Thomas Nicely, a relatively unknown American mathematics professor, found a fault with his three Pentium-powered computers. Intel had been so well branded, he knew exactly who to blame. A crisis was about to unfold.

At first Intel denied there was a problem. 'With Intel inside, you know you've got unparalleled quality' ran the company slogan, and the Intel directors saw no reason to suppose this may not be entirely true. But the bad publicity did not go away, as Nicely decided to share his views on the Internet. Once again, thanks to modern technology, a minor complaint quickly became an international incident.

When IBM announced it was halting shipment of Intel-powered PCs and developing a microprocessor of its own, things started to get serious. In a major oversight on IBM's part, it had decided to concentrate on developing computer hardware, leaving the software and microchips to Microsoft and Intel. That proved a mistake, as IBM realized too late that it is software capability and processing speed that the customer is really buying - not the grey plastic box they come in. Now IBM had an excuse to switch to its own processor.

The technical fault was minor. Intel estimated it might affect the average user once every 27,000 years! IBM countered that with companies running networks of thousands of PCs, problems could occur at any time - they were taking no chances. Andrew Grove, Intel's CEO and author of the aptly named 'Only the Paranoid Survive', summed up his feelings at the time: "We are quite clearly anxious to have this event behind us, but given that this has become a major event in the mass media involving people who are not accustomed to dealing with sophisticated mathematical terms ... quite frankly we don't know what to do."

Part 2

Intel's first mistake was to regard the criticism of its chips as unfair. It certainly was unfair - the Pentium was still far more reliable than earlier processors - but that was not the point. Having spent 80 million dollars persuading the market to upgrade to the new Pentium machines and a further 70 million on the famous 'Intel inside' campaign, it had raised customer expectations to the point where any fault, however small, would not be tolerated. Intel had, in effect, promoted the excellence of its product too well and now had to take the consequences.

The company's initial response was to play the whole thing down. Only a few users with very special needs would be likely to be affected. So if customers could prove they might have a problem, their microchip would be replaced. This strategy proved to be a disaster. It only made Intel look unsympathetic and arrogant. Presentations to reassure corporate users also backfired.

Intel was left with no choice. It decided to offer free replacements to anyone who wanted them. Andy Grove himself admitted: "Maybe we have been thick-headed ... but we finally figured it out." This damage limitation strategy was undoubtedly costly, but it worked - restoring consumer confidence in the world's number one microprocessor.

Presentation Skills Page 85 Listening

Good morning everyone. My name is Janet Wilkins, Marketing Director at Joy Toys, and I'm here to talk about the growing "tweens" market. I'll begin by outlining an overall profile of the typical tween and his or her general tastes. I'll then look at some of the challenges that this blossoming market presents, as well as go into what opportunities exist, and I'll finish by looking at some case studies of companies who have had some success in that market (including our own, of course), and maybe even learn from a few that haven't been so successful. There'll be some time at the end for questions and any other comments.

Does everybody have a handout? Good. So, to start off, let me ask you: What is a 'tween' anyway? I guess the best way to answer that question is to look at what a tween likes to do. The 8 to 12 year-olds of the 1960s contented themselves with playing with dolls, building model cars and helping Mum round the kitchen. For the 8 to 12 year-olds of today, that just won't do. Today's child in this age-bracket, the tween, isn't playing with dolls – she's playing with hearts, and breaking a few. A tween won't be building a model car, he'll be building his own website. And a tween is much more likely to be helping Mum choose a new outfit than help her round the kitchen. In short, today's 8 to 12 year-old children – our tweens, are kids with an edge: they're cool, they're flirtatious, they're trendy, they're savvy and, what's especially relevant for our talk today, they're hard to reach. If you look at this graph, you'll notice how the spending habits of kids in that age bracket has changed dramatically over the last decade. We see a steep rise in …

Unit 11 Language Focus
Page 101 Discrimination

1. Systems Analyst

Well, obviously, after three years, I suppose I may need some in-service training to get me back up to speed. But I did actually do a refresher course at my local technical college about a year ago, which was really useful. I think I'm a fairly quick learner and I certainly wouldn't have a problem reporting to someone younger than me. I also like working as a part of a team – that's one of the things I've missed most, actually. My husband and I are planning to have another child in a few years. We'd like a little brother or sister for Harry. But right now my main priority is to get back into the kind of work I really enjoy, which is computer services. And this is the company I want to work for.

2. Marketing Director

Of course, I realise that working in a country like this presents a number of cultural problems, especially for a woman. But, to be honest, I've always found in the past that once people get to know and respect you as a manager, any prejudice they may have had starts to disappear. For example, you know from my CV that I worked quite closely with a Korean advertising agency during the 2002 World Cup and I can honestly say that I had no problems whatsoever. At least, I never experienced any real prejudice at all. It's true that one of the directors was a little too er …'enthusiastic' about my presence, as you know. But that's a completely different kind of problem - which I dealt with.

3. Production Manager

I think working on the production side for as long as I have – getting my hands dirty, as it were – I've come up against a certain amount of prejudice from male colleagues. It's pathetic, really, but quite a few of them still seem to think that I can't possibly know what I'm doing. Frankly, I'm as good at what I do as any man - have to be, really. I've got a first-class degree in mechanical engineering, I've always been extremely highly-driven in everything I do, both at work and in my free-time, and I've always worked quite happily in a field that's still dominated by men. So for me, gender is not an issue. If other people think it is, that's their problem, not mine.

4. Management Trainer

Well, I can see that it might seem strange for a man to be running courses in assertiveness targeted specifically at women. I mean, how do I know what it's like for a woman trying to get on in a male-dominated business, you might say? But the way I see it is I'd be bringing another dimension to the training your female consultants offer. Kind of, the view from the other side. And anyway, as far as I'm concerned, assertiveness is not a feminist or even a female issue. Surely both men and women can benefit from the same basic approaches and techniques. As for working with a team of women. Well, why would I complain about that?

Unit 12 Fluency Work
Page 110 Simulation: Takeover Battle

Announcer: And the time is just coming up to seven o'clock. Here's Robert Barron with 'The Business Breakfast Interview'.

Barron: We live in the age of merger mania. Corporate acquisitions and strategic alliances are regularly splashed all over the front pages of our national newspapers. And the sums of money involved just get bigger and bigger. But what happens to those companies after all the media excitement has died down? When two different corporate cultures meet, is the result more often failure than success?
With me in the studio this morning is Corinne Sheldon, an M&A specialist for Marshall-Rivers Bank, who's spent ten years financially structuring some of the biggest takeovers in the global media business. Corinne, welcome. Why is it that some acquisitions work and others don't?

Sheldon: Well, Robert, obviously there's no single answer to that. But I'd have to say the single biggest factor in transnational acquisitions, which is what I've mostly been involved with, is culture - do the two companies fit culturally. Take two companies which were recently taken over - *StarLink* satellite TV and the Italian general interest magazine *Tutto Bene*.

Barron: Right, both taken over in the last twelve months.

Sheldon: Exactly. Whereas *StarLink* has done incredibly well, it's share price soaring by 44%, *Tutto Bene* is in all kinds of trouble. In fact, it looks as though it may even be closed down.

Barron: Yeah, so we've heard. Why is that?

Sheldon: Well, *StarLink* adapted well to the structural and cultural changes that followed the takeover and *Tutto Bene* didn't. It's as simple as that. The Italian management resisted just about every change the parent company wanted to make.

Barron: But wasn't that also because *Tutto Bene* is a very traditional family business?

Sheldon: Well, that certainly didn't help. But it's more a question of flexibility, I think. Palace Cinemas, for example, was also a private business, and they've done extremely well since they were taken over, modernizing and even adding 30 new cinemas to the chain.

Barron: Right. Goodwill and adaptability on both sides is important, but what about something like Wild West World? A cowboy theme park in the Ukraine, if you can believe it! They've done amazingly well. Nobody expected them to break even and it looks like they'll make a two million dollar profit this year.

Sheldon: Yes, well, if I remember correctly they were bought very cheap. Of course, if you take over a company when it's in real financial difficulty, provided you don't take on too much debt and the basic business plan is good, you can often turn it around very quickly. Look at e-scape.

Barron: Oh, yes, the Croatian computer games geniuses. They were having trouble repeating the success of one of their early products, were bought out and have now come up with another blockbuster, haven't they?

Sheldon: They certainly have. At Huckster, however, it's a different story. Their business plan seemed like a great idea until they got into legal difficulties. Now it looks like they'll just sell off their technology and close down the business. That's if their technology hasn't already been copied by their competitors.

Barron: Hm. That's the problem, isn't it? Hi-tech companies are always risky. Carte Mondiale is struggling too, I hear.

Sheldon: Well, they're having some of the same problems credit card companies had thirty years ago, but I still think they'll be very successful in the long-term. They're a very strong company with a fabulous business concept.

Barron: We'll watch them closely. Finally, Jade Tiger Productions. I know you were involved in this takeover deal yourself, Corinne, so you must be pleased with it how it's working out.

Sheldon: Yes, I am, Robert. The film business has always been enormous in India and it was just a matter of time before global media companies saw the potential there. Advertising and merchandising is where the real profits will come from though. I think the JTP acquisition is a perfect example of a good transnational acquisition - a solid company with an excellent track record, a history of profit and dynamic flexible management.

Barron: Corinne, thanks for joining us.

Sheldon: My pleasure.

Barron: That was Corinne Sheldon of Marshall-Rivers Bank talking to us about transnational mergers in the global media business. Just time for some last-minute news now. Tsunami, the Japanese surf and sportswear company is reporting record profits of $17 million after opening no fewer than twelve new stores across the United States. But it's bad news at the headquarters of Gulp! The Australian soft drinks company seems so far unable to equal its success in the Far East with its range of comically named fruit drinks. Americans and Europeans, it seems, just don't like the sound of mango-flavoured Roo Juice. Can't say I blame them...

Negotiating Skills Page 111 Listening

Amanda: And here's our proposal: it's of course open to discussion.

George: OK. Hmm. Well, ...

Amanda: And here's our proposal: it's of course open to discussion.

George: OK. Hmm. Well, that's not exactly what we had in mind.

Amanda: Oh really? And why is that?

George: Well, we're not really prepared to pay that much, frankly. I don't know. We're... we're going to need some time to think it over.

Amanda: Right. I see. If we adjust the price to something more to your liking, will you accept the rest of the proposal?

George: Well, actually, there are a few points I don't feel totally comfortable with.

Amanda: I see. Could you give me an example of what you mean?

George: Well, what we're agreeing to is 3 years using you as our main supplier of keyboards and accessories – I don't feel comfortable with that long a commitment.

Amanda: Right, I see no problem in changing that if you like. Would you be happier with a 2-year contract?

George: Yes, I think so.

Amanda: Excellent, consider it done. In return, we'd like a clause in the contract giving us rights to first refusal on renewal. How does that sound?

George: I think that's fair. I'll just need to see it in writing, if that's OK.

Amanda: No problem. All right. So then we're all agreed on that?

George: Yes.

Amanda: Excellent, then it's settled.

George: Well, not yet. There's still the matter of price.

Amanda: Oh, yes. Of course. Sorry. How would you feel about $178,000 instead of $180,000?

George: To be honest, I was hoping for a bit less.

Amanda: $177,500?

George: I'm afraid that's still not good enough. Would you be willing to reduce that figure? Say, $160,000? Or...

Amanda: Hmm. Let me ask you this: What would you like to see happen? What will it take to reach an agreement today? I'm open to suggestions.

George: I've told you. Reduce that figure to $160,000.

Amanda: Well, to be frank, we're not prepared to go below $177,000, really, but we would be willing to offer a 5% across the board discount on all our printer accessories. And that's the best we can do right now.

George: Hmm. Make it 10% and you've got yourself a deal.

Amanda: You drive a hard bargain, George. It's a deal.

Unit 13 Language Focus
Page 118 Business Grammar 3

1

Tom: Right, as you know, we're getting a lot of bad publicity about the rates of pay and working conditions in our Asian factories. We're front page news in all the major papers. Frankly, I think we should pull out of Asia altogether.

Enrique: You can't be serious!

Tom: I'm deadly serious, Enrique.

Enrique: But those factories are some of the most cost-effective we have. And, besides, we have a responsibility to our employees out there.

Tom: I can understand how you feel, but there's no option, I'm afraid.

Anne: Wait a minute. There must be a way round this.

Tom: Well, what do you suggest, Anne?

Anne: Well, I could be wrong, of course, but I'd say the main problem in those factories is not what we pay but the way the local managers treat their workers.

Tom: I couldn't agree more.

Anne: So why don't we simply put our own managers in there?

Tom: You must be joking! You think we 've going to get our people to go and work in those places?

Anne: Hm, you may have a point there. Well, then what if we train the local managers instead, get them to run their factories to the same standards we set here.

Tom: There wouldn't be any point, I'm afraid. There's no way we could impose our corporate culture over there, Anne. Believe me, it just wouldn't work.

2

Alan: OK. I'm afraid I have some very bad news. We've just heard one of our tankers has broken up off the coast of Galicia in Spain.

Jack: Oh, my God!

Alan: You can say that again, Jack. It's a disaster. This will be our third wreck in fifteen years. The ship concerned is The Illustrious.

Diane: I might have known! The Illustrious must be at least 25 years old. I said it should have been withdrawn from service years ago.

Jack: What's the state of the damage, Alan?

Alan: At this stage, we can't be certain. But it looks like the ship's leaking about 125 tonnes of fuel a day. With a total cargo of 70,000 tonnes, what we have to worry about is the ship sinking and taking all that fuel to the bottom of the sea.

Jack: Can't we prevent that?

Alan: We'll have to wait and see. But, frankly, I shouldn't think so. There wouldn't be time. The storm that wrecked the ship is making it difficult to get a rescue team in. Fortunately, we got all the crew off safely and a massive clean-up operation has already started.

Diane: You realise if the ship sinks, it could continue to leak fuel for another four years?

Alan: You don't have to tell me, Diane. That's what I'm worried about.

Jack: Are we insured for what this is going to cost us?

Alan: That shouldn't be a problem. We're covered for up to $20 million.

Diane: Well, let's just hope that turns out to be enough.

Unit 14 Language Focus
Page 124. Expressions with Money

1
Speaker 1   What do you think of the plan to install an executive gym?
Speaker 2   To be honest, I think it's a complete waste of money.

2
Speaker 1   Why don't we just inject some more cash into the project if it's still underfunded?
Speaker 2   Because there's no point in throwing good money after bad.

3
Speaker 1   Can't we pay off the loan with the money that's coming in from our subsidiaries in the Gulf?
Speaker 2   Well, most of that money's tied up, I'm afraid.

4
Speaker 1   So why aren't we investing in a new plant?
Speaker 2   Because I'm afraid money's a bit tight at the moment.

5
Speaker 1   How much of that money's liquid?
Speaker 2   Very little. In fact, hardly any of it can be turned into cash for over a year.

6
Speaker 1   Look, we can't just throw money at the problem.
Speaker 2   No, but it wouldn't hurt to spend a bit more on advertising, would it?

7
Speaker 1   We've made a pretty good profit for the last three years running.
Speaker 2   In that case, shouldn't we be channelling some of that money into R&D?

8
Speaker 1   I don't suppose you could lend me a couple of hundred pounds, could you?
Speaker 2   What do you think I am … made of money?

Page 134. Abbreviations & Acronyms

1. UN 2. NATO 3. IMF 4. GNP 5. GDP 6. GATT
7. VAT 8. NAFTA

Glossary

agenda (noun) the items to be discussed during a meeting

applicant (noun) a person applying for a job

aptitude test (noun) a test to see if an applicant is good for a job

asset (noun) money, equipment, property or other item that increases the real value of a company or person's wealth

B2B (noun) business to business; usually Internet companies selling to businesses; compare to B2C, business to consumer

backfire (verb) when a plan has an unexpected and negative result

background (noun) the professional history of a person or entity

bad debt (noun) money owed that hurts cashflow

bargain (noun) something purchased that is good value for money paid

billboard (noun) an outdoor advertisement meant to be seen by people in the street

boardroom (noun) the place where shareholders meet, also used to refer to where important decisions are made

bottom line (noun) the minimum a person will accept when negotiating a deal

bounce back (verb) to recover from losses or a negative business trend

brainstorm (noun/verb) an idea that occurs suddenly; to think of ideas or solutions individually or in a group

brand loyalty (noun) the idea that a consumer will always use the same product/service

brand name (adjective) of a well known brand; opposite: generic, off-brand

brandstretching (noun) using a brand name that is known for one particular kind of product on other products

breakthrough (noun) an event, invention or idea that solves a problem or causes positive change

bribe (noun/verb) money or gifts used to persuade a person; to persuade a person using money or gifts

broke (adjective) having no money

cashflow (noun) the money a company makes and spends

catch on (verb) to become popular, esp. an idea or product

commodity (noun) traded raw material, such as precious metals and food

corporate ladder (noun) the hierarchy that exists within an organization

cost-effective (adjective) an expense with little or no negative financial impact

cross-cultural (adjective) an idea or product that is relevant to two or more cultures

cutting-edge (adjective) using the latest methods, techniques or technology

cyberbuzz (noun) excitement about a product or service generated on the Internet

cyberspace (noun) the virtual space that exists on the Internet

dead-end (noun/adjective) no exit; having no positive outcome, limiting

dedication (noun) a kind of desire decided commitment to work hard and consistently

drive (noun) a feeling that makes a person want to continue

entrepreneur (noun) person who builds businesses

e-tailer (noun) person or business based in the Internet

extravagant (adjective) unnecessarily expensive

forecast (noun/verb) a prediction based on current conditions, such as a sales forecast; to try to predict future circumstances based on current conditions

forward-looking (adjective) always trying to improve, evolve or advance

glass ceiling (noun) imaginary barrier to reaching high positions in a company, especially for women

go under (verb) for a business to fail

green (adjective) in business, to be friendly to the environment and nature

ground-breaking (adjective) completely new and revolutionary

guts (noun) courage

headhunter (noun) a person who tries to find talented new talent employees for companies

high flier (noun) a successful business person

high-yield (adjective) usually used to describe a kind of investment, often a high-risk bond

hired gun (noun) person with special qualities or skills hired on a temporary basis, usually in a crisis situation

homework (noun) in business, to do ones homework is to do the necessary research in order to be prepared, e.g., (for negotiations or, competition)

household name (noun) a brand name that is so common that everyone has heard of it

hype (noun) excitement created in newspapers or other media about a new product or service

ingenuity (noun) ability to think of new approaches or solutions

initiative (noun) doing things without being asked or told to

innovative (adjective) describing something that is new;, a fresh approach

junk bond (noun) a high-yield bond usually sold to finance takeover bids

killer instinct (noun) in business, the desire to crush competition

lateral thinking (noun) the ability to think in unconventional ways, often in order to solve a problem

Glossary

lay off (verb) to let go of an employee or employees because of a company's financial crisis

lookalike product (noun) a product launched which is similar to another already existing and successful in the marketa successful existing product

market saturation (noun) when so much of the same product or /service exists in a specific market that there is no room for more competition

market share (noun) the portion of one given market a company controls, often expressed in percentages

market-driven (adjectivenoun) when a company company that makes business decisions based on market trends and needs

marketing mix (noun) the different means and strategies used promote a business, product or service

meltdown (noun) a sudden and complete failure

me-tooism (noun) the practice of doing what the others are also doing

middle-of-the-road (noun) in business, the largest group of consumers, with the most typical demographics

mission statement (noun) a sentence or more that is the official company business philosophy, especially about what it wants to achieve

morph (verb) a business that turns into another, often an internet Internet company that becomes a "brick and mortar" (real) business

networking (noun) communication between professionals to exchange ideas and build useful business relationships

no-win situation (noun) a situation in which there can be no positive result, no matter the action taken

outsource (verb) when a company uses a third party for certain specific tasks

outstanding debt (noun) money owed, especially after a long time

poverty line (noun) an amount of money, often expressed in dollars, which is the minimum amount decided by a government that a person can earn in order to survive

press release (noun) a kind of article or report written to attract the interest of media like newspapers and television, usually for the purpose of marketing and promotion

price-sensitive (adjective) when a market will suffer if a product is priced too high or too low

privatise (verb) when a state-owned enterprise is sold to private interests

profile (noun) a product or service has a high profile if it is widely recognized by consumersconsumer recognition of a product

rat race (noun) expression used to describe the fast pace and competition of modern urban life

restructure (verb) when a business changes its management structure in order to make operations more efficient

rough figure (noun) an inexact but approximate figure

self-starter (noun) a business or person that requires little effort to get started

self-employed (nounadjective) when a person who is or has his or her own business

speculate (verb) to guess what the future value will be of a stock or commodity

subliminal advertising (noun) a kind of advertising which manipulates basic human feelings, such as fear and desire, in order to attract consumers

supply and demand (noun) the economic force which controls price

sweatshop (noun) a kind of factory, sometimes illegal, where workers are paid very low wages

synergy (noun) a positive energy that exists between two entities, such as between a market and a business, and that works to increase the two entities' strength

takeover bid (noun) when one company makes an offer to buy another

team-spirit (noun) good-natured cooperation among employees

track record (noun) in business, the significant events in the history of a company or individual

trade barriers (noun) an obstacle, such as a high tax, that a government imposes to restrict the importation of certain goods

trade gap (noun) when a country imports much more than it exports

trendy (noun) something that is in fashion, or that is changing behavior

upmarket (adjective) a product or service that appeals to people in high income brackets

user-friendly (adjective) a product or service that is easy to use or understand

venture capital (noun) money invested in new projects

wage slave (noun) person who earns just enough to survive

word of mouth (noun) when positive comments are made about a product or service from one consumer to the next, usually based only on the good quality of the product or service itself

job

apply for a job – to fill out a form or send a CV to try and get a particular post

be out of a job – to be fired or laid off

be sacked from a job – to be fired

quit ones job – to decide to leave a job

hold down a job – to work at keeping the same job for a long time

go job-hunting – to look for a job

change jobs – to work at a different company

get a job offer – when a person receives an offer of employment

sale

make a sale – to make a customer buy your product or service

boost sales – increase sales

sales have dropped – when sales decrease

sales have picked up – when sales increase

sales figures – the report of how much has sold

sales forecast – prediction of how much will be sold

sales force – the people selling your product/service

sales target – the desired amount to be sold by the end of a given period of time

deal

close a deal – to make a customer buy

make a deal – to make a customer buy

negotiate a deal – to make a customer buy after much discussion

strike a deal – to come to a business arrangement

the deal is on – when two parties agree to a business arrangement, such as a contract

the deal is off – when, often due to bad circumstances, a deal is canceled

the deal fell through – when a deal is close to being closed but in the end fails

a shady deal – a deal that may not be legal

contract

be in breach of contract – when one or both parties to a contract do something which goes contrary to that which has been agreed on in the contract

be under contract – when a person or people are doing a specific job for a company, usually with the understanding that the service is exclusively for that company

break a contract – to end an agreement that has been written in a contract, usually without all parties agreeing

(re)negotiate a contract – when, after some time, one or more signatories decides he or she wants to change a part or parts of a written contract

renew a contract – when a company agrees to begin a new term of service with a business or service provider after the previous contract term has expired decides that it still needs the services provided by the person or person who has been providing a service for that company even after the time provided in the contract for the project has already expired

sign a contract – to make a contract official by writing in one's legal name when a contract becomes official by signing your legal name on a contract

terminate a contract – when one or both parties to a contract decide to end the contractual agreement

contract out – to hire a third party to do a specific task

market

break into a market – to penetrate a market, often one that is difficult to sell to

corner a market – when one company gains total or nearly total control of a market

flood the market – when one company sells a high volume of one particular product

market research – to do research such as conduct surveys and focus groups in order to better understand a market

market share – how much of one market a company controls

market value – how much a product is worth when sold

buyers' market – when there is more supply than demand

risk

be worth the risk – when there exists a risk, but that risk is small compared to the positive outcome that can be achieved

run a risk – when a risk exists

calculated risk – a risk that is taken after planning

low risk – when little risk is involved

high risk – when there exists some danger in a particular course of action

no-risk – when no or virtually no negative outcome is possible

risk management – when steps are taken to avoid major problems

risk factors – the elements of danger that exist in a particular decision that is made

capital

capital asset – property or money that increased the value of a business

capital expenditure – the money needed in order to keep a business running or expand a business

capital gains and losses – value of a business made or lost

capital intensive – a business investment that requires large amounts of money that is not liquid

capital spending – money spent on fixed assets

long-term capital – money spent on property and fixed assets that will be used for several years or used as reserves for future operations

venture capital – money used as investment in new projects and that represents a risk, but which may bring high returns

start-up capital – the money and assets needed in order start a business

success

achieve success – to reach success

bring about success – when an action taken is rewarded with success

Glossary

ensure success – taking action to be sure success occurs

guarantee success – when success is certain to occur

meet with success – when something is successfully attemted

a sure(-fire) success – a guaranteed success

business

business plan – the initial plan of how one intends to start and run a business

business unit – one individual operation, often part of a larger organization

business card – a card which contains your contact and other relevant professional information, such as job title, name of company with which you are affiliated

business lunch – a lunch which is also a business meeting

run a business – to operate a company

go out of business – when a business fails

go into business – to start a business

"we're in business" – when the circumstances are acceptable to begin to take action

profit

profit and loss statement (P&L) – a report which shows the figures of that which has been made and spent during given period of time

profit-sharing plan – a scheme a company offers its employees so that they too can enjoy the benefits of a company's successes

profit margin – the percentage difference between income and the cost of operations

make a profit – to make money after expenses are covered

bring in profit – to attract money

generate profit – to make money, to sell

net profit – the money that is left after overhead costs are covered

gross profit – money made before overhead costs are accounted for

shares

sell shares – to sell stocks on the open market

buy shares – to buy stocks

issue shares – when a company goes public and sells stocks on the open exchange

offer shares – when a company goes public and sells stocks on the open exchange

blue chip shares – low-risk stocks in good companies

"tech" shares – stocks sold by companies dealing in technology, such as computers and other electronics

foreign shares – stocks and bonds issued by foreign companies and governments to attract investment and hard currency

cash

pay cash – to pay in real currency

cash advance – to get cash from a credit card, or in advance of a pay cheque

cash cow – a product, service or subsidiary company that consistently generates strong profits

cash on delivery (COD) – delivery costs to be paid by person receiving shipment

cash on hand - liquid assets available at any given moment

cash-poor – company with little liquid assets

cash-strapped – company going through a temporary period of cash shortage

brand

brand loyalty – when a person or consumer group always buys the same brand

brand management – the task of keeping a brand fresh in consumers' minds and with a positive image

brand name – a brand that is well known

brand awareness – a condition that describes consumers who are concerned with the name of the product or service they use consumer familiarity with a product or service

brand association – the image or style that one related to a particular brand

brand identity – a brand that has a strong image

off-brand – a brand that is not well known and so is usually a cheaper option

costs

cost control – trying to keep costs down

cost of living – how much it costs to live in a given area, including the cost of housing, transportation and food

bear the cost – to assume costs

cut costs – to try and reduce costs

minimise costs – to make costs as low as possible

offset costs – to make the costs incurred less hurtful by making them as beneficial to overall operations as possible or by making other adjustment within a company in order to compensate for those costs

sell at cost – to sell a product without expecting to lose or make money from it, often for the purposes of promotion

operating costs – how much it costs to keep a business running

price

asking price – when selling a product, where one expects to set the selling price; the price point

bargain price – an unusually low price for a particular product price control – being careful to keep prices attractive to consumers

price war – when two or more companies offering the same product reduce prices in order to gain or retain market share

price range – the minimum to maximum price at which a product can be sold

price-sensitive – when a market will suffer if a product is priced too high or too low

mark up prices – to increase the profit margin

cut prices – to make prices lower, often during a sales promotion

product

develop a product – when a product is being planned

discontinue a product – when a product is no longer selling or is obsolete and is terminated

launch a product – to alert the media about to begin promotion and sales of a new product or service

product design – the planning phase of the look of a new product

product line/range – all the products offered by a company

product life-cycle – how long a product will last before it is discontinued because it no longer is profitable to keep in the range

best-selling product – the product which is most profitable for a company

spin off product – a product which is a variation of a successful product which already exists on the market and which was very successful

budget

set a budget – to decide on a budget

draw up a budget – to agree on a budget

keep to a budget – to not exceed a budget

overstep ones budget – to exceed a budget

go over budget – to exceed a budget

balance the budget – to plan income and expenditure so that they balance

budget restraints – to have a limited budget or to not be able to invest in new projects because of limited cash flow

budget cuts – to reduce certain features of a business, such as employee benefits, in order to keep a company profitable

competition

come up against competition – to meet competition

face competition – to meet competition

beat the competition – to outperform the competition

outsmart the competition – to think of a better strategy than the one the competition has or had

be one step ahead of the competition – to plan ahead in such a way that the competition can only imitate you

cut-throat competition – competition with little or no business ethics

fierce competition – when a market it close to saturation or businesses or products fight to defend or improve their positions in the market when the existing competition in a market is ready to do all to defend its market position

stiff competition – when a market is close to saturation

customer

put the customer at ease – help a customer feel good about spending his or her money

regular customer – a customer who always returns to the same business, or buys the same product

tough customer – a consumer that is not easily convinced that he or she should purchased the product being offered

satisfied customer – a customer that walks away from a deal feeling happy about the money she or he spent

irate customer – a customer who is angry about something that the company did

return customers – satisfied customers who return because of the company's positive qualities

customer service – the way a customer is treated by a company's employees

customer satisfaction – how happy a customer feels post-after a purchase

Fluency Work

Simulation: Takeover Battle

Possible Acquisition Targets.

StarLink   Market Valuation: $5bn

The StarLink satellite TV company is based in Buenos Aires, Argentina, and beams 24-hour programming in Spanish and Portuguese into most parts of Central and South America. High start-up costs have meant that it has taken seven years to see a profit, but future prospects are good.

Huckster   Market Valuation: $1bn

This internet company based in Seattle, USA, actually gets more hits than AOL! Using MP3 technology, Huckster offers free downloads of music CDs. Once valued at $3bn but now involved in a court battle with recording companies over copyright, the company could still be turned into a very profitable subscription business.

PALACE CINEMAS
Market Valuation: $1.5bn

Based in London, UK, Palace Cinemas is a chain of one hundred cinemas located throughout Britain. In business for over 50 years, Palace has lacked effective leadership since the death of founder Sir Adrian Appleby eighteen months ago. Many of the company's cinemas were originally theatres and lack a full range of modern facilities.

Tutto Bene
Market Valuation: $1bn

Owned by the Minucci family and based in Milan, Italy, tutto bene magazine specializes in celebrity news, fashion and gossip. Unable to compete with the likes of Hello, it has tried to reposition itself as a teen-magazine with only partial success. Readership dropped to 1 million last year, but, thanks to a strong editorial team, is now recovering.

e-SCAPE   Market Valuation: $0.5bn

This computer games company is based in Zagreb, Croatia. Started by three 17-year-olds in a spare bedroom three years ago, e-scape became famous overnight when it developed the bestselling game, Moon Racer. It hasn't produced anything quite as successful since then, but has high hopes for its new fantasy game, Valhalla.

Jade Tiger Productions   Market Valuation: $2bn

JTP is based in Delhi, India, and is one of 'Bollywood's oldest film studios. Film-going is a national obsession in India and the market is obviously huge. JTP blockbusters include Night of Desire and Fires of the Heart starring matinée idol Ravi Kumar. A large part of JTP's revenues now come from product placement.

Wild West World
Market Valuation: $0.25bn

This adventure theme park is based in Kiev, Ukraine, and offers rides and attractions with a Wild West flavour. Very popular when it first opened, the park has suffered from cashflow problems in recent years and now attracts only half the visitors it used to. This year it reported a loss, but new corporate events and conference facilities are proving successful.

Carte Mondiale   Market Valuation: $3bn

CM is a smart card company based in Lille, France. The company pioneered electronic money, which replaces cash as well as credit cards and allows you to buy anything from a coffee to a car using one simple microchip. Very popular with young professionals, the cards need to be more widely accepted before the idea can really take off.

Tsunami   Market Valuation: $1bn

Tsunami, based in Kagoshima, Japan, both manufactures and retails surfer sportswear as well as distributing to other clothes stores. The Tsunami brand has gained a kind of cult status in the Japanese youth market and the grand opening of the new megastore in Miami, Tsunami's first outside Japan, was a major media event.

GuLP!   Market Valuation: $3bn

This soft drinks company based in Perth, Australia, has successfully positioned itself as the Down-Under alternative to all-American Coke and Pepsi. By using healthy natural ingredients and giving their products crazy names like Gator Guzzler, Roo Juice and Peach Melbourne, Gulp! has managed to take 15% of the soft drinks market in the Pacific Rim.